'Highly recommended for upper-division undergraduates through professionals, this book contains an excellent, extensive bibliography that will provide the advanced student or scholar with numerous resources for in-depth analysis of many important contemporary issues.'
– G.M. Greenberg, *Choice*

'*Gender and Colonialism* provides an excellent overview of liberation psychology from a feminist perspective. In the fashion of a Psychological Bulletin article – extended to book format – it gives a meaningfully organized, well-written, systematic and creative summary of the literature in this research domain.'
– T. Teo, *Theory and Psychology*

'It is a wide-ranging reference text, excellent for teaching purposes.'
– M. McDermott, *Women's Studies International Forum*

'Moane's book makes a significant contribution to a necessary discussion of oppression and liberation in psychology.'
– S. Austin, *Feminism and Psychology*

'Moane's book will appeal to a wide audience...her book is thus both practical and visionary.'
– B. Bayer, *Irish Journal of Feminist Studies*

Also by Geraldine Moane

CARE PROVISION AND COST MEASUREMENT: Dependent Elderly People at Home and in Geriatric Hospitals (*co-author*)

SUPPORT SERVICES FOR CARERS OF ELDERLY PEOPLE LIVING IN THE COMMUNITY (*co-author*)

Gender and Colonialism

A Psychological Analysis of Oppression and Liberation

Geraldine Moane
University College Dublin, Ireland

Foreword by Mary Daly

First published 1999
This revised paperback edition published 2011 by
PALGRAVE MACMILLAN

Palgrave Macmillan in the UK is an imprint of Macmillan Publishers Limited,
registered in England, company number 785998, of Houndmills, Basingstoke,
Hampshire RG21 6XS.

Palgrave Macmillan in the US is a division of St Martin's Press LLC,
175 Fifth Avenue, New York, NY 10010.

Palgrave Macmillan is the global academic imprint of the above companies
and has companies and representatives throughout the world.

Palgrave® and Macmillan® are registered trademarks in the United States,
the United Kingdom, Europe and other countries.

ISBN: 978-0-333-69966-9 hardback
ISBN: 978-0-333-99429-0 paperback

This book is printed on paper suitable for recycling and made from fully
managed and sustained forest sources. Logging, pulping and manufacturing
processes are expected to conform to the environmental regulations of the
country of origin.

A catalogue record for this book is available from the British Library.

A catalog record for this book is available from the Library of Congress.

10 9 8 7 6 5 4 3 2 1
20 19 18 17 16 15 14 13 12 11

Printed and bound in Great Britain by
CPI Antony Rowe, Chippenham and Eastbourne

Contents

Figures

Foreword

This is an important book for all who want to face and understand the dilemmas posed by living in patriarchy, the state of possession. It is about the struggle to survive and thrive on the Boundary, to Realize a New Reality that is based on biophilia, or love of life, that is in harmony with the Dance of the Universe. This involves understanding that patriarchy is characterized by oppression, repression, depression, with increasingly destructive forces bringing us nearer to global ecological collapse than ever before.

This state of possession stultifies women, who have layers of crippling thought-patterns comparable to the footbindings which mutilated millions of Chinese women for over one thousand years. These thought-patterns are mindbindings comprised of masterminded myths and ideologies meant to mummify the spirit and maim the brain. Women must break out of these mindbindings, for at a time when life on this planet is threatened it is increasingly clear that the cause of women and the cause of ecology are profoundly connected.

What Geraldine Moane succeeds in doing is showing women how to cast off these mindbindings. She manages to do this first by creating an awareness in the reader of how the state of possession infiltrates and permeates the lives and experiences of women. She describes in a scholarly and thorough manner how the overarching myths and structures of patriarchy enclose and stifle the impulse to liberation. She suggests specific and practical steps for moving to the Boundary – the new time/space created by women surviving and thriving. Following the methods described by Geraldine Moane, women can learn to realize their own power and communicate contagious courage and pride even in the midst of oppressive conditions. Drawing on the cauldron of women's experiences, she aims to shatter the casings that keep women from discovering the source of deep purposefulness that makes possible growth, adaptation and creation. Her goal is to cause volcanic eruptions in women's psyches so that they can whirl away in all directions from the death-march of patriarchy.

I am particularly impressed by the practicality of her book. She identifies the important interconnecting mechanisms of patriarchal control, including violence, political exclusion, economic and sexual exploitation and dissemination of phallocratic ideology. She specifies in detail how patriarchy grinds women down physically, mentally, emotionally and spiritually. Standing firm in her belief that 'You can't keep a good woman down', she proposes and spells out strategies which can spark a tremendous uprising of women, such as building self-confidence, developing a sense of history, cultivating creativity, making connections and fostering solidarity. These strategies can enable women and all who resist the state of possession to join together, to overcome separation and fragmentation, to realize our connectedness and powers of creation, to craft the New Reality that we long for so deeply.

Geraldine Moane's analysis and directives are based on years of experience in the Irish and American women's liberation movements. Recalling the powerful events of the seventies and beyond, she reminds wild women of our great and ancient heritage. Refusing to be defeated by the doldrums of the 'millennial times', she catches the torch passed down by her foresisters through the ages. She urges her readers to wake up and continue the struggle for liberation.

MARY DALY
Crystal Lake,
Newton Center, MA

Mary Daly, who died in January 2010, was a leading radical feminst who published eight books, describing herself as a Positively Revolting Hag and a Crafty Pirate/Voyager.

Acknowledgements

This work began with what seemed like a simple question, asked a long time ago, namely, why is it that a small number of people can keep a large number of people in a state of oppression? Over the years, this led to the related questions of what is involved in breaking out of oppression and how can we bring about the radical social transformations that are now so badly needed. While these questions are of concern to a great number of people in different locations, this book focuses particularly on the role of psychology, and of psychological understanding, in addressing these questions.

The first edition of this book was the outcome of a long period of engagement with questions about oppression and liberation that began in the post-colonial Irish context of the 1970s, a period of economic underdevelopment combined with the (re)emergence of liberation movements informed particularly by socialist and feminist ideas. Teaching in the fields of psychology and women's studies along with political activism provided a crucial catalyst for clarifying the ideas and for furthering the analysis. Writers who were particularly influential in the development of the analysis include Mary Daly, Jean Baker Miller, bell hooks, Frantz Fanon, Mary Robinson and Steve Biko, along with numerous other writers in feminist and post-colonial theory and psychology. I adopted the phrase 'liberation psychology' which at the time had origins in several different contexts and has since been increasingly associated with the writings of the Latin American psychologist Martín Baró and colleagues.

Publication of the first editon in 1999 coincided with the flourishing of women's studies in Ireland and internationally, and also with increasing efforts to develop psychologies that would engage with oppression, liberation and social justice issues. Writers in these areas that were particulalry helpful include Erica Burman, Rose Capdevila, Michelle Fine, Lisa Goodman, Sheila Greene, M. Brinton Lykes, Maritza Montero, Isaac Prilleltensky, Ral Quiones Rosado, Rhoda Unger, and Sue Wilkinson.

Along with many others in Ireland and internationally, I have had the opportunity to put liberation psychology into practice in several different contexts, and these experiences have contributed immeasurably to greater understandings of oppression and liberation that have been incorporated into this second edition. I would particularly like to acknowledge the rich experiences, insights and challenges that course and workshop participants brought to bear in exploring oppression and liberation.

Feedback from readers of the first edition from a wide range of backgrounds has consistently indicated that the book provides personal insights and political understanding in an accessible way, and that it has often been inspirational and even life-changing. The book has been cited in a wide variety of sources and is acknowledged by many as a pioneering and valuable contribution to understandings of oppression and liberation. All of these factors provided the motivation to produce a revised paperback edition that would hopefully retain the strengths of the first edition while also reflecting developments since then.

This second edition, like the first, is dedicated to my parents whose commitment to fairness and equality has been evident throughout their lives. I especially acknowledge Sonya Mulligan for her constant love, inspiration, courage, strength and creativity. I would also like to thank all my family members. Friends, colleagues, students, political allies and many others have provided support, inspiration and challenge. It would be impossible to name everyone who contributed over so many years. I would like to acknowledge John Baker, Kathy Barry, Ursula Barry, Eimear Burke, Teresa Burke, Helen Burke, Sara Cantillon, Martina Carroll, Maeve Casey, Sally Clifton, Mary Condren, Kay Conroy, Joni Crone, Claire Cullen, Margaret Daly, Mary Daly, Tricia Darragh, Marie Davis, Kay Ferriter, Vivienne Glanville, Sheila Greene, Celine Leonard, Kathleen Lynch, Margaret MacCurtain, Mary McAuliffe, Eunice McCarthy, Rhona McCarthy, Mary McDermott, Irene McIntosh, Evelyn Mahon, Gerardine Meaney, Joan Mullan, Pat O'Connor, Monica O'Connor, Katherine O'Donnell, Mary O'Sullivan, Jackie O'Toole, Carolyn Phinney, Patricia Prendiville, Sean Ruth, Finn Reygan, Claire Sawtell, Eilis Stanley, Hilary Tierney, Mary Paula Walsh, Niamh Wilson and Olive Wilson.

Colleagues and students in University College Dublin, particularly in the School of Psychology, the School of Social Justice (Women's Studies and Equality Studies), the Egalitarian World Initiative, and other schools in Arts, Celtic Studies and Human Sciences have provided a supportive and stimulating environment for the development and implementation of liberation psychology. Additional insights were gained by collaborations with colleagues in Trinity College Dublin, University College Cork, National University of Ireland Maynooth, University of Brighton, Boston College, Boston University, Harvard University, University of California Berkeley, University of Prince Edward Island and University of Fort Hare.

I would also like to thank a variety of allies from various political groups – Irish Women United, Dublin Rape Crisis Centre, Dublin Lesbian Line Collective, Women's Coalition, Lesbians Organizing Together, Psychologists for Freedom of Information, Freedom from Pornography Campaign, Hanna's House and Women's Aid. The Sexual Diversity and Gender Issues Special Interest Group of the Psychological Society of Ireland and Organizations for Survivors of Institutional Abuse have encouraged further analysis. The Irish Institute for Counselling and Psychotherapy Studies and the Irish Centre for Shamanic Studies have also been important sources of inspiration.

Material support is a vital component in providing time and resources for writing and research. I would like to acknowledge the many sources of fellowships and scholarships that contributed to the work of this book. These include the Economic and Social Research Institute Dublin, University College Dublin, University of California Berkeley, Fulbright Commission, American Association of University Women and the Marie Curie Transfer of Knowledge Programme.

I would finally like to thank the staff at Palgrave Macmillan, and particularly the late Jo Campling who commissioned the first edition of this book.

1
Women, Psychology and Society: The Personal is Political

The phrase 'the personal is political' is one which has resonated through the women's movement, and other liberation movements, for many years. It continues to be relevant today. In the globalized world of the twenty-first century we are experiencing dramatic changes linked to large scale economic and political forces that can often appear to be beyond our control. The downturn in the global economic system and climate change are two examples that are global in scale, and have significant impact on our daily lives. Traditional political methods can seem limited in the capacity to shape these patterns. Yet consumer choices and technological advances allow for new forms of social networking and political mobilization that may provide opportunities to shape the political in diverse ways.

The insight that the personal and the political can shape each other is at the core of this book, in which I wish to explore the connections between psychological patterns and the political and social conditions associated with oppression and liberation. In order to do this I will draw primarily on writings in the psychology of women, colonialism and feminist theory, and on women's experiences of personal and political change. My aim is first to develop an understanding of how social conditions, particularly oppressive social conditions, can create debilitating psychological patterns, often referred to as 'internalized oppression', and secondly to identify processes and practices which can aid in transforming oppressive psychological and social patterns and attaining liberation. A practical objective is to gather and consolidate a comprehensive body of theory and a range of positive practices in a presentation which will be useful to women and minorities, whether they wish merely to be informed or seek to actively participate in the search for liberation and full equality at the personal and political levels.

1

My analysis of oppression and liberation is at two levels. One is the sociological level, identifying patterns of society associated with oppression which are particularly relevant for understanding psychological development. In particular, society is seen as hierarchical, and the first part of this analysis draws on feminist writers and writers on colonialism to identify the social mechanisms by which hierarchy is maintained and controlled. The second level is the psychological, focusing on psychological and behavioural patterns, the realm of individual thoughts, feelings and actions. A psychological analysis of oppression identifies the psychological and behavioural patterns associated with being relatively dominant or subordinate in a hierarchical system, while a psychological analysis of liberation explores the psychological processes involved in developing the capacities to take action to bring about social change. A psychology of liberation, or a liberation psychology, aims to use these insights to facilitate personal and social transformation.

The analysis was motivated by observing the striking parallels between what feminist psychologists such as Jean Baker Miller (1986) have written about the psychology of women, and what writers on the psychology of colonialism such as Frantz Fanon (1967a; 1967b) have written about the psychological effects of being colonized. Additionally, both feminist social psychologists and writers on colonialism seek to understand the processes involved in breaking out of oppression. My ultimate goal is the development of what may be called a feminist liberation psychology. Such a psychology would engage with thoughts and feelings, as do traditional psychologies, but would clearly link these to structures of power, as do radical psychologies. It would emphasize the histories and communities which form contexts of development, rather than focusing primarily on family of origin. It would strive for building of bonds, fostering of solidarity, releasing anger, cultivating creativity and engaging in collective action, rather than the individual and private exploration of thoughts and feelings. It would emphasize action and engagement, rather than self-absorption and disengagement. In short, it would clearly integrate the personal and the political.

The analysis offered in this book is quite different in its aims and content from traditional psychological analyses, which have rarely addressed questions related to oppression, as feminist and other radical critiques of psychology have emphasized. It aims to provide a systematic elaboration of the insight which is fundamental not only to feminist theorizing, but also to other emancipatory analyses, namely that personal and psychological factors as well as social conditions play a role in both oppression and liberation. This book aims to build on the insights which have already been offered by the many writers on feminism and colonialism to be reviewed below by developing a model which will systematically link areas of psychological functioning to structural features of oppression. It will then develop an analysis of liberation by drawing on the experiences of women involved in the women's liberation movement to chart the processes involved in transforming the psychological patterns associated with oppression and taking action to bring about change. Further insights will be gained from liberation psychologies that have been emerging around the world, particularly in the last ten years, offering theoretical and practical insights into personal and social transformation. This chapter will provide a historical overview of the themes of this book drawing on key writers, and an outline of how the developments of the last ten years have been incorporated into this revised and expanded paperback edition.

'The personal is political'

The phrase 'the personal is political' was coined in the early days of the women's liberation movement in the United States (Hanisch, 1971; Freeman, 1975). It developed out of the realization that experiences which were thought to be purely personal, such as those to do with sexuality, emotions and relationships, were actually shaped by the social and political forces of society. By describing their experiences in rap or consciousness-raising and other groups, women gained the insight that their own individual experience was shared by other women. The following quotation regarding consciousness-raising, from Jo Freeman (1975, p. 118), illustrates many of the central themes of this book:

> From this public sharing comes the realization that what was thought to be individual is in fact common; what was thought to be a personal problem has a social cause and a political solution. The rap group attacks the effects of psychological oppression and helps women to put it into a feminist context. Women learn to see how social structures and attitudes have molded them from birth and limited their opportunities. They ascertain the extent to which women have been denigrated in this society and how they have developed prejudices against themselves and other women. They learn to develop self-esteem and to appreciate the value of group solidarity.

In this quotation there is an identification of psychological oppression and its links to social conditions, an acknowledgement of the importance of building self-esteem and fostering solidarity, and the recognition that political and social change is essential for personal change.

Feminist analysis and research continued to document the connections between the personal and the political over the following decades in areas previously either ignored or regarded as the isolated personal experiences of particular individuals. Documentation of the prevalence of rape and violence against women, and examination of the laws and institutions of society, clearly demonstrated that violence against women was socially structured and played a role in upholding power differences between men and women (Brownmiller, 1975; Dworkin, 1981). Women's experiences of sexuality were linked to legal, religious and economic institutions of society which controlled and regulated sexual, emotional and economic relationships (Faderman, 1981; Koedt, 1973; Rich, 1980). The understanding of motherhood was extended to encompass the economic, ideological and religious forces which shaped the individual mother's experiences of joy, love, anger, dependency and isolation (Chodorow, 1978; Rich, 1976).

Feminist analyses, and the emerging area of the psychology of women and feminist psychology, extended the analysis to mental health and to areas such as the self, identity, emotions, friendships and sexual relationships, creativity and spirituality. The social construction of gender, and concepts such as sex roles, became central in explaining women's psychology. As later critiques noted, these concepts, while successfully linking personal experiences to social conditions, were both too general in assuming that sex roles operated similarly across different social groups, and too narrow in failing to link sex roles with broader economic and cultural forces. Feminist psychologies aim to address this by placing power differentials at the centre of their analysis. Thus while an early 'psychology of women' approach to depression might link it to the restrictions of sex roles, a feminist approach would place it in the context of women's economic dependency, negative cultural stereotypes, or sexual violence (Kaschak, 1992; Unger and Crawford, 1992; Wilkinson (ed.), 1996; Ussher, 1991).

While the emphasis in the early women's liberation movement was on the impact of the political on the personal, there was also an acknowledgement of the impact of the personal on the political. This was an important development for women who were excluded and alienated from traditional political processes. It challenged the traditional meaning of 'political' as 'that concerned with government and the state', a meaning which had also been challenged by civil rights and other activists. It asserted that actions ranging from an insistence on using

[margin handwritten note: The sexual structures controlled emotional and economic relationships]

non-sexist language to challenging heterosexuality could be seen as political and could contribute to social change (Douglas, 1990).

As the phrase 'the personal is political' permeated different areas of discourse and analysis, a number of different interpretations developed, some of which undermined the potency of the original slogan. The belief that all aspects of the personal were linked to the political could lead to crippling self-awareness and constant guilt over the way that everyday actions could be supporting the status quo. The idea that everything at the personal level could somehow influence the political meant that personal change itself, even in a therapeutic context, could be seen as political. Differing interpretations of the link between the personal and the political became more complex and fluid over time as new understandings of identity, power and politics emerged (Bhavnani and Phoenix, 1994; Landrine and Russo, 2009).

Obviously there are difficult and complex issues which lie within the scope of the phrase 'the personal is political'. What will be kept clearly in the mind for the present is the insight that the personal is influenced and shaped by the political and social context. In order to understand the personal, it is therefore necessary to focus on the political and social context. Furthermore, if psychological patterns are shaped by social conditions, then psychological change must be linked to changes in social conditions. Facilitating personal and political change is therefore an important goal for a liberation psychology.

Psyche and society

The phrase 'the personal is political' is one of the many which recognize the essential interconnectedness of psyche and society. The premise that psyche and society shape each other is fundamental to this book. Indeed it is a premise of almost all contemporary approaches in psychology. Even the most extreme biological determinist acknowledges that environmental factors play an important role in influencing individual psychological development. The importance of the environment in relation to genetic and biological factors has been highlighted in debates about cloning, where it is acknowledged that an individual cloned from a mature adult, although genetically identical, could not turn out to have identical psychological characteristics, because she or he would develop in a different family and cultural context. Conversely, approaches which view psychological development as shaped primarily by environmental and cultural factors agree that the individual plays an active role in mediating their effects. Individuals actively construct their understandings of the world, and shape the environments in which they develop. Thus two individuals in an identical environment will, to some extent, experience and be shaped by different aspects of that environment, and will also shape aspects of the environment themselves.

This basic premise, that psyche and society shape each other, is elaborated in diverse ways by the many theoretical frameworks – psychoanalytic, social constructionist, discursive, cognitive behavioural, feminist, evolutionary – which inform contemporary theorizing in psychology. Various phrases such as constructionist, interactionist, dialectical and ecological are used to capture the dynamic relationship between the individual and the social context. For the purposes of this book I will draw on a framework which is widely used in developmental psychology and elsewhere, namely that presented by Bronfenbenner (1979) in his book *The Ecology of Human Development.* Bronfenbrenner used the word 'ecology', borrowed from biology, to refer to the biological and social systems in which humans develop across the lifespan. He recognized the importance of the immediate environment, as most approaches in psychology do, and developed the concept of a social ecology to encompass the broader social system in which the immediate environment is embedded. He proposed a model of the person as placed in a series of four concentric circles of influence from the immediate personal level to the broader socio-political level. The ecological model, and other forms of dynamic systems theory, became influential in many areas of psychology, and are particularly useful for understanding the links between psyche, society and the natural ecology. It also acknowledges the ongoing mutual influences of humans and environments over time (Bronfenbrenner, 2004).

Bronfenbrenner suggests that society at large impacts on the individual through its influence on the microsystem or the immediate settings in which individuals live their lives. The immediate settings are the household, neighbourhood, school, workplace, leisure centres and other physical arenas in which individuals are physically placed. In the course of a day, and across their lives, individuals move from one micro setting to the next. It is within the micro setting that social interaction takes place, whether it be face-to-face interaction, or interaction with culture, mass media, and so on. Bronfenbrenner referred to society at large as the exo and the macro level. The exosystem level consists of social structures – politics, economics, education, mass media, art, religion – while the macrosystem consists of their products – culture and ideology. For the sake of clarity, and in line with common usage in sociology, I will combine the exosystem and macrosystem and refer to both of them as the macro level (Giddens, 2006). In between the micro and the macro level is an intermediate level, the meso level, which corresponds primarily to the community or organizational level of society. The meso system is the collection of settings in which individuals operate, and it is also shaped by social structures and ideology. All of the levels influence each other and shape and are shaped to varying degrees by the individual. Individuals are often relatively unaware of the macro level – it impacts on the individual through shaping the immediate settings (micro level) and organizations (meso level) in which the individual is embedded. The majority of individuals exercise their influence most directly at the micro level. It is primarily through organizing at the meso level that they have an impact on the macro level.

The example of education will illustrate these three levels. At the micro level, educational settings consist of the specific physical settings – classrooms, libraries, and so on – in which the individual is physically present. These settings are characterized by place, resources, activities and people. At the meso level, education consists of the organizations – schools, universities, community colleges, daytime education centres – which contain these settings, and it also consists of organizations such as trade unions and parent organizations. At the macro level, education consists of political structures, educational policy and ideology.

The micro level is the immediate level at which the individual both shapes and is shaped by society. Individuals are born into and develop in particular settings which shape them, and within these settings they make particular choices of who or what to interact with. For example, particular family dynamics will influence individual psychological development, but individuals also have an influence on the families into which they are born, or which they form later in life. Mass media and discourse generally, which are at the macro level, shape individual development, but individuals can choose (within limits) the types of discourses to which they are exposed, and also interpret and otherwise mediate the impact of mass media and other cultural inputs. Psychological development and psychological change are not privatized individualized processes which happen regardless of social context, but are intrinsically and dynamically related to the individual's specific social context. Indeed, it is one of the fallacies of many models in psychology and psychotherapy and also of the self-help movement that it is possible to change the individual without changing the social context (McLellan, 1995; Rapping, 1996; Smail, 2001).

Both the nature of the settings and the choices available to individuals are influenced considerably by their status in society: for example, gender and class. Individuals growing up in poverty will spend their time in settings characterized by deprivation – poor housing, inadequately resourced schools, deprived neighbourhoods – while individuals growing up with privileged backgrounds will spend their time in enriched settings. Gender will also shape individual settings – within the household girls will often have fewer resources than boys, girls' schools may offer a narrower range of subjects, girls lack access to sport and other leisure activities, girls receive less and different kinds of attention from teachers and other figures. Resources and choices at the micro level will influence life opportunities such as access to higher education and employment. In adulthood, class and gender will continue to influence the choices and opportunities available to individuals (Bronfenbrenner, 2004).

This discussion highlights the fact that the social context is shaped by class and gender. Other social statuses such as race, ethnicity, disability and sexual orientation also influence the social context. The interaction between the individual and society is not one of equal reciprocal influence, as many psychological theories assume. Individuals with privileged status in society are favoured by more enriched environments, have more choices in their lives, and have more opportunities to influence society, while those from underprivileged backgrounds are disadvantaged by deprived environments, have fewer choices in their lives, and have more limited opportunities to shape society (Nelson and Prilleltensky, 2004; Queralt, 1996). The importance of power and status differentials in shaping individual development is highlighted by this discussion, and is implicit in the phrase 'the personal is political'.

Patriarchy

Power differentials, that is, differences in access to power and resources, are a central feature of the social context from a feminist perspective (Richardson and Robinson, 2008; Tong, 2009; Walby, 1997, 2009). In modern Western societies power differentials are systematically related to gender. Men are more likely to be favoured by power differentials, or to be dominant, while women are more likely to be disadvantaged by power differentials, or to be subordinate. Power differentials are also related to social categories such as class, race, ethnicity, religion, sexual orientation and other social statuses. Feminists have elaborated the concept of patriarchy to capture the systematic manner in which power is concentrated in the hands of men, whether this involves political or economic power, or the capacity to shape dominant social discourses or worldviews (Daly, 1978; Millett, 1970; Walby, 1990).

An enormous body of research both by feminists and by national and international agencies has now accumulated, documenting patterns of male domination. Globally, for example, women hold around 6 per cent of cabinet seats and around 10 per cent of seats in parliament (United Nations, 2005). In Western societies the percentage of women in parliament ranges from a high of over 40 per cent in Norway, Sweden and Finland to around 15 per cent in Ireland, the United Kingdom and the USA, and to a low of less than 10 per cent in France and Belgium (Seager, 2003; Walby, 2004). Economically, women earn around 10 per cent of the world's wages and own around 1 per cent of the world's property (United Nations, 2005). In Western societies, including the United States, women's earnings are around 80 per cent of men's earnings (Seager, 2003; Walby, 2004). These figures are general indicators – a great deal of feminist research in sociology, politics and economics is oriented towards documenting changes and variations as well as analysing underlying patterns associated with these indicators (Richardson and Robinson, 2009; Tong, 2009; Walby, 2009).

The term 'patriarchy' was borrowed from anthropology and sociology, where it was used to refer to societies characterized by patrilineage (tracing ancestry through the father) and rule of women and younger men by older men through their positions as head of the household. The term captures two themes of importance to feminists. One is the theme of domination of women by men, or a gender analysis. The other is the theme of differential access to power by men, or a class analysis. Historical and cultural variation is also acknowledged around the central theme of male domination. Millett, one of the first feminists to elaborate the concept of patriarchy, points out that 'While patriarchy as an institution is a social constant so deeply entrenched as to run through all other political, social, or economic forms, whether of caste or class, feudality or bureaucracy, just as it pervades all major religions, it also exhibits great variety in history and locale' (1970, p. 46).

The concept of patriarchy has provoked much discussion and debate among feminists (Tong, 2009; Whelehan, 1995). Some argue against viewing male domination and female subordination as systematically patterned and institutionalized. This counter-argument is made by liberal feminists who acknowledge that there is inequality between men and women in society, but who view women's subordination as the outcome of a number of small scale inequalities. It is also made by post-modernist and post-structuralist feminists, who see power as dispersed rather than located in social structures, and who challenge the unity of the categories 'man' and 'woman'.

These counter-arguments challenge a monolithic concept of patriarchy as involving the domination of all women by all men. Critiques by women of colour, Native women, lesbians and poor women that the concept overlooks differences among women, especially along the lines of race, class and sexual orientation, have also contributed to a more complex elaboration of the term (Collins, 1990; Mohanty et al., 1991; 2003; Penelope, 1994). The term still captures the widespread acknowledgement that women's subordination is patterned and socially institutionalized. Walby (1990, p. 20) refers to patriarchy as a 'system of social structures and practices', and notes that 'The use of the term social structure is important here, since it clearly implies rejection both of biological determinism, and the notion that every individual man is in a dominant position and every woman in a subordinate one' (p. 20).

Patriarchy in the Western context can thus be viewed as a social system which is first of all hierarchical: that is, it can be characterized as a pyramid where a small percentage of people have access to most of the wealth and power, while large numbers have little access to wealth and power. It is secondly male dominated, in that it is mostly men who have access to power. It is also the case that those who have access to power in Western societies are most likely to be white and heterosexual. It can be seen as a global system, in which global as well as local positions of power are held primarily by men. Thus there are class, race and gender dimensions to patriarchy, and there are also, as noted above, historical and cultural variations. A great deal of feminist theorizing has been devoted to clarifying these dimensions of patriarchy, and also to addressing questions regarding the origins, dynamics and development of patriarchy.

The question that will be addressed in this book is how psychological development is influenced by patriarchy, which is viewed as a hierarchical system. Feminist research on patriarchal patterns will be combined with writings on colonialism to provide an analysis of how power differentials are institutionalized and maintained at the macro or societal level and to highlight how this has implications for day-to-day life, or the micro level. This will then provide the basis for an analysis of the psychological patterns associated with hierarchy.

Colonialism

Historically, colonialism has referred to a system whereby one country implants settlers in a distant country with the aim of economically exploiting and/or politically dominating that country. More recently, the word 'colonialism' has been used in a variety of settings to encompass political, economic, cultural and psychological colonization, political and cultural decolonization, neo-colonialism, post-colonialism, imperialism and post-imperialism. At the heart of these concepts is a relationship of domination – subordination. Colonialism is of interest in this work because many explorations of colonialism have focused considerable attention on gender, power and domination, and therefore offer fertile ground for insights into the workings of hierarchical systems (McLeod, 2007; Said, 1993).

In the context of Western Europe and the USA, colonization refers to the conquest and settlement of territories by European countries, especially by Britain and France, but also by Spain, Portugal, Belgium, Germany, Sweden, Italy and the Netherlands (Ferro, 1997). By 1914, over three-quarters of the globe, including most of Africa, Asia, South America and the Caribbean and Pacific Islands, was economically and/ or politically dominated by Western powers, including the United States. Colonial domination was supported by military force, by economic ties, and by cultural control, and was justified by an ideology which emphasized native inferiority and the benefits of colonization. As in the case of patriarchy, there has been considerable debate about the systematic nature of colonization, about the extent of domination and exploitation, about the role of colonized people in seeking or colluding with colonization, and about the legacies of colonialism.

The Irish example highlights many of these debates (Caherty, 1992; Carroll and King, 2003; Kinealy, 2008; Lee, 1989). Systematic colonization of Ireland by the English through military conquest and land plantations began in the sixteenth century, offering a considerable period of time for the study of colonial patterns which has been the subject of voluminous research. During this time there were a number of military invasions and defeats by the British, yet in many cases some of the native Irish allied with the invaders. Irish land was appropriated and settled by the British, yet some of the descendants of these settlers became allies in the Irish struggle for independence from Britain. Irish political and economic structures were replaced and sometimes subsumed by British structures, but some natives turned this to their own advantage. Resistance to colonization was often undertaken by a minority whose efforts were undermined by apathy and betrayal.

The aim here is not to deny the reality of colonial domination – Irish history includes slaughter and rape by British armies, penal laws which deprived natives of land and political rights, economic policies which resulted in mass famine and emigration, and cultural policies which resulted in the virtual erasure of the indigenous language (Curtis, 1994; Kinealy, 2008; Lee, 1989). It is rather to acknowledge that systems of domination rarely involve total domination of one group as a whole by another group as a whole.

Decolonization historically referred to national movements to resist colonization and to gain political independence. It expanded to refer to economic, political, social and cultural transformations that might be required to obtain freedom from colonial patterns and the attainment of a level of self-definition and self-determination (Chinweizu, 1987; Ruane, 1986; Thiongo, 1986; Trask, 1993). These transformations may begin in a colonial context, and continue into the post-colonial period, where 'post-colonial' refers to a situation in which national political freedom from colonial rule has been achieved. The word 'imperialism' can refer to political, economic or cultural domination, usually of formerly colonized countries by colonizer countries, but also to refer to new attempts at military domination, such as by the US under the Bush adminstration (Enloe, 2007). Whether the analysis is political, economic or cultural, it is clear that there are largescale inequalities of power and resources between countries that have been historically colonized and those that have historically been colonizers. The current global economic system, dominated by the International Monetary Fund and the G8 (Canada, France, Germany, Italy, Japan, Russia, Britain and the United States) is clearly linked to colonialism, involving continuing exploitation of global planetary resources, increasing concentration of wealth in the elites of the G8, and increasing impoverishment of the global majority. The collapse of the global financial system may ultimately exacerbate global inequalities, and/or may create opportunities for new economic, political and cultural forms. Such new forms may arise from bottom-up mobilization for change, which is a central focus of this book.

Colonialism is of interest in this book primarily because it is a system whose explicit aim is one of domination and exploitation, and because it also offers models of liberation from domination and exploitation through the processes of decolonization which have occurred in the Irish and other contexts. While it is probably most accurate to see colonialism as a form of patriarchy, I would prefer to view them as separate though interlocking systems in this work. Clearly, the experience of colonization is gendered: that is, it is experienced differently by men and by women. Furthermore, constructions of gender have served the interests of colonial domination,

and colonial domination has produced ideologies and cultural practices which buttress patriarchy.

Psychological analyses of oppression

So far it has been argued that the social and political context shapes
psychological development, that a central feature of the social and
political context is that it is hierarchical, and that hierarchical systems
involve domination and subordination. Subordination may be regarded
as oppressive when it involves an individual or group being controlled
against their will, and when systematic patterns are used to enforce
subordination. In this book oppression is used to refer to patterns of
poverty, marginalization, prejudice, violence and discrimination that
are linked to economic, political and cultural structures of inequality in society. These structures are considered in detail in Chapter 2.
Oppression is associated with repression, suppression, isolation, marginality, social exclusion, poverty and powerlessness.

A psychological analysis of oppression involves a systematic explor-
tion of the links between oppression and areas of psychological
functioning such as emotions, sexuality, identity, self-concept and self-
esteem, psychological distress and madness, and interpersonal relationships. In a broad sense, psychological analyses of oppression have been
undertaken from a variety of perspectives. They include fictional and
autobiographical accounts of the experience of oppression, historical
and political commentaries which allude to psychological patterns,
and explicit theoretical analyses by psychiatrists, psychoanalysts, psychologists and psychotherapists. They may be derived from a variety
of social contexts, influenced by race, class, gender, ethnicity and sexual orientation. Early examples of writers who discuss psychological
aspects of oppression include Miller's (1986) analysis of the impact of
domination–subordination on women, Fanon's (1967a; 1967b) description of the damage of colonialism, hooks' (1993; 2002b) account of the
impact of racism and sexism on black women, Maracle's (1996) writing
about the experience of being a Native woman, and Pharr's (1988) discussion of homophobia.

There can be little doubt from even a cursory examination of these
authors that oppression has a profound impact on psychological functioning. Exemplary themes include loss of identity, fear, powerlessness,
suppression of anger, isolation, ambivalence and sense of inferiority.
Such patterns clearly undermine the capacity of those in situations
of oppression to resist domination, and to take action to bring about

not everyone is oppressed (margin annotation)

change. Of course, as the foregoing discussion of psyche and society would imply, not every individual in a situation of oppression is a passive victim of oppression, nor does oppression affect everyone in the same way. On the contrary, as many of the above writers emphasize, individuals and groups often resist oppression with great tenacity, and both oppression and resistance are also associated with qualities such as courage and perseverance (Martín-Baró, 1994). Nevertheless, oppression creates considerable psychological difficulties for oppressed groups as clearly demonstrated in research in psychology (McAuliffe, 2008) and the social sciences (Wilkinson and Pickett, 2009).

Psychological analyses of liberation

Changes in the Personal is political social & psychological (margin annotation)

The concept of a liberation psychology, or a psychological analysis of liberation, emerged from contexts of resistance to patriarchal and colonial oppression (Bulhan, 1985; Martín-Baró, 1994; Starhawk, 1987). Although many of those who have provided a psychological analysis of oppression have also turned their attention to liberation, few have explicitly discussed the concept of a liberation psychology, or described the actual psychological processes and practices involved in liberation. It follows from the interrelationship between the personal and the political that liberation must involve psychological change as well as changing social conditions. A psychological analysis of liberation involves identifying psychological processes and practices which will transform the damage associated with oppression, and which will facilitate taking action to resist domination and bring about social change.

Early writers on the psychology of oppression offered extensive critiques of traditional psychologies, viewing them as part of the status quo and as often operating in oppressive ways. Critiques, which will be discussed more fully below, ranged from fundamental epistemological and methodological problems to the ethnocentrism, classism, racism and sexism of traditional psychologies to outright dismissal of any attempt to bring a psychological analysis to bear on what are seen as political issues. The US based African writer Bulhan, who provides a quite scathing critique of racism in psychology, summarizes some of these problems (1985, p. 256): 'Underlying much of prevailing psychological theory and practice are the ethic of individualism, the ideal of individual autonomy, a particular conception of basic human needs, as well as an exclusive emphasis on individual change, which together reflect fundamental cultural as well as class biases.'

As these critiques suggest, it is not sufficient merely to apply existing psychological theories to formerly neglected groups, or to attempt to remove racist, sexist and other biases. There is a need, for example, to redress the fundamental individualism of psychology, its emphasis on adjustment, and its neglect of powerlessness, inequality and marginality. The need for an emphasis on a collective rather than an individual focus is emphasized by Bulhan (1985, p. 259): 'A psychology tailored to the needs of the oppressed would give primacy to the attainment of "collective liberty" and, since such liberty is attained only by collectives, would emphasize how best to further the consciousness and organized action of the collective.' It is also captured by feminist psychologist Starhawk, one of the first to use the phrase 'liberation psychology' (1987, p. 23):   *Personal political*

> A psychology of liberation is one whose primary focus is the communities we come from and create. Our collective history is as important as our individual history. A liberation psychology is more concerned with how structures of power shape and bind us than with the particular events of our individual childhoods.... a liberation psychology is more concerned with ways of creating communal healing and collective change.

Fortunately in the last ten years there have been developments all over the globe of psychologies that aim to engage directly with oppression and liberation (e.g. Lykes and Moane, 2009; Montero and Sonn, 2009). Although still marginal to established North American and European psychology, these include feminist, post-colonial, critical and liberation psychologies that will be reviewed throughout this book, and especially in Chapter 8. These developing psychologies are based in feminist, political and community psychology, but insights about social justice and diversity issues are also developing in clinical psychology, psychotherapy and counselling. There is a converging understanding that psychological patterns are linked to political and social patterns, that is, to the macro level of society, and that to alleviate psychological distress and foster psychological growth and development requires social as well as psychological transformation. It is thus essential for a liberation psychology to acknowledge social and political conditions and their link to psychological patterns and to explicitly emphasize taking action to change social and political conditions. This will inevitably require a discussion of social and political change, as well as personal change, as writers on liberation psychology have argued.

a bridge

Bridging the gap between personal change or personal development and political change or political activism remains a challenge for feminist and other emancipatory movements. This analysis will therefore focus on change not only at the personal and political levels, but also at the interpersonal or meso level of relationships and community, which is a bridge between the personal and the political. The process of liberation will involve change at the personal, the interpersonal and the political levels, and this may be seen as a cycle of liberation. Changes at the personal level, such as developing identity, can facilitate interpersonal changes such as support and solidarity which in turn can assist in taking action to bring about change at the political level. Taking action itself can lead to more changes at the personal and interpersonal levels such as increased confidence, which facilitate further action, creating a cycle in which change at one level feeds into changes at the other levels. One of the fundamental aims of this book is to identify the processes and practices which will facilitate change at all three levels.

Critiques of psychology

The problems of individualism and of sexist, racist and class bias in psychology have already been alluded to. While many contemporary theoretical approaches in psychology acknowledge the importance of social context, and of the interaction between the individual and the social context, they may still be criticized for focusing on the individual and for failing to analyse adequately the impact of social conditions, and in particular, the impact of power differentials in society. Early critiques noted that psychological theorizing has tended to focus on the individual and provide accounts of psychological patterns such as depression or creativity which involve individual factors such as personality characteristics, or family dynamics, ignoring broader cultural and social factors (Bulhan, 1985; Fox and Prilleltensky, 1997; Wilkinson, 1996).

A classic example of this trend is the development of Freud's psychoanalytic theory. Freud's theorizing was based in part on women patients whose psychological distress manifested itself in the form of physical symptoms such as vomiting, paralysis or loss of speech, a condition diagnosed at the time as 'hysteria'. In pursuing the origins of these symptoms, Freud found that many of his patients recalled having been sexually abused as children, and he formulated the hypothesis that hysteria was caused by early childhood trauma. The publication of his hypothesis resulted in a storm of controversy familiar to contemporary readers. In the face of this Freud reformulated his hypothesis to suggest that children had fantasies of sexual contact with adults, and that it was the repression of these fantasies that lay at the root of adult hysteria. This then led to his exploration of the inner workings of the mind, to the neglect and indeed distortion of societal dynamics (Chodorow, 1994; Herman, 1981; Masson, 1984).

This episode in the history of psychoanalysis has of course been the subject of intense discussion and debate over the years. My purpose in recounting it is to highlight the pattern of exclusively focusing on the person, and also to draw attention to the political context of psychological theory. In this instance, a form of psychological distress which was found primarily in women was explained as a function of intrapsychic dynamics. The actual reality of child abuse was erased, and gender and power dimensions were ignored. The implications of this for psychological practice were profound. Women's accounts of childhood sexual abuse were dismissed as fantasy, psychiatrists and psychotherapists believed themselves to have greater access to women's consciousness than women themselves, and the cure for women's psychological distress was, at best, to focus on women's 'feelings about their feelings', and, at worst, to institutionalize women in psychiatric hospitals (Chesler, 1972; 2006). Psychoanalytic theory established the basic assumption that both the cause and the cure for women's psychological distress lay in women's own thoughts and feelings, rather than in the social context in which women lived their lives, an assumption which continues to dominate psychological and psychiatric practice. Its influence on public discourse is illustrated by debates over 'false memory', where women are accused of manufacturing memories of childhood sexual abuse (Brown and Burman, 1997; Haakin and Reavey, 2009).

Another example of psychological theory which has been widely influential in society generally is that of humanistic psychology, or the human potential movement, which owes its origins to Abraham Maslow and Carl Rogers. In focusing on the creative and growthful aspects of psychological functioning, Maslow and Rogers provided an important counterpart to the emphasis of psychoanalysis on sexuality and aggression. Yet neither theorist paid attention to the ways in which the social context would foster or inhibit psychological growth and development. Growth and development, or what is now quite often called personal development, was seen as a process involving primarily personal practices – exploration of dreams and fantasies, release of emotions, affirmations and various other individual and group practices.

Critics of psychoanalysis and the human potential movement viewed this emphasis on the person and on private individualized experience as a form of mystification which obscures the role of social conditions in creating psychological distress, reflecting racist, sexist and class bias (Rapping, 1996; Smail, 2001).

Feminist critiques of psychology and psychiatry initially focused on the treatment of mental illnesses in psychiatric settings. Chesler's (1972) groundbreaking work *Women and Madness* placed the treatment of women's mental illness firstly in the context of radical views which emphasized the social construction of madness and the destructive effects of institutionalization, psychosurgery, electric shock treatment and drug treatment (Laing, 1961; Szasz 1972). Chesler documented the double standards and abuses which were applied to women in psychiatric settings. Psychological distress in women was more often attributed to biological factors which supposedly rendered women intrinsically weak and prone to mental illness. Women were admitted in much larger numbers to psychiatric hospitals, often by their husbands or male relatives and often against their will. Women were kept in psychiatric hospitals for longer periods, were more likely to receive electric shock treatment, and suffered sexual abuse and sexual harassment in psychiatric hospitals and other settings. The misogyny and mystification of the psychiatric system is manifested most obviously perhaps in the profusion of 'blame the mother' theories which have been invoked to account for deficiencies in both male and female development. These theories coexisted with the assumption of women as intrinsically weak and inferior, an assumption which was evident in discourses about women's psychological distress, and women's psychology generally.

In a classic critique of psychology which is still widely read, Weisstein (1968, 1970, 1993) summarized the assumptions about women which were found in traditional psychological theory. Women were viewed as 'inconsistent, emotionally unstable, lacking in a strong conscience or superego, weaker, "nurturant" rather than productive, "intuitive" rather than intelligent, and, if they are at all normal, suited to life in the home and the family. In short, the list adds up to a typical minority group stereotype of inferiority' (Weisstein, 1970, p. 244). Psychological theorizing about women has frequently been based on research and theory developed with male samples or with males as the model, and then modified to apply to women. This produces a fundamental double standard identified by many writers – men are seen as the norm, women as deviant, and somehow almost always deficient or defective. From its foundation, psychological theory and research has provided support for the exclusion of women from public life based on women's inferior psychological capacities (Bohan, 1992; Sherif, 1979; Unger 1998).

Not only theory and research, but also the organization of the discipline of psychology itself reflects its embeddedness in patriarchal society. Like most disciplines, positions of power in psychology – heads of departments, editorships of journals, memberships of funding committees, officers in professional associations, senior positions in health services – are most often held by men, despite the enormous increase in women in psychology. Women researchers and theorists continue to be erased and omitted from 'the canon', and topics of central interest to women, such as menstruation and motherhood, receive relatively little attention (Denmark and Paludi, 2007).

Feminist critiques of psychotherapy and counselling have focused on similar themes of mystification, abuse and exploitation. Psychotherapy focuses attention on individual and private experiences without attending to the broader social context. In an early critique of psychotherapy, Mary Daly argues that the language and methods of psychotherapy constitute a system 'of creating and perpetuating false needs, of masking and maintaining depression, of focusing/draining women's energy' (1978, p. 280). She sees it as a form of social control, keeping women 'supine, objectified and degraded' (Daly, 1978, p. 229).

As psychotherapy, counselling, personal development, twelve-step and other programmes proliferated, feminists became increasingly critical of the obsessive preoccupation with the self and with feelings that these practices engendered (Kitzinger and Perkins, 1993; Rapping, 1996). They argued that too often women entered therapy for feelings such as depression, alienation and exhaustion, which could clearly be linked to oppression, and ended up focusing on their childhood and enmeshed in endless analysis of their feelings which left them feeling inadequate and confused. Friendships and communities were undermined as women sought support from therapists rather than from each other. The quest for the 'real' or 'inner' self left women 'locked into perpetual cycles of "self-discovery"' (Kitzinger and Perkins, 1993, p. 107). Kitzinger and Perkins argue that among many American and British lesbians (those, it must be added, who are middle class), psychotherapy and personal development have become substitutes for political action, concluding that 'we do not need psychology. Psychology is, and always will be, destructive of the lesbian/feminist enterprise' (p. 198).

It is clear then that there are very strong grounds for adopting a critical stance towards psychology as a discipline, a discourse and a practice. The oppressive nature of psychological theories and practices has also been noted in the context of racism and colonialism. Writing of the impact of colonialism, Bulhan (1985) charts the support that psychological research on intelligence and individual differences has provided for racist assumptions of white superiority. He argues that by developing hegemonic psychological models based on white middle-class samples (Bulhan did not attend to gender in his critique), psychology denies the existence and value of diversity. Treatments of psychopathology emphasize control and adjustment, and in their neglect and obfuscation of deprivation and oppression deny the reality of people's lives and render them silenced and helpless. These critiques led some to reject psychology and psychotherapy completely.

However, another response has been to try to develop radical or feminist approaches which are overtly political and which aim to illuminate women's oppressions and change social conditions (Brown, 1992; Burman, 1990; 2008; Wilkinson, 1986). In the editorial of the first issue of the journal *Feminism & Psychology*, Wilkinson writes that feminist psychology is committed to 'developing a psychology which properly represents women's concerns in all their diversity... and to the deployment of such a psychology to address a range of social inequalities (including, for example, race and class, as well as gender)' (Wilkinson, 1991, p. 5). Feminist psychology involves 'the acknowledgement and analysis of power differentials as central to social life' (p. 9). The diversity of feminist psychology grew to encompass a range of key topics for women that had been marginalized or absent in traditional psychology, for example sexual violence, racism, lesbian identity, homophobia, pornography, femininity, the body and social class (Clarke and Peel, 2007; Hesse-Biber, 2007; Landrine and Russo, 2009). As feminists in general developed their analysis to account for diversity and difference, feminist psychologies have developed in many directions theoretically and practically. Thus while feminist psychologies have in common a challenge to the oppressive nature of psychology and the aim of ending inequality and oppression, they may disagree over the means of achieving this.

This book presents a psychological analysis which clearly locates itself within the broad framework of feminist psychology. I would disagree with the complete rejection of psychological analysis advocated, for example, by Kitzinger and Perkins (1993). Internalized oppression is a theme which recurs in writings on women, racism, colonialism, homophobia and heterosexism, and other experiences of oppression. It is associated with psychological patterns which include self-hatred, sense of inferiority, helplessness and despair, mutual distrust and hostility, and psychological distress and madness. Internalized oppression is an obstacle to political activism, along with the obstacles posed by political and social forces, and oppressed groups have developed methods for confronting internalized oppression and diminishing its harmful effects. Radical and feminist psychological approaches which are self-critical and politically aware can offer insights and strategies for transformation in a variety of contexts. Rather than offering psychological explanations for the political, this book seeks to develop political explanations for psychological phenomena, and to harness psychological insights for political purposes.

Scope and aims of the book

When the first edition of this book was published in 1999, although there was a rich historical tradition, there was still relatively little work in psychology directly addressing oppression and a small emerging body of work that focused on liberation. The first edition of this book was one of the earliest to develop liberation psychology, and to integrate psychological writings in feminism and colonialism. Fortunately, since then the literature in psychology on oppression, liberation and social justice has gathered enormous momentum, producing a rich and diverse body of work from around the world, particularly in feminist, liberation, postcolonial, critical and community psychologies which will be reviewed in Chapter 8. As psychologists increasingly engaged with more diverse and sometimes marginalized and impoverished communities, the fields of clinical psychology, counselling and psychotherapy also developed their analysis of social justice issues, with feminist psychotherapy and counselling psychology playing a lead role.

There has been a growing recognition of the connections between psychological distress and social conditions such as poverty, racism and homophobia. Conversely, psychological well-being or wellness has been increasingly linked to social cohesion, equality and social justice, that is, to aspects of society as a whole, rather than just to individual personal history. Society itself has been conceptualized more fully as involving not only local and national levels, but also the global or transnational level. There has been a convergence in many fields on some of the central themes of this book, namely: that psychological patterns are shaped by social conditions; that social conditions must be conceptualized at the macro level as well as at the community and micro levels; that practices that aim to be transformative are more effective if they address, directly or indirectly, all three levels.

There have also, of course, been enormous social changes over the last decade. What began as an economic boom that held the promise of greater equality and better standards of living locally and globally has become an economic meltdown that threatens even greater levels of impoverishment and inequality. These dramatic economic events have highlighted the global nature of the economic system, and particularly the role of multinational corporations and financial and economic elites who operate across national boundaries and have enormous influence on national and transnational political, economic and cultural policies and practices. Political, economic and cultural power seem to have become more concentrated than ever in global consortia, with the G8 countries and increasingly China established as global economic and military powers. The exploitation of planetary resources has become completely unsustainable, threatening to push climate change to catastrophic levels (Enloe, 2007; Shiva, 2009).

Along with these indicators of structural domination have of course been movements of resistance and transformation that vary from UN global Human Rights initiatives to worldwide social movements to local subversive direct action. For a variety of reasons power has been recognized as dispersed beyond traditional political systems and has been exercised in many different contexts in many different ways. This has been discussed particularly in poststructuralist, post-modern and constructionist approaches in and beyond psychology. These approaches argue that individuals and groups may have multiple or complex identities that are constructed in specific contexts where gender, ethnicity, class, sexual orientation and other influences interact, sometimes in contradictory ways (Mohanty, 2003; Hesse-Biber, 2007). This highlights the complexity of everyday life at the individual level. Individuals are seen as moving through different spaces where power and subjectivity may be fluid, rather than (or along with) belonging to fixed categories embedded in a hierarchy. This book aims to provide a structural and systemic analysis that allows for these complexities, reflecting hopefully the creative tension that is also a feature of (post-)modern complex societies.

Irish society has also undergone enormous changes in the last decade, much of it linked to global economic developments that seemed to have shifted the Irish economy from a serious depression through the 1980s to the creation of a wealthy economy. A remarkable feature of the late 1990s through to 2008 for Irish society was a shift from a homogeneous culture with large scale emigration to a multi-ethnic and multicultural society with considerable immigration, especially from Eastern Europe but also from around the globe. There were other dramatic changes, many of them linked to legacies of Ireland's colonial history described more fully in Chapter 9. A negotiated agreement involving Northern Ireland, the Republic of Ireland and Britain reshaped political and economic relations and brought an end to armed conflict. The Catholic Church, whose dominance could be traced to colonialism, experienced severe collapse and total loss of credibility as patterns of physical and sexual abuse were documented along with a longstanding church policy of cover up and denial. Women gained economic, legal and reproductive rights, and equality legislation provided rights to many minorities.

In addition, following publication of the book I used the framework developed in the book and the theory and research that was available to deliver courses and workshops in liberation psychology in several community settings in Ireland (Moane, 2009). These courses and workshops were participatory, creating a space where students and workshop participants were involved in the course content and where knowledge and understanding were created based on their own viewpoints and experiences. This allowed for more detailed and specific elaboration of society as a system, of domination, of its impact on daily lives, of psychological patterns linked with oppression and liberation and of the factors involved in making changes on the path to liberation. Feedback from the courses highlighted the value of having a clear social analysis that took a systems perspective for understanding the dynamics of oppression and identifying the processes involved in personal and social transformation. It illustrated the negative psychological patterns for which the phrase internalized oppression has been used, but also highlighted psychological strengths that could be linked to oppression. The benefit of focusing on personal, interpersonal and political change through the cycle of liberation was evident. This new edition thus addresses psychological transformation and also builds further towards an understanding of social transformation, and of the role of individuals, groups and communities in bringing about social transformation.

This new edition retains the logic and structure of the first edition, and has been updated throughout to reflect developments. The book aims to contribute to the development of a liberation psychology that emphasizes personal and social transformation. Such a psychology presupposes an understanding of psychological and social patterns associated with oppression. Since psychological patterns are linked to social conditions, this approach starts with a social analysis of oppression. Understanding of psychological patterns associated with oppression and liberation is provided by reviewing key writers in feminism and colonialism who have elaborated their understanding of the psychological impact of oppression, and of the processes involved in liberation.

As noted above, liberation is seen as a cycle of change involving three levels, the personal, the interpersonal and the political.

Chapter 2 provides a historical and contemporary analysis of society as a system of domination and provides evidence for identifying patterns associated with oppression that function to maintain domination. Chapter 3 reviews writings on the psychological patterns associated with oppression and domination identified by selected feminist writers and by writers on colonialism. Chapter 4 continues the psychological analysis by identifying processes and practices which feminist writers and writers on colonialism have seen as liberating, or facilitating personal and social transformation. The following three chapters (5–7) provide elaboration of these processes and practices, expanding on the cycle of liberation based on further theory and research, and exemplified through experiences of those involved in liberation movements in Ireland and globally. Chapter 5 focuses on the level of personal change, identifying areas such as self-worth, sexuality, spirituality and sense of history that can contribute to personal strength. Chapter 6 explores the interpersonal level of making connections and developing solidarity especially in groups and communities, incorporating much new material on these topics. Chapter 7 addresses the political level through developing an understanding of social change and exploring options for action, again based on historical and contemporary examples. A new Chapter 8 provides a more in depth review of recent developments in feminist and liberation psychologies and related areas, with examples of applications of liberation psychology, including my own work. Chapter 9 continues a discussion of personal and social transformation. The analysis is further broadened to highlight the interconnections between different experiences of oppression and strategies for liberation. Since liberation ultimately involves an end to oppression and inequality it includes an exploration of some of the ideals and visions for liberation that have been articulated in the Irish context and globally by selected feminist and other writers on liberation, ranging through liberation psychology, transpersonal psychology, human rights and egalitarian worldviews.

While this book presents a general account of internalized oppression and of some of the processes involved in breaking out of that, it does not aim to provide a general theory, or a mechanistic cause and effect model with supposed universal applicability. Obviously oppression is experienced very differently by different individuals, who in turn respond in distinct ways. While the emphasis in the book is on the way social conditions shape psychological patterns, there is also a fundamental recognition of individual uniqueness, and of the fact that each individual, whether dominant or subordinate, negotiates, within limits, their own stance *vis-à-vis* their status.

Obviously the book will touch on psychological distress and madness, since this is clearly one possible outcome of being oppressed. In particular, patterns of depression and addiction recur in the writings reviewed in this book. However, the book does not focus exclusively on psychological distress, or aim to explain psychological distress. Psychological distress and madness are among the wide range of themes which arise in both feminist writings and writings on colonialism, themes which relate to the self and identity, emotions and interpersonal relationships. The aim is to describe these patterns, and to suggest that under conditions of oppression, individuals may experience some or all of them, at different times, and in different ways.

The focus of the book is on women, but it is not the intention to draw an analogy between 'woman' and 'colonized', and between 'men' and 'colonizer'. Certainly there is an argument to be made for such an analogy – analogies involving colonialism have been made in many contexts, ranging from the literary to the biological. Early examples include Robin Morgan, who writes that 'Women are a colonized people. Our history, values, and cross-cultural culture have been taken from us – a gynocidal attempt manifest most arrestingly in the patriarchy's seizure of our basic and precious "land": our own bodies' (1978, p. 161). Kathleen Barry (1979) uses the model of colonization in her book *Female Sexual Slavery* writing that 'Sex colonization is insidious. Not only are women dominated as a group – socially, politically, and economically – but unlike any other colonized group, they must share the homes and beds of their colonizer' (p. 195). In the Irish context, Lynch and O'Neill (1995) apply the concept to education and social class, arguing that 'the "colonized Other" in education must surely be the working class. It is the one about whom most has been said but who never speaks back' (p. 310).

I would prefer, for the purposes of this book, to confine my discussion of colonialism to the actual historical colonial domination of one country by another. The writings of and about women who have had this experience of colonialism will be discussed throughout the book. As outlined above, colonialism is regarded as an example of a system of domination, writings on the psychological aspects of colonialism are used to illuminate psychological patterns associated with domination and subordination, and decolonization provides insights into the processes involved in gaining liberation from such oppressive patterns at both the personal and the political level.

A vast array of writers from a variety of disciplines and from no disciplines have addressed the themes discussed in this book. I have chosen to confine myself to writings in feminist theory with a political orientation, to feminist and liberation psychologies and to writings on colonialism which provide a psychological perspective. I have departed from this primarily in the case of Irish writings, where I have drawn on a wider range of writers. One of the main strengths noted by readers of the first edition of this book is that it is written in a clear and accessible manner. I have aimed to maintain this accessibility by limiting references, for the most part, to key historical figures and contemporary publications that provide up-to-date material. The exception to this is in Chapter 8, where a detailed review of recent academic publications in liberation psychologies is provided. The book thus provides extensive up-to-date bibliographic material, key theoretical writings and many practical examples of liberation psychology in action.

2
Hierarchical Systems: Patriarchy and Colonialism

A key argument of this book is that hierarchy is a central feature of the social context, and that hierarchical systems have specific implications for psychological development. To understand fully the implications of hierarchical systems for psychological development, it is first necessary to consider the characteristics of hierarchical systems in greater detail. This chapter will outline the relationship between hierarchies and the dynamics of domination–subordination, and identify social patterns by which hierarchy is implemented and maintained through a historical analysis of patriarchy and colonialism. These patterns will then be documented as they are manifested or, more specifically, insititutionalized in modern Western society. Consideration of their implications for everyday life, or for the micro level, will lay the basis for analysis of the psychological patterns associated with hierarchy.

white women

Hierarchy as a feature of the social context

A hierarchy involves graded ranks marked by differences in power and resources. Hierarchies are often shaped as pyramids, with small numbers near the top of the hierarchy, and large numbers at the bottom. Society as a whole is hierarchically organized, or stratified: societies can be seen as consisting of 'strata' in a hierarchy, with the more favoured at the top and the less privileged nearer the bottom. Inequalities are a feature of hierarchies, in that those near or at the top have more power and resources, while those at the bottom have relatively little. Gender, class and minority group status are of key importance in influencing position in the hierarchy and the possibilities for mobility (Giddens, 2006).

Hierarchy operates at the three levels of the social context outlined in the previous chapter. At the macro level, society as a whole is stratified in a class structure (using class in the broadest way to refer to structured inequalities in society as a whole). At the community or organizational level, almost all organizations, whether they are large bureaucracies or small lobby groups, have a hierarchical structure, involving varying numbers of layers. At the micro level, many settings, including the family, are structured hierarchically. Indeed hierarchy is such a central feature of organization in modern Western society that it has become the 'taken-for-granted', and is often regarded as both inevitable and desirable (Beteille, 1983; Miller, 1986).

Almost all of the major systems of society – politics, economics, religion, education, mass media, art and culture – which are hierarchically organized are male dominated. The political system is an obvious example already alluded to in Chapter 1. At the top of most political systems is a head of state, who is almost always male, and a cabinet, of which rarely more than 15 per cent are women (Seager, 2003). The structure of state and local government is hierarchical, as is the public service, the judicial system and the security and defence systems. Comparative studies in Europe and the USA show that there are very few women in top positions in these hierarchies, and that there are usually only between 5 per cent and 15 per cent of women at the second or third levels. Ireland ranks in the middle band for most of these comparisons, with Scandinavian countries showing the highest percentages, Britain and USA around the middle, and France, Portugal and Greece ranking lowest (Seager, 2003; Walby, 2004; 2009).

Male domination has also been documented in other systems of society. In the economic system, top positions in financial institutions, in business, even in trade unions representing female-dominated occupations, are held primarily by men. All religious hierarchies are male dominated. In the world of art, literature and mass media, top executives, editors of magazines and newspapers, owners and directors of publishing houses are almost all men. In the areas of health and education, while females may predominate in some areas, senior public servants and chief executives in educational and medical institutions and organizations are predominantly male (Seager, 2003). Indeed there is hardly a single case of a mixed-gender social institution that is hierarchically organized where women predominate at the top of the hierarchy. Even in such an obvious area as women's magazines, it is apparent that while the editors and writers are mostly female, the content of the magazines is heavily influenced by the advertising industry, which itself is male dominated. In the case of the family, it will be recalled that the term 'patriarchy' is based on 'male as head of household'; the degree of male domination in households will be discussed more fully below.

This discussion has emphasized male domination, particularly at the top levels of hierarchies. Echoing the themes discussed in Chapter 1, it must also be stated that these positions are primarily held by men of a particular race, religion, class background and sexual orientation, which in the Western context is white, Christian, middle-class, heterosexual – and also able-bodied and settled (that is, not belonging to a nomadic group such as gypsies or travellers). Obviously some women, particularly of a similar background, also occupy some positions of power, although, as the above discussion indicates, it is rare for women to attain positions at the top of the hierarchy. And it is also possible, although difficult, for people with other disadvantages – disabled, lesbian or gay, working-class – to attain positions of power. It is also the case that marginalized groups themselves are stratified by gender and other variables (McAuliffe, 2008; Oliver, 1996).

Hierarchy and the dynamics of domination–subordination

There are certain dynamics which are almost inevitable once a hierarchical system is in place. For example, even where a group of individuals on an equal footing appoint or mandate a representative or group of representatives to act on their behalf in a particular situation, it is likely that over time the representatives will end up knowing more about the situation. The representatives will probably interact more with each other than with those they represent, and will often have to make decisions without full consultation. In this instance, although the group is fully committed to consultation, briefings, equality and so on, and a hierarchical structure has been agreed upon, it has created inequalities in communication patterns, access to information and decision-making.

Feminist psychologist Jean Baker Miller (1986) provides one of the first examples of a feminist psychological approach to hierarchical systems. She argues that a dynamic of inferiority–superiority is inevitable even in those hierarchical situations that she describes as temporary, such as that between parent and child or between teacher and student, whose purpose is to foster development to the point where the inequality ends. Miller (1986, p. 5) writes 'The reality is that we have trouble enough with this sort of relationship... Above all, there is great difficulty in maintaining the conception of the lesser person as a person of as much intrinsic worth as the superior.' In writing about permanent inequality, Miller argues that once a group is defined as inferior, the superior or dominant group judges them to be incapable of performing roles that the dominants value highly, and assigns them roles such as providing services which are poorly valued. The inferior capacities of the subordinates are seen as innate or natural. Stereotypes of the subordinates include 'submissiveness, passivity, docility, dependency, lack of initiative, inability to act, to decide, to think' (Miller, 1986, p. 7). These stereotypes obviously reinforce and justify inequality.

A second dynamic which Miller (1986) identifies is the control by the dominant group of the cultural outlook. The dominant group has the most influence on the cultural outlook, and it legitimates and obscures inequality through myths such as the biological inferiority of the subordinate group, or in the case of women, arguments about the natural place for women. Dominants define what is 'normal'. They seek to convince both themselves and subordinates that 'the way things are is right and good, not only for them but especially for the subordinates' (Miller, 1986, p. 9). They will use their control to suppress conflict, since any questioning of the status quo is seen as threatening.

Miller thirdly suggests that in order to preserve the myth of superiority, dominant groups have to deny their vulnerabilities and weaknesses. Areas to do with dependency and helplessness, or with passion, sexuality and intimate relations are deeply threatening to those in dominant positions, and are relegated to the unconscious: 'These parts of experience have been removed from the arena of full and open interchange and relegated increasingly to a realm outside of full awareness' (p. 23). In the case of gender, Miller points out that 'In Western society men are encouraged to dread, abhor, or deny feeling weak or helpless, whereas women are encouraged to cultivate this state of being' (p. 29). This denial of vulnerability also extends to all functions associated with the fostering of growth and development. These functions have been assigned to women, and because women are subordinate, have been seen as without value.

Similar patterns have been described by writers on patriarchy and on colonialism. Both Simone de Beauvoir (1961) and Frantz Fanon (1967b) write of the control of cultural outlook, and assumptions of superiority on the part of men, and of colonizers; women, and the colonized, are thus faced with cultural products not of their making, and which include stereotypes of them as inferior. De Beauvoir and Fanon both invoke the concept of 'Other' to describe how characteristics of men, or the colonizers, become the norm, and areas of vulnerability are projected onto women, or the colonized. De Beauvoir (1961, p. xvi) writes that woman is 'defined and differentiated with reference to man and not he with reference to her; she is the incidental, the inessential as opposed to the essential. He is the Subject, he is the Absolute – she is the Other.'

The discussion so far illustrates a fundamental point – that hierarchies have dynamics, and these dynamics have implications for psychological functioning. The dynamics of hierarchies have received considerable attention in Ireland and internationally as the Catholic Church has come under increasing scrutiny for the occurrence of systematic abuse in institutions run by the Church and of sexual abuse by Catholic priests in parishes and communities. Two government sponsored investigations in the Irish context document the extent of this abuse (Ryan, 2009; Murphy, 2009). The Ryan report on abuse in reformatory and industrial institutions from 1930s to 1970s documents an occurrence of physical, sexual and emotional abuse over decades that was so extensive that Ryan concludes that it was clearly systemic. The Murphy report focuses on sexual abuse in the Dublin archdiocese and concludes unequivocally that in failing to report known abusers and in moving abusive priests from one location to the next, the archdiocese placed the protection of the Church at all costs over the welfare of children. Both reports link abuse to the hierarchical structure of the Catholic Church with an emphasis on authority, obedience, secrecy and control. Both reports also note the interest of the Church in covering up abuse in order to protect its own reputation and assets. The devastating impact of such abuse on survivors has been documented in the Ryan report and in accounts by survivors (Fahy, 1999). As Miller's discussion suggests, such a top-down hierarchy will create social and psychological pressures that will almost inevitably result in abusive behaviour.

Psychological patterns will be discussed in the following chapter. What is needed for a full understanding of the social context is an analysis of the structural nature of domination–subordination, that is, the way in which domination–subordination is institutionalized. For this, I would like to undertake a closer examination of the historical development of patriarchy and colonialism. Both of these systems involve institutionalized domination, and may therefore be called systems of domination. A historical analysis will help to clarify how it is that systems of domination become established and maintained, and aid in identifying patterns or dynamics which are characteristic of systems of domination. This will provide a framework for describing patterns which are characteristic of contemporary Western society.

The evolution of patriarchy

The work of historian Gerda Lerner (1986; 1997) provides one of the earliest analysis of the historical development of patriarchy. Arguing that patriarchy is a social system that evolved over time, rather than an unchanging biologically determined social system, Lerner illustrated her analysis with a detailed account of the development of patriarchy at a particular time and place, namely in ancient Mesopotamia from the third to the first millennia BC. This period of history in the Ancient Near East is considered exemplary by many feminist historians because of the actual historical process and also because 'the major gender symbols and metaphors of Western civilization were largely derived from Mesopotamian and, later, from Hebrew sources' (Lerner, 1986, p. 11). Obviously the historical process described here is specific to this time and place; the purpose of the presentation is to illustrate the evolution over time of a system of domination.

In discussing theories regarding the origins of patriarchy, which range through biology, anthropology, archaeology, psychoanalysis and economic theory, Lerner (1986) notes that many theories either assume that male domination is biologically based and therefore inevitable and universal, or look for a single cause such as the discovery of agriculture to explain the emergence of male domination. In contrast, she argues that patriarchy evolved over time: 'patriarchy as a system is historical: it has a beginning in history' (p. 6). She asserts that: 'The period of the "establishment of patriarchy" was not one "event" but a process developing over a period of nearly 2,500 years, from approximately 3,100 to 600 BC. It occurred, even within the Ancient Near East, at a different pace and at different times in several distinct societies' (p. 8).

In Europe and the Middle East, prior to the discovery of agriculture around 10,000 BC, humans for the most part lived in hunter-gatherer societies for which there is very little evidence of systematic stratification or hierarchical organization, either from the archaeological record or from anthropological studies of contemporary hunter-gatherer societies. The earliest evidence of villages and towns which developed following the discovery of agriculture indicates that they were relatively egalitarian, were often matrilinear and matrilocal, and engaged in ritualistic activities that centred around earth-mother symbolism (Gimbutas, 1991). While these societies could not be called matriarchal because they were not clearly female dominated, some feminist writers have suggested terms such as matricentred or matristic to convey the central role that women played in artistic and ritualistic life (Eisler, 1987).

With the development of agriculture and other historical developments between 10,000 and 3,500 BC, society became increasingly hierarchical. Lerner (1986) suggests that the development of male dominance was not necessarily consciously planned: 'Things developed in certain ways, which then had certain consequences which neither men nor women intended' (p. 51). A key element in this process was the recognition and control of women's reproductive capacity. The capacity of women to bear children was a valuable resource; it became increasingly valuable as agriculture, with its emphasis on labour and surplus, developed. Women became commodities not just as labourers, but as bearers of children who could contribute labour and who would inherit surplus. The control of women's reproduction became central to the development of patriarchy.

A detailed historical analysis becomes possible with the establishment of the archaic state in the Near Middle East with its protohistorical and later historical records. By then, society was highly structured, with a propertied class and a division of labour based on class and gender. Focusing on Mesopotamia in the first phase, 3,100 to 2,000 BC, Lerner (1986) concludes that women exercised considerable power in the economic, political and religious spheres, although they came increasingly under men's power in the family. They were active in politics as diplomats and representatives with political power, they managed their own estates and engaged in business and legal transactions in their own right, they participated in the labour force and were active as artisans, they were active in cultural and religious life as scribes, poets, priestesses and prophetesses. This is in contrast to the later period, after 2,000 BC, when women were increasingly excluded from political, economic, cultural and religious life (Hamilton, Whitehouse and Wright, 2006).

For Lerner (1986), the most important development at this time was the emergence of slavery, that is, the creation of a class of human beings who could be deprived of freedom and forced to labour against their will. Slavery marked a new level of domination–subordination beyond that created by social stratification and the division of labour. It required the explicit development and institutionalization of a set of practices which involved marking a group as different, excluding them from participation in the social order, treating them as commodities for sale, and extracting their labour through violence and economic dependency. A key element in this is the process of 'dishonouring', whereby the individuals who are to be enslaved are deprived of dignity and autonomy. Lerner suggests that the fact that women were already subordinate within kinship systems, were obviously physically different, and could readily be shamed through rape, made them vulnerable to slavery, and she notes that the evidence suggests that there were more women than men among those for whom the first historical evidence of slavery exists. From the beginning, women's enslavement involved sexual slavery, that is, female slaves were forced to provide sexual services (as were some male slaves) and to bear children.

Lerner (1986) argues that it is the development of slavery that is most important in tracing the history of domination not only of females by males but of males by other males. Slavery provided a model for other forms of domination at both the social and psychological level. Legal and social practices were developed, and symbols of domination–subordination were elaborated. The power of dishonourment or of stigma was recognized:

> stigma becomes a reinforcing factor which excuses and justifies the practice of enslavement in the minds of the dominant group and in the minds of the enslaved. If this stigma is fully internalized by the enslaved – a process which takes many generations and demands the intellectual isolation of the enslaved group – enslavement then becomes to be perceived as 'natural' and therefore acceptable (p. 100).

Along with the emergence of slavery came other distinctions between women. In particular, prostitution and the concubine system became highly developed, again both involving the sexual control and exploitation of women. In a detailed analysis of the legal codes of the time, Lerner (1986) documents the increasing control of women by defining them in terms of their relationships to men – to father, husband-to-be or other male relative. There was increasing state regulation of sexual matters in the creation of laws which were maintained in Europe up until the twentieth century – rape became a crime against the husband or father, self-induced abortion was punishable by the severest penalties, and a double standard applied to adultery.

Finally class divisions between women on the basis of their sexual status became codified in laws which created the wearing of the veil as a status symbol available only to married women. More accurately, the law made the wearing of a veil available only to women who were under the domestic protection of a man as a wife, concubine or daughter, and made it a crime for prostitutes or slave girls. Lerner (1986) notes that one of the effects of such a law was to create a distinction between 'respectable' (mothers, virgins under male protection) and 'non-respectable' (prostitutes, women not under male protection) women.

During this time there was also increasing exclusion of women from spheres of public life. By the turn of the first millennium BC, women were excluded from political and economic roles, and were deprived of education. However, women were still prominent as priestesses, and goddesses played powerful roles in the pantheon of deities celebrated in ritual and mythology. Complex changes in religion and cosmogony took place over a long period of time and involved a shift from polytheism to monotheism, the ascendancy of a single male god, and the exclusion of women from the temple and from religious life. The end result of this was an all-male priesthood who mediated the relationship between humans and the divinity, and the investment of all creative powers, including procreative powers, in a male god. Women were thus excluded not only from political and economic life, but also from the symbolic and religious systems (Condren, 2002; Lerner, 1997).

Lerner's (1986) account of the evolution or development of patriarchy illustrates the manner in which male domination became established over a long period of time. It was not necessarily systematic or planned; different elements were put in place at different times, which combined over time to form an interconnected system of domination. This involved the institutionalization of male dominance in political, economic, cultural and religious spheres. It was accompanied by the use of coercion – the shaming of women through rape, and physical and military force. It led to the control and exploitation of women's economic, reproductive and sexual resources. It required the establishment of ideologies which justified male dominance. And it involved the creation of divisions between women based on their economic and sexual status.

Colonialism as a system of domination

Based on this sample and on contemporary and historical analyses of patriarchy and colonialism, I would suggest that systems of domination (that is, hierarchical systems which are not consensual and which involve institutionalized domination and inequality) rely in part on modes of control for their maintenance. The use of violence is a fairly brutal and obvious mechanism. However, over generations of domination, modes of control become more pervasive and more subtle, focusing on control of economic, political and symbolic systems. Over time, the modes become institutionalized and shrouded by ideology such that it becomes difficult for both the dominants and the subordinates to recognize them. If these modes are working well, they not only succeed in keeping the subordinates in their place, they convince the subordinates that they deserve their position, or that indeed their subordination is natural and actually good for them.

More specifically, I would propose six modes of control which are characteristic of systems of domination, and which have important implications for psychological functioning. These are: violence, political exclusion, economic exploitation, cultural control, control of sexuality, and fragmentation or 'divide and conquer'. These patterns can be clearly seen in Lerner's analysis of the creation of patriarchy. They appear in varying forms in systems which involve domination and subordination, whether domination is based on race, class, sexual orientation, religion or other categories. They are referred to frequently in writings on oppression, as the reviews in Chapters 3 and 4 indicate, and they recur in writings on social control. For example in a classic analysis Young refers to the 'five faces of oppression' (Young, 1990, p. 241), which involve violence, politics, economics, culture and marginalization. Bartky (1990, p. 23) sees 'stereotyping, cultural domination and sexual objectification' as central to oppression. Apfelbaum explores the impact of similar patterns in systems of domination on intergroup relations (Apfelbaum, 1979; 1999). Political, cultural and economic structures are described by Baker et al. (2009), Mullaly (2002) and Ruth (2006). Here I will elaborate on these modes through the example of colonialism.

Colonialism, the systematic domination of one territory by another, is itself a form of domination which has evolved and changed historically, and which has taken different forms geographically and culturally (Ferro, 1997; McLeod, 2007). Colonial domination relied, of course, on military force, but also employed various levels of political, economic and cultural control. Like other systems of domination, colonization maintained itself not just through political, economic and cultural control, but also through psychological conditioning. Writing in the Indian context, Nandy (1983, p. 3) states that 'a colonial system perpetuates itself by inducing the colonized, through socioeconomic and psychological rewards and punishments, to accept new social norms and cognitive categories'.

Given that colonialism operates in a patriarchal context, it is clear that colonialism is itself a gendered process. In a colonial context, violence, political exclusion, economic exploitation, sexual exploitation, control of culture and divide and conquer are patterned differently for men and for women. Furthermore colonialism and patriarchy reinforce each other as systems of domination. Mechanisms of domination developed for patriarchal control could be applied in a colonial context and vice versa. For example, as colonialism restricted the economic opportunities for the population generally, women were restricted to ever decreasing spheres of economic activity. In turn, the limitations on women's economic activity made them more dependent and powerless in society. Another example is in the area of discourse, where a common pattern of regarding the colonized country and the colonized people as 'feminine' occurs. Discourses of femininity involving weakness and emotionality were invoked to reinforce the inferiority of the colonized country and people. The juxtaposition of the colonized 'feminine' country or people with the colonizing 'masculine' country or people asserted the dominance of men over women (Nandy, 1983; Meaney, 1993).

The history of Western colonization can be placed in the context of the development of patriarchy and capitalism, with the systematic colonization of South America, Africa and much of Asia as the next step in the development of patriarchy following the historical developments described by Lerner (1986). Colonization aided in the systematic accumulation of capital, linked the sexual division of labour to the global division of labour, and enabled the further elaboration of ideologies of white and male superiority. Legacies of colonialism may be seen in global economic, political and cultural patterns which continue to shape the contemporary world order (Ashcroft et al., 2006; Enloe, 2004; 2007; McPhail, 1987; 2009).

In the following discussion the aim is not to provide a systematic analysis of colonialism, but rather to elaborate on the dynamics of systems of domination by illustrating the use of the six modes of control (violence, political exclusion, economic exploitation, cultural control, control of sexuality and fragmentation) and highlighting other dynamics in the Irish context during a specific historical period. This is between 1650 and 1850, when English colonial domination of Ireland was being established (Curtis, 1994; Kinealy, 2008; Moody and Martin 2001; O'Brien and O'Brien, 1995). Prior to this, Irish society had undergone a number of invasions by Vikings and Normans, but while these invasions had created different social groupings, they had left the native Irish (or Celtic) society, which had its own laws, language, literature, religion and cultural practices, largely intact. In the sixteenth century, Elizabethan colonial expansion was more systematic, involving military campaigns and land plantations. Later, religious conversion became an important factor in colonial policies in Ireland. Thus unlike the Indian case, for example, where British colonization was primarily concerned with politics and economics, in the Irish case, colonization also involved systematic efforts to replace the indigenous Gaelic (Celtic) culture and to impose the Protestant religion. From the sixteenth century onward, as O'Brien and O'Brien (1995, p. 61) assert: 'A pattern had now established itself that was to prove enduring: Catholic Ireland dominated by the superior force of Protestant England.'

The use of *violence*, involving military invasion and occupation, is obvious in the colonial context. Examples of the use of violence in the Irish context during this period include systematic military campaigns such as the Elizabethan wars of the sixteenth century and Cromwell's campaigns in the seventeenth century (both of which involved seizure of land). Troops were used systematically to suppress resistance groups such as the Whiteboys (1760s). A nation-wide armed rebellion was suppressed by troops in 1798, and troops were used to enforce the banning of a mass political meeting in 1843. There was also a continuous garrison presence, indicating that violence is pervasive not just through warfare but as a back-up to political and, as will be apparent below, economic control, and it obviously permeated the day-to-day lives of the colonized.

Colonialism is maintained through control of the political system, and especially through *political exclusion*. In Ireland, between 1650 and 1850, Penal Laws were introduced with the aim of solidifying Protestant (and English) control of the country, and included cultural restrictions which will be described below. The Penal Laws barred Catholics from parliament, from holding any government office, or from entering the legal or military professions. Restrictions were placed on the many popular movements which sought change through political means, and secret societies were suppressed through force. Various efforts were also made to restrict parliamentary representation and to control the Irish parliament, which became subordinate to the government in London, and was finally abolished in the Act of Union of 1800.

Economic exploitation occurred in a variety of forms from seizure of land to taxation systems. In Ireland, by the end of the seventeenth century, 80 per cent of land had been transferred by force from natives to settlers (Curtis, 1994). This involved enforced migration of many natives and the loss of land and power by the Gaelic aristocracy, resulting in massive disruption of the social system. The above-mentioned Penal Laws barred considerable numbers of native Irish from receiving education or the means for advancement in the professions. Restrictions on trade and economic development were also used to limit economic competition. Examples of this included banning the export of Irish cattle, and restrictions on the export of wool to countries other than England. By the time of the Great Famine (1845–48), millions of peasants lived on small rented holdings and sold all but their potato crops to pay their rent. Rent payment itself was a form of economic transfer to landlords living in Britain (Curtis, 1994; Kinealy, 2008).

Sexual exploitation refers to the exploitation of sexual and reproductive resources. The most obvious example of this is in the area of prostitution. Where there was a military presence there was also prostitution, with enforced pregnancy through rape occurring during military campaigns. Another example of sexual exploitation is that of the female house servant, from whom the master of the house expected and received sexual favours. A well-known commentator on the eighteenth century writes: 'Landlords of consequence have assured me, that many of the cottars would think themselves honoured by having their wives or daughters sent for to the bed of their master; a mark of slavery that proves the oppression under which such people must live' (Young, 1780, pp. 127–8, quoted in Curtis, 1994, p. 23). Prostitution is related to economic exploitation, in that the more restrictions there are on women's economic activities, the more likelihood there is of women becoming prostitutes. Indeed, it illustrates the interlinkage of the six mechanisms: violence is used in the context of prostitution, prostitutes are excluded from power because of their illegal status, discourse represents them as shamed and inferior women, and they are divided from each other and from other women.

Systematic policies to *control culture* included the outlawing of the Irish language, and the exclusion of Irish language, history and music from the school curriculum. As English increasingly became the language of politics and commerce, the use of the Irish language became increasingly restricted to the private domain. The suppression of the native culture was accompanied by a discourse which justified the status quo, and a major element in this was the generation of negative stereotypes about the Irish. The Irish were presented as barbarians as early as the twelfth century, with common stereotypes including lazy, stupid, bestial, amoral, emotional and superstitious, stereotypes which recur in many colonial and racist contexts (Curtis, 1996; McVeigh and Rolston, 2009). The aim, among others, was to establish the Irish people and Irish language and culture as inferior, and to blame the Irish for their condition. The following quote from the London *Times* illustrates the use of stereotypes during the Great Famine (due to which 2 million people died and a further 2 million emigrated). The *Times* wrote of 'the astounding apathy of the Irish', stating that the Irish are 'a people born and bred from time immemorial in inveterate indolence, improvidence, disorder and consequent destitution' (Póirtéir, 1995).

Fragmentation (divide and conquer), or the creation and/or exploitation of divisions is the final pattern characteristic of systems of domination to be discussed here. Historically, the fact that Irish society consisted of separate and autonomous kingdoms, often in competition with each other, opened the way for successful Viking and Norman invasions. The later imposition of divisions between Catholic and Protestant and the racial/ethnic and cultural differences between the two groups was a further barrier to united opposition. Class interests intersected with religious and cultural differences to further fragment Irish society. As in other colonial situations, the ruling class allied with the colonizing power to further their mutual interests. Explicit colonial policies such as military campaigns and plantations led to social disruption, breaking up families, tribes and historical social units. The greater economic and political power of the colonizer was an incentive to collusion among the colonized, creating competition and distrust among them. These examples illustrate the considerable pressures, ranging from coercion to self-interest, which prevented unity and created divisions among the colonized.

This account of colonization illustrates the modes of control where there is a clear and overt intention to impose domination through their explicit use. Some further points may be made about systems of domination based on this analysis. One is that the modes of control are interconnected with each other – this was already alluded to in the example of prostitution – and they are underpinned by violence or the threat of violence. For example, economic exploitation and sexual exploitation were facilitated by violence and political exclusion, and were justified by an ideology of inferiority. Fragmentation, or divide and conquer, created obstacles to political unity, and divisions were exacerbated by economic and sexual exploitation and by an ideology of inferiority. These in turn created further divisions.

Another point which arises in the colonial situation is that of the interrelationship or interdependency of dominants and subordinates: in this instance, the colonized and the colonizer. The colonizer and the colonized became enmeshed in a system in which both were participants, and in which each influenced the other, albeit unequally. For example, in the economic case, English wealth was enhanced by the appropriation of Irish land and other economic resources, while the Irish economy became dependent on the English economy for markets and investment. Like other aspects of domination, this interdependency benefits the dominant group, and it also undermines the independence of the subordinate group. Another pattern with obvious psychological implications that is frequently discussed in the case of colonialism is the ideology of inferiority–superiority. In this example, the dominant group, the English, assert their superiority in contrast with the inferiority of the subordinate group, the Irish.

It is also evident that those in positions of subordination offer a range of resistance to domination. Parliamentary strategies and mass rallies were among the more conventional forms of resistance. Another obvious form of resistance which has received considerable attention in Irish history is armed resistance. Tactics such as hunger strikes, which have their origin in ancient Gaelic society, or boycotting (a practice of social and economic ostracism first practised against a historical figure, Captain Boycott) were developed in the face of political exclusion. Secret societies abounded at various points. Along with these more overt forms of resistance were the tactics which Scott (1985) refers to as 'the weapons of the weak' – non-cooperation, false compliance, secrecy, feigned ignorance, sabotage. Cultural resistance in the form of poetry, music, drama, folklore and even religious affiliation are all evident from Irish history (Curtis, 1994; Kinealy, 2008), and are found in other systems of domination.

Finally, it is clear that some groups or individuals among the subordinates collude or cooperate with the dominant group. In the case of Irish colonization, various individuals colluded with the English in a variety of ways – joining the English army, becoming informers, taking positions in colonial administrations, acting as agents for landlords and business people. More generally, sections of the ruling class and of the middle class cooperated as a group with the English, to their own benefit. Collusion has to be seen in the context of a system of domination, and may often be enforced cooperation, or an outcome of the greater economic and political power of dominators, but it may also obviously arise out of self-interest.

Dynamics of patriarchy in Western society

Modern Western society may be seen as part of a global system which has developed in part through the interconnections of patriarchy and colonialism (Enloe, 1989, 2007; Mies, 1986). This global system may be analysed as a system of domination; indeed there is now an enormous amount of international research on women, documenting patterns related to violence, politics, economics, sexuality, culture and fragmentation in a variety of countries (Agarwal, 1988; Barry, 1995; Seager, 2003; Walby, 2009). While there have obviously been considerable changes in these patterns, in part from the influence of the women's movement, research on both Western societies, and globally, continues to document male domination, and indeed domination by countries which have been colonizers. The aim of the present discussion is firstly to highlight the degree to which modes of control are institutionalized in modern Western society, and secondly to illustrate how these mechanisms permeate the micro-level or the day-to-day lives of women. This will further facilitate making links to the psychological level, which will be the focus of the following chapter.

Violence

Violence against women takes a number of forms in Western societies generally. It obviously includes rape, and also battery and sexual assault. Physical violence includes beating up, pushing, bruising, kicking, strangling or choking and even murder. It is often perpetrated in a sustained way over a long period of time, resulting in serious bodily injuries, and physical and mental health problems. Mental abuse includes verbal attacks, emotional outbursts, threats of violence, withholding of money and interrogation. Over half of such violence, including rape, takes place in the context of an intimate relationship, and such violence is found across class, urban–rural and other social contexts (Dobash and Dobash, 1992; O'Connor, 2008).

It is extremely difficult to establish the extent of such violence because of a lack of research and because of the very strong pressures on women to keep silent about such crimes. For example, in the case of rape, international research estimates that overall only about 10–15 per cent of rapes are reported to police, positioning rape as the most unreported serious crime, while conviction rates are also lower than for other crime rates, with comparative studies showing that only 6–10 per cent of reported rapes lead to conviction (Kelly and Regan, 2003). Figures on reported violence or on conviction rates are therefore completely inadequate in assessing the extent of violence against women.

The use of survey research can be problematic in part because it encounters the problems of disclosure mentioned above. However, American research based on crime–victim surveys provides evidence that prevalence of rape among adult women is between 14 per cent and 25 per cent, with considerable regional variation (Crawford and Unger, 2004). An Irish study involving a random representative sample found that 7 per cent of women reported having been abused in the previous year by a partner or ex-partner and 18 per cent had been subjected to violence at some time by a current partner (Kelleher and O'Connor, 1995). A majority of those surveyed knew a woman who had been subjected to violence by a partner. These findings were confirmed by a national study of sexual assault and violence in Ireland using a representative sample (McGee et al., 2002). McGee et al. found that 10 per cent of women reported experiencing penetrative abuse over their lifetimes, with 21 per cent reporting non-penetrative contact abuse, and a further 10 per cent reported noncontact abuse. Thus fully 42 per cent of women experienced sexual abuse over their lifetime. Furthermore, McGee et al. found that some 50 per cent had never reported their assault to anyone, and less than 10 per cent engaged with the legal system.

Violence against women may be said to be institutionalized to the extent that the major institutions of society that are charged with preventing such violence not only fail to do so but actually create barriers to women attempting to enlist their help. Walby (1990, p. 143) states: 'Male violence against women is sufficiently common and repetitive, with routinized consequences for women and routinized modes of processing by judicial agencies to constitute a social structure.' Women have written extensively of the difficulties they encounter in disclosing the crime and in undergoing legal proceedings (O'Connor, 2008). This is because violence against women occurs in a cultural context in which both ideology and legal and other services tend to support the view that women deserve to be violated ('asking for it'), that women will make false claims, and that men are not responsible. Fear, the threat of further violence, the shame and stigma attached, and economic dependency are among the factors which prevent women from disclosing experiences of violence. Many women report that gardai and social workers do not believe their stories, and subject them to intrusive and humiliating interrogation. In its summing up and sentencing policy, the judicial system continues to reflect considerable ambivalence about the responsibility for sexual violence (O'Connor, 2008).

Violence against women has also been institutionalized through the growth of the sex industry, which has become a highly profitable international industry taking many different forms. These include trafficking of women, mostly from very poor backgrounds to wealthier countries, military prostitution, sex tourism and pornography, with the sex industry now rivalling sport and video entertainment in profitability (Jeffreys, 2009). The sex industry provides another arena in which violence against women is enacted through sex trafficking, prostitution, and pornography. Trafficking in women, which involves imprisonment and forced labour is itself a form of violence, and is enforced through repeated sexual assault. Both Irish and international research provide extensive evidence of the use of violence and drug pushing to coerce women into prostitution and pornography (Jeffreys, 2009; O'Connor, 2008). The sex industry provides an example of the interconnections of violence and economic exploitation, with profits from the sex industry almost entirely in the hands of men. It also contributes to control of sexuality and to cultural control through representations of women and of sexuality that emphasize power and control, frequently depicting sexual violence as enjoyable, and women as bodies for sale. Pornography and prostitution thus contribute to a context in which violence against women is pervasive and where the judicial system continues to fail to hold men responsible for violent behaviour.

Such attitudes to women are also reflected in another form of violence or coercion, namely sexual harassment, where women are subject to bullying, harassment and humiliation of a sexual nature. Surveys show that over 60 per cent of women have experienced such harassment, in the workplace, in public places, or in the home (Crawford and Unger, 2004; Rollins, 1996). Research on sexual harassment highlights the role played by power differences, showing that such harassment more often occurs in relationships such as that between a boss and a subordinate or a lecturer/professor and a student, which are marked by power differences.

Finally, although not all women may be direct victims of violence or sexual harassment, almost all women experience problems because of the pervasiveness of violence and harassment. Studies in Europe and the USA find that up to 80 per cent of women worry about sexual assault, and restrict their behaviours out of fear of sexual assault (Crawford and Unger, 2006; Gordon and Riger, 1989). This fear is reinforced through depictions of high levels of violence against women, and of women as victims, in mass media, popular culture and pornography (Ussher, 1997).

A variety of factors converge, then, to make violence a serious problem for women, and one which permeates their everyday life, imposes restrictions and prevents them from participating fully in society. These factors include cultural attitudes which are highly ambivalent about violence against women and which maintain a considerable degree of silence about the problem. Social and legal systems, from which women have been excluded historically, reflect these attitudes, and fail to recognize or respond appropriately to the problem. Women's economic dependency on men and their isolation within the home, has made it extremely difficult for women to resist violence. The end result is that the vast majority of women have directly experienced sexual violence and/or harassment, and the vast majority of women restrict their behaviours out of fear of sexual violence. Furthermore, women live in a climate in which sexual violence against women is constantly depicted through pornography, mass media and advertising.

Political exclusion

The exclusion of women from power was documented earlier and is illustrated for the case of colonialism in a variety of policies which were adopted in the newly emerging post-colonial state in Ireland (Coulter, 1993; Tweedy, 1992). Women were excluded from jury duty and from certain areas of employment, married women were barred from access to jobs in the public service, contraception and abortion were illegal and information about them was banned, divorce was illegal, married women were domiciled with their husbands and were dependent on their husbands for access to social welfare, to child benefits and to financial services. Despite these restrictions, women did continue to mobilize between the 1920s and the 1960s, drawing on histories of resistance to colonization, to organize outside mainstream political structures, putting their energies into community-based organizations. This pattern of exclusion from mainstream politics and involvement in community organization is found in many post-colonial countries (Jayawardena, 1986). Indeed legacies of resistance to colonialism can be seen as strengthening women's movements in the late twentieth century (Coulter, 1993; Moane, 1996).

As the economic and other changes of the 1960s and 1970s opened up Irish society, women were well placed to make the most of whatever opportunities for women became available, and to mobilize and form a strong women's movement. This and other factors led to changes in legislation, welfare and social policy, labour force participation, and a host of other areas, culminating in the election in 1990 of the first woman President of Ireland, Mary Robinson. These developments illustrate the existence of resistance and the possibilities for subordinate groups, in alliance with those in more dominant positions, to bring about change.

While there have been enormous changes in Western societies generally as a result of the women's movement and a variety of other factors, it is still the case that traditional politics continue to be highly male-dominated in most Western countries, as figures provided earlier in this chapter indicate. Undoubtedly, women will continue to participate more fully in institutionalized political and public life, and also in other forms of political activity. However, many structural features of the economic, political and legal, systems, as well as women's responsibilities in the domestic sphere impinge on women's involvement in public office. Women politicians themselves have spoken of such factors as 'the old boys club', attitudes to women, the organization of the political system requiring evening and weekend availability, sexual harassment and other overt attempts to keep women out of political power which continue to create obstacles to women's political participation (O'Connor, 1998).

Feminist analyses of women's political exclusion have tried to explain not just women's exclusion from traditional politics as discussed above, but also differences in women's political values and political participation. This has led to efforts to broaden what is considered conventional politics, whose concerns often do not include 'women's issues', and to challenge the very structuring of politics, highlighting the democratic deficit – aspects of the political system which present obstacles to grass-roots participation, especially by those in marginalized positions in society. This is manifested in evidence of greater political alienation among women compared with men (and among most marginalized groups), and this alienation is greater among women who are full-time in the home or who lack education (Unger, 2004).

Women's exclusion from political life thus involves a convergence of structural and attitudinal factors, and has an important psychological impact on women's sense of political agency. Many women do not see a way to take action either to improve their immediate conditions or to bring about change at a broader level. This exclusion means that women do not have a full say in decisions that affect their day-to-day lives, and furthermore, that political issues that are of greater concern to women are neglected or judged to be unimportant. This is evident in the neglect of local and community concerns and, most obviously, in policies regarding birth control and childcare which will be discussed more fully below. Frustration, anger and feelings of powerlessness are among the psychological reactions to political exclusion.

Economic exploitation

Global indicators on women's economic exploitation were cited in Chapter 1, with United Nations figures indicating that women own around 1 per cent of the world's wealth and earn around 10 per cent of the world's income. In Western societies, women's incomes range between 60 per cent and 80 per cent of men's incomes (Barry, 2008; Walby, 2009). While the gap between women's and men's earning has narrowed in many Western countries, this narrowing has not occurred for part-time workers, where there has been a big increase in the percentage of women.

There is thus evidence of discrepancy in earnings between men and women even when hourly incomes for full-time workers are compared. Overall earnings for men and women show much greater discrepancy because there are a number of differences in the pattern of employment for men and women. In particular, women are more likely to be segregated into certain sectors of employment, such as services, which are low-paying relative to other sectors such as industry. Women are also much more likely than men to be working part-time, which is less well paid and has fewer fringe benefits, including pensions. Although there has been a large increase in women in the labour force in European countries, much of this can be accounted for by the increase in women in part-time employment. As Barry (2008, p. 2) points out: 'most of the temporary, part-time casualised and precarious workers are women.'

These figures show that women are disproportionately less likely to be in secure and high-paying jobs than men, although obviously there are some areas, particularly professional and public services, where these disparities are not so great. Conversely, women are more likely to be in insecure and low-paying jobs, including temporary and part-time jobs. Other factors such as differential access to training and education, biases against women in evaluation and in promotional procedures, and differing patterns of benefit and payment-in-kind contribute to widening the gap between men and women, and create obstacles to women's equal participation in the labour force. Within a sector, the higher the level on the hierarchy, the smaller the percentage of women, relative to their overall proportion in that sector. In other words, women are far less likely to be found at the top of career structures, a phenomenon still referred to as 'the glass ceiling' (McCarthy, 1995).

These factors obviously have an enormous impact on the day-to-day working lives of women. A further implication of these labour market trends is that a disproportionate number of women have income levels which place them in poverty. Research on poverty has shown consistently that, however it is conceptualized and measured, more women than men live in poverty, a trend which has been consistent both historically and internationally (Barry, 2008; Cantillon, 2005; United Nations, 2005). Factors which contribute to women's poverty include

the above labour force trends, the fact that women are primarily responsible for children – which creates economic demands – the absence of
childcare, and the fact that (in households with a male earner) male
earners do not always share income or resources adequately or evenly.
Research in Ireland, Britain and elsewhere shows that even in households with two earners, income and resources in households are not
shared equally, that men have more leisure time per week, and women
do more of the housework than men (Barry, 2008; Cantillon, Gannon
and Nolan, 2004).

A final area to consider is women's unpaid labour in the home. This
includes the support that women provide to male partners to engage
in income-earning and entrepreneurship, and also services such as
cooking, house-cleaning, laundry and childcare, which can be and are
provided on a commercial basis in modern society. It also includes caring for the elderly and others such as those with developmental disabilities who would otherwise require social or health services. Such
labour is unpaid, and indeed is not classified as work. Here feminist
analyses emphasize the vital contribution that such work makes to the
economy and to society generally, while noting that there have rarely
been attempts to describe such work, to assign a value to it, or to consider it as contributing to wealth. Since individual men, and society
generally, benefit from women's unpaid labour, feminists argue that
this is economic exploitation (Delphy and Leonard, 1992; Lynch, Baker
and Lyons, 2009). Research shows that women do more domestic work
than men even where there are dual earners or where both partners
are retired. Women in paid employment do less household labour than
full-time mothers, but still retain primary responsibility for household
management and childcare, creating what feminists have called 'the
double shift' – a first shift of paid work, followed by a second shift of
unpaid work. Further analyses of women's activities as upkeepers of the
family, kin, neighbourhood and communities, highlights women's vital
contribution to the interpersonal fabric of society or to the building
of bonds. Lynch, Baker and Lyons (2009) provide a detailed analysis
of women's involvement in unpaid care and love labour, showing that
women have primary responsibility for caring for children and dependent adults, and linking this to the patriarchal division of labour and
undervaluing of love and care.

It is clear from the research presented here that there are substantial
patterns of economic exploitation specific to women. These patterns
mean firstly that women have considerably less access to wealth, and
that more women are impoverished. Women's jobs are more likely to be

routine and insecure, and women's labour in the home is not afforded any economic value. Women are more likely to be economically dependent and, if they are employed, to be in insecure jobs. Economic dependency, insecurity and impoverishment are much more likely to be features of women's day-to-day lives, while at the psychological level, insecurity, anxiety, worry, lack of self-worth and dependency are related to these conditions.

Cultural control

The control of established discourses through domination of mass media, art and culture, education, religion and other sources has already been briefly described, with the important implication that those in subordinate positions are exposed to discourses about the world, and more specifically about themselves, which are not of their own making, and yet which have profound implications psychologically. Two themes which will be illustrated below are the absence of women's voices and indeed the erasure of women from literature, history and intellectual discourse, and the ways in which representations of women serve to maintain women's subordination (Richardson and Robinson, 2008).

Specific examples from the Irish context illustrate the connections between language and representation. Nuala Ní Dhomhnaill, a writer in the Irish language, is one of many who link language with psyche, writing that the Irish language offers access to dimensions of imagination which go back to ancient times, dimensions which include the 'otherworld' of magic and divination, the world of Mother Earth: 'Mar is an nGhaeilge teanga na Mórmáthar' ('For Irish is the Great Mother tongue') (Ní Dhomhnaill, 1994, p. 24). She suggests that the Irish language affords greater expression for women's experiences of sexuality, mothering and connection with nature. Linking patriarchy and colonialism, she writes that the loss of the Irish language deprived the Irish of culture and identity, but also of access to a way of thinking and feeling which was more characteristic of pre-enlightenment Europe.

Writing of erasure in ways which echo a number of women poets, Irish poet Eavan Boland describes some of the difficulties for the woman poet when faced with a language (in this case the English language) and a poetic tradition in which women's voices, and indeed women's concerns, are largely absent (Boland, 1995; 2007). She writes: 'I began writing in a country where the words woman and the word poet were almost magnetically opposed' (1995, p. xi). The themes of women's lives were not reflected in poetry: 'being a woman, I had entered into a life for which poetry has no name' (1995, p. 18). Furthermore, she felt alienated by men's use of women in poetry: 'The majority of male poets depended on women as motifs in their poetry. They moved easily, deftly, as if by right among images of women in which I did not believe and of which I could not approve. The women in their poems were often passive, decorative, raised to emblematic status. This was especially true where the woman and the idea of the nation were mixed' (Boland, 1989, p. 12). Boland finds this linkage deeply offensive: 'Once the idea of a nation influences the perception of a woman then that woman is suddenly and inevitably simplified. She can no longer have complex feelings and aspirations. She becomes the passive projection of a national idea' (Boland, 1989, pp. 12–13). Meaney (1993) links this equating of women with the nation to control of sexuality: 'They [women] are not merely transformed into symbols of the nation. They become the territory over which power is exercised' (p. 233).

The representation of the nation in the form of a woman (Mother Ireland, Mother India) lies at the intersection of gender and colonialism, and gender and nationalism. Representations of famine are another example of such an intersection, in an analysis from the Irish context. Several analyses of representations of women in Irish mythology show how changes in representations of women over time disempower women. These analyses also find that representations of women's reproductive capacities, and in particular of menstruation and motherhood are often either absent, or represent women as being victimized (Condren, 2002; Casey 2007). Casey in particular points out that 'representations of the blood mysteries are near absent, and when, if rarely present, are denigrated or pathologised' (Casey, 2007, p. 1).

Kellegher (1996) explores the complex ways in which female images are used in famine literature. She firstly notes the frequency with which male writers use the female form to depict the horrors of famine: 'The spectacle of famine ... is thus frequently constructed through female figures, its traces inscribed on hunger-ravaged, unclothed bodies' (p. 29). The use of the female form, Kellegher suggests, allows the expression of the 'unspeakable', the appalling suffering and primal horrors of famine, and can thus be powerful and evocative. But it also individualizes, and indeed feminizes, the experience of famine. Kellegher argues that 'The characterization of famine mothers ... allows the author to move the discourse on famine away from political and economic spheres into a moral register' (p. 38). In much of this discourse, the portrayal of famine reinforces the prevailing (colonial) political ideology – of famine as an act of nature, as inevitable, and as due to the moral weakness and idleness of the natives, and also reinforces mythic views of woman as bad mother and as helpless victim. Even twentieth-century famine literature contains recurring female themes: 'the famine mother, the ministering angel, the sacrificial victim' (Kellegher, 1996, p. 111). Both representations – Mother Ireland and famine victim – are powerful images which echo mythic themes of woman. They reinforce narrow cultural constructions of gender, equating femininity with nature, with passivity, with maternity, with victimhood, often in a sexualized way, while masculinity is associated with reason, with activity, with power and often with sexualized aggression. Furthermore, they are representations of women created by men, and used by men for evocative or political purposes. Women are objectified, their bodies depicted as raped or ravaged, providing a vehicle for the male writer's emotional expression.

Control of discourse extends to art, literature, mass media, popular culture, religion, education and even language itself (Cole and Henderson, 2005). Feminist research consistently shows that women are either absent, often through erasure, or representations of women reinforce narrow and stereotypic views, most often of women in domestic and maternal settings, in positions of lesser power or of subordination, characterized by docility, emotionality and subservience to men, and conforming to particular standards of beauty and attractiveness (Orbach, 2007). In their everyday lives women are thus rarely exposed to representations of women as strong, independent, competent and powerful. At the psychological level, control of discourse is directly related to the construction of self and identity, to feelings of self-worth and self-esteem, to the capacity for self-expression, to imagination and to the sense of belonging in society.

Control of sexuality

A variety of institutions, including judicial, medical, religious and educational are involved in the regulation of sexuality both nationally and internationally. The most obvious form of sexual exploitation which was discussed above is the sex industry, which operates on a global scale (Jeffreys, 2008). Sexual exploitation extends to include the sexualization and objectification of women in advertising and promoting of consumer goods.

Control and exploitation of reproductive capacities range from population policies to reproductive technologies and the institutionalization of motherhood (Kennedy, 2004; Raymond, 1994). Control of women's reproductive functions encompasses not only women's capacity for reproduction, but of health care surrounding this. In her historical study of the (male-dominated) medical profession in

Ireland, Murphy-Lawless argues that the medical profession has been a source of an ideology which viewed women in childbirth as 'poor, weak, feeble, in a word incompetent to undergo childbirth without male intervention' (Murphy-Lawless, 1993, p. 16). She argues that the maternity hospital is 'the institutional expression of a series of economic and philosophical arguments about the importance of women as reproducers'.

The control of sexuality under the guidance of the Catholic Church has been a central feature of Irish society since before the foundation of the present state, and provides a historical example of sexual exploitation in practice (Smyth (ed.), 1992). Catholic Church teaching was that women's function in marriage was to bear children, and that sexuality itself served the function of procreation. Women were seen almost exclusively as bearers and rearers of children, defined almost solely in terms of their reproductive function. These views were enshrined in the Constitution, in an article which states that the woman's place is in the home, in a prohibition on divorce, and later in an article which equated the life of a mother with that of a foetus. Contraception, abortion and sterilization were illegal and unavailable until campaigns began in the 1970s; women who became pregnant outside a marriage relationship were subject to severe ostracization, rejected by their families, often sent to do unpaid work for religious orders. Restrictions on women's participation in the labour force outlined above were informed by these views. Women were legally as well as ideologically confined to the home, and, in the absence of contraception, had little choice but to bear children, a situation which amounted to enforced motherhood. These policies have led to a litany of tragedies, including both the deaths of women in childbirth, the murders of unwanted new-borns, and the confinement of women to church-run Magdalen laundries where they were coerced into providing unpaid labour (Smith, 2007).

There have been enormous changes in these areas in Ireland under the influence of the women's movement, again an example of the capacity of social movements to bring about change (Connolly and O'Toole, 2005; Kennedy, 2004). Contraception is now widely available but there are no abortion facilities with the result that around 5,000 women travel annually to Britain for abortions (Rossiter, 2009). Debates and politics in Ireland about reproductive rights have been the most intense and sustained of any, and have exposed the role of the Church, state, medical and legal professions in maintaining control in this area. These debates go to the heart of sexuality itself, challenging the narrow view of sexuality which equates sex with heterosexual intercourse for the purposes of procreation, a view which is also enshrined in attitudes and laws regarding, homosexuality (O'Carroll and Collins (eds), 1995; Quiery, 2002).

The particular pattern that sexual exploitation takes is enormously influenced by religious views, and will therefore vary from one country to the next. In the Irish context there has been exploitation of reproductive capacities along with control and suppression of sexual capacities, which may be seen as an outcome of the interaction between Catholicism and colonialism. Experiences of sexuality, the body, childbearing and motherhood are all aspects of psychological functioning which are directly affected by the institutions and discourses surrounding sexuality.

Fragmentation (divide and conquer)

Fragmentation, or divide and conquer, involves a process whereby differences between women are created or exacerbated in socially structured ways. Obviously in modern society there are considerable differences between women based on class and other variables. Indeed acknowledgement of difference or diversity among women has been a central theme of modern feminist writings, and this has been partly due to the increasing strength of feminist women of colour from North America, Africa, Asia and Latin America, with their sensitivity to differences between women based on race, ethnicity, religion, region and class (Collins, 1990; Mohanty, 2003). In discussing differences among women, feminists not only exhibit self-criticism and conflict, but also seek to engage radically with such differences in order to construct understandings and interventions which are more pluralistic. This is the opposite of a strategy of control, which seeks to exploit such differences in order to maintain domination.

In this section the emphasis is on factors specific to women which create further divisions, mainly through increasing isolation and competition among women. In the discussion of colonialism it was noted that enforced migration and competition were two of the ways in which people were separated from each other, and by which close ties were disrupted. A specific form of enforced migration which applies to women is the practice of obliging women to leave their family of origin and settle with their husband's family and community. Obviously such enforced migration is no longer the practice in many countries, but feminist analyses of marriage and the family continue to highlight the ways in which the institution of marriage and the family have the effect of isolating women in the home, often at a distance from their family of origin.

The institution of heterosexuality exacerbates female competition through a range of factors which include an emphasis on women's physical attractiveness and dependency on men. Upon marriage, the custom whereby women change their surnames to those of their husbands separates women from their own life and family history. Within the family cycle, motives for moving are often related to career moves on the part of husbands. The experience of isolation reported by women who become full-time mothers and home-makers, which is exacerbated by the absence of childcare, has been well documented (Crawford and Unger, 2004; Rollins, 1996).

In the labour market, isolation and competition are exacerbated by the particular patterns of women's labour-force participation. Women are more likely to be in temporary and insecure jobs which are located in physically dispersed settings, factors which have long been recognized as creating difficulties in organizing them into trade unions or other interest groups. These features, combined with women's childrearing responsibilities, have the effect of making women's career paths more often disrupted, involving frequent job changes or periods of absence from the labour market. Other patterns include the absence or low percentage of women in top positions in the labour force which intensifies competition between women. Tokenism, the practice of appointing women to one or two positions of power in response to demands for gender equality, has the effect of both isolating the token woman, and creating envy and competition among her former peers. Thus structural features of the labour market, in particular the kinds of occupations in which women predominate, and the limits on women's upward mobility, increase isolation and competition among women (Barry, 2008).

A variety of cultural patterns also increase divisions between women, including the patterns of erasure and representation discussed above. The absence of a shared cultural tradition through the erasure of women from history and literature, and the distorted representations of women as powerless and inferior, undermines a sense of collectivity and identification with other women. Other examples of patterns which create distrust and alienation among women are those of blaming the mother, or blaming the victim in the case of sexual assault. This is exemplified in Daly's (1978) analysis of the many forms of institutionalized violence perpetrated against women globally, which range from the burning of witches in medieval Europe to genital mutilation in modern Africa. Daly (1978) notes that in many cases women are the ones who actually perform the violent acts, or who collude or cooperate in their performance. Women become 'token torturers', so-called because the power structure of the situation leaves women with little choice but to perform the roles assigned to them. This both erases the fact that the beneficiaries are men, and creates a pattern of scapegoating women, creating hostility and mistrust among women. The idea of women as tokens or scapegoats is also present in the pattern of placing women in the front line as receptionists, secretaries, shop assistants and so forth, where they become the targets of frustration and anger.

Fragmentation, or divide and conquer, is a mechanism of control which is essential to the maintenance of domination, and which can be linked to particular social structures, although it has received relatively less attention than the other mechanisms discussed here. Isolation, competition, erasure, false representation, tokenism and scapegoating are patterns which are present in women's everyday lives through family, work and cultural and social institutions. One of their most important effects is to prevent women from making connections with each other and feeling a sense of identification with other women. These patterns create feelings of isolation and powerlessness, obscuring the social origins of such feelings. They create distrust, hostility and ambivalence among women, and deprive them of a sense of solidarity, thus furthering their sense of dependency on men.

Systems of domination and psychological functioning

Western societies have been characterized by a series of institutionalized patterns or modes of control: namely, violence, political exclusion, economic exploitation, cultural control, control of sexuality and fragmentation. These mechanisms maintain domination, legitimate and mystify it, and permeate everyday life. These patterns are historical and changing. They have their origins in the historical development of patriarchy over 3,000 years ago, have evolved and changed in the context of colonialism and the development of the current global system, and have been affected by, among other things, contemporary women's movements. They permeate everyday lives or the micro level, and have implications for psychological development.

Before proceeding to the psychological level, it is necessary to reiterate the points about the individual level made in Chapter 1 and elaborated in this chapter. Systems of domination rarely involve unmitigated domination by one group and total subordination of another, but rather involve varying degrees of systematic and intentional domination by the dominant group along with levels of both cooperation and resistance by the subordinate group. Since most individuals in a system belong to multiple groups which may be relatively dominant or subordinate, individuals may gain or benefit by the degree to which power differentials favour them or disadvantage them. As individuals they may vary in the degree to which they intentionally exercise domination, collude with domination, or resist domination. Individuals favoured by power differentials may reject the benefits of whatever privilege they have, or take action to rectify inequalities. Individuals disadvantaged by power differentials may seek to overcome the obstacles and attain positions of power where they can benefit by power differentials, or, likewise, take action to resist or change the situation.

Individuals are therefore embedded in a system in which they can exercise some degree of choice, although the amount of choice is related to their status in society. However, it is also clear that the patterns described in this chapter will have considerable implications for psychological functioning. The psychological impact of domination or subordination will vary from one group to the next and from one individual to the next, and will also change across the life-span. What a psychological analysis of oppression can do is identify the many psychological patterns which may develop in response to domination or oppression, while a psychological analysis of liberation can identify processes and practices which can transform these patterns.

3
Psychological Patterns Associated with Hierarchial Systems: The Cycle of Oppression

From a psychological perspective, it is clear that there are enormous societal forces operating to produce considerable psychological difficulties for oppressed groups. Some of these difficulties may be directly related to modes of control. For example, violence is associated with fear and restriction, economic dependency may be associated with psychological dependency, and negative stereotypes can create a sense of inferiority. Patterns identified in the previous chapter included fear, restriction, powerlessness, insecurity, distortions of sexuality, sense of inferiority and isolation, and these patterns have been discussed by writers on both feminist psychology and psychological aspects of colonialism. Furthermore, writers have also explored, although most often in passing, the psychological effects of domination, where patterns such as anger, arrogance, rigidity and unwillingness to admit vulnerability or emotional weakness have been described.

This chapter will explore selected writings in feminist psychology and the psychology of colonialism with the aim of gaining a richer description of the psychological patterns associated with oppression, and of the interrelationships between these patterns. The chapter will focus on writers who have explicitly linked psychological patterns to the social conditions such as violence, economic deprivation and control of culture which were discussed in the previous chapter. The writers reviewed in this chapter highlight the damaging psychological effects of oppression, which is the focus of this chapter. Their insights into the processes involved in liberation will be reviewed in Chapter 4. For the most part, they may be criticized for failing to make distinctions within the groups they discuss, whether those groups be women as a whole, black women or lesbians, or a particular colonized group. It has already been stated, and may be reiterated, that an ecological or systems framework understands psychological patterns to be the outcome of a complex interaction over time between individuals and the multiple dimensions of the social conditions in which that individual develops. Thus the aim of the review is not to make generalizations about groups, but to elaborate on psychological patterns that may develop under oppressive social conditions.

Feminist psychologists and writers

Feminist psychologies have their origins in the women's liberation movements, particularly in their challenges to psychiatry and psychotherapy, and to the construction of psychology as a discipline. One of the earliest works to emerge from this movement, Phyllis Chesler's *Women and Madness* (1972), exposed the abuse and control of women within the psychiatric system. Chesler argued that what is labelled 'madness', particularly depression, is either an inevitable outcome of conformity to the prescribed female role, or a label applied to women who refuse to conform to the female role. She suggested that at the heart of female conditioning is pressure to attend to others and gratify others' needs, and argued that this must be transformed into identities 'forged out of concern for their own survival and self-definition' (p. 301). Chesler also saw the need for institutional and structural change. As the field of 'psychology of women' emerged, it built up extensive empirical research on many aspects of women's experiences and psychological patterns, alongside the more theoretically oriented feminist psychology, which makes more explicit links between patriarchal social conditions and psychology and behaviour (Crawford and Unger, 2004; Denmark and Paludi, 2007; Wilkinson, 1997).

The authors to be reviewed below vary in the extent to which they draw on this work, and in some cases do not have psychological training. What they have in common is an analysis, either from an empirical basis or from clinical or personal experience, of psychological patterns associated with structural features of oppression. They may be considered foundation writers in feminism and colonialism, in that they were among the first to provide an in-depth discussion of psychological aspects of oppression, often in very personal ways. This chapter reviews specific writings by each of them in which they link oppression to specific structural features, namely colonialism (Maracle, 1996), domination–subordination (Miller, 1986; Kasl, 1992; Herman, 1997), racism (hooks, 1993; 2002b), poverty (O'Neill, 1992) and homophobia (Pharr, 1988). By selecting writers who vary considerably in voice and background, and who address diverse social conditions, it is hoped to both acknowledge specificities and highlight common themes in the different experiences of oppression.

Lee Maracle

Lee Maracle, a Native American activist and writer (Maracle, 1990) who lives in Canada, has provided a deeply personal and insightful account of the oppressions of colonialism and sexism in her book *I am Woman* (Maracle, 1996). She identifies the aims and mechanisms of colonialism, placing some of the negative patterns and behaviours of Native Americans in the context of their history of colonialism and their current condition as one of the poorest sectors of North American society. Where at first her political consciousness focused on the Native movement as a whole, she became increasingly aware of the role of sexism and misogyny within Native culture, which she saw as themselves a legacy of colonialism, racism and patriarchy. Maracle (1996) writes that: 'Until March, 1982, feminism, indeed womanhood itself, was meaningless to me. Racist ideology had defined womanhood for the Native woman as nonexistent' (p. 15). Women themselves had internalized the sexism which permeated the Native movement: 'As women we do not support each other. We look at males when they speak and stare off into space when a woman steps assertively into the breach of leadership' (1996, p. 18). For Maracle, claiming her identity as a woman, and developing her awareness of sexism and misogyny in the Native community was essential: 'I woke up. I AM WOMAN! Not the woman on the billboard... But a woman for whom mobility, muscular movement, physical prowess are equal to the sensuous pleasure of being alive' (1996, p. 17).

In describing colonial patterns, Maracle (1996, pp. 93–4) focuses on control and erasure of culture, on the loss of power, and on fragmentation:

Destruction and expropriation of knowledge, particularly language, medicine (science) and culture is a prerequisite for the unabated persecution of pockets of resistance. The aims of the colonizer are to break up communities and families, and to destroy the sense of nationhood and the spirit of cooperation among the colonized. A sense of powerlessness is the legacy handed down to the colonized people. Loss of power – the negation of choice, as well as legal and cultural victimization – is the hoped for result. It can never be wholly achieved. At every juncture in the history of colonization, we have resisted domination. Each new prohibition was met with defiance, overt and covert.

A sense of powerlessness, pain, shame, anger, hopelessness and despair are among the emotional reactions which Maracle (1996) describes. There is a need to remain invisible, as 'the colonizers erase you, not easily, but with shame and brutality' (1996, p. 8). Native men are labelled as lazy and drunk, while Native women are regarded as being stoic and without feelings – 'Do they have feelings?' (1996, p. 17). Spirituality, which Maracle regards as 'natural to us all' is 'obstructed and even crushed' (1996, p. 115). Creativity is distorted, its products appropriated, and cultural expression is altered without regard for Native aspirations. Sexuality is permeated by sexism and racism, as Native women are erased, and both men and women suffer the humiliating awareness of the respect and sexual attraction each has for whites, especially white women who are presented by popular culture and pornography as sexually powerful and available. While anger and rage are natural reactions to the oppressions of Native Americans, Maracle (1996) writes that too often anger and rage are directed within the community, rather than towards the colonizers. She uses the phrase 'lateral violence' to refer to the violence and aggression which Native people direct towards each other:

> The anger inside has accumulated generation by generation, and because it was left to decay, it has become hatred. By its very nature, racism only permits the victimized race to engage that hatred among its own. Lateral violence among Native people is about our anticolonial rage working itself out in an expression of hate for one another (1996, p. 11).

Further, she links the abuse of alcohol to the continued frustrations and defeats of the Native movement: 'It is our history of losing that keeps us locked to the bar stools, not our fear of fighting' (1996, p. 95). Lateral violence permeates intimate relationships: 'I have brought pain and terror into our bedroom. My lover has brought pain and anger' (1996, p. 31). It is acted out on Native women by Native men in the violence of battery and rape, and in the sexism of Native men, sexism which Maracle contrasts with the respect held for women in indigenous Native culture.

Jean Baker Miller

Jean Baker Miller's (1986) book *Toward a New Psychology of Women*, first published in 1976, continues to be one of the best-known books on women's psychology. It was an early and groundbreaking attempt to link women's psychology to the social conditions of their lives and, in particular, to the dynamics of domination–subordination. Miller, a white North American psychiatrist, based her analysis on her clinical practice, and while she acknowledges variations based on class, race and ethnicity, her work has been criticized for the homogeneity of its case base, and in particular for its exclusive focus on heterosexuality. Miller tried to address these criticisms in the revised edition of the book (1986), and in her later work (Jordan et al. 1991; Miller and Stiver, 1997). While the later development of relational psychology (Jordan, 2004; Robb, 2006) forged new understandings and practices for psychotherapy and psychology, Miller's insights into the dynamics of domination–subordination were most clearly stated in her 1976/1986 book. These insights were introduced in Chapter 2, where the dynamics of inferiority–superiority, control of cultural outlook, and denial of vulnerabilities and weaknesses were described. These dynamics have a number of implications for psychological functioning for those in dominant and subordinate groups.

A major theme of Miller's is that subordinates are oriented towards others: 'anyone in a subordinate position must learn to be attuned to the vicissitudes of mood, pleasure and displeasure of the dominant group' (Miller, 1986, p. 39). Subordinates may be more attuned to the dominants than they are to themselves, to the point where they are unaware of their own needs. Emotional sensitivity is also developed through the subordinate role as carriers of emotional vulnerability, which makes it easier for subordinates to admit weaknesses and fears. In the case of women, emotional sensitivity to others is heightened by their role in fostering growth and development. Carried to excess, this orientation to others can lead to emotional weakness and dependency. However, Miller argues that emotional sensitivity and attunement to others are capacities which could become strengths if society placed a higher value on fostering growth and development (Miller, 1986; Miller and Stiver, 1997).

This focus on others creates problems with self-knowledge – there is a difficulty for subordinates in obtaining a realistic assessment of their own needs. Problems with self-knowledge are compounded because of the myths about subordinates that are inherent to systems of domination. There is a conflict between the understanding of self that subordinates develop based on their own experience, and the myths which are presented in the culture, creating an inner tension for subordinates.

The orientation towards others means that women tend to value themselves and what they do in terms of giving. They define themselves and obtain self-worth by how much and how well they satisfy others' needs. Women's self-worth is also undermined by myths of inferiority. The activities of subordinates are not valued by society, and therefore subordinates tend to be seen as 'not doing anything' (Miller, 1986, p. 52). The emotional work involved in fostering development is not seen as activity, while the work that women do in the household, in fostering their husbands' careers, and in creating community, is invisible.

The capacity for direct action is another area which is undermined by subordination. Subordinates wish to remain as hidden as possible, and resort to disguised and indirect ways of acting and reacting which often appear as manipulating. They avoid direct action for their own interest: 'Such actions can, and do, literally result in death for some subordinate groups. In our own society, a woman's direct action can result in a combination of economic hardship, social ostracism, and psychological isolation – and even the diagnosis of a personality disorder' (Miller, 1986, p. 10). Direct action is also blocked by subordinates' lack of power, and by the way in which the use of power is affected by subordination. Miller defines power as 'the capacity to produce a change' (1986, p. 98) and argues that women are most comfortable with power when they are using it in the service of others.

The construction of anger in women has an inhibiting effect on women's capacity for direct action. As Miller points out, 'any subordinate is in a situation that constantly generates anger. Yet this is one of the emotions that no dominant group ever wants to allow in subordinates' (1991b, p. 183). Anger is blocked through fear of retaliation by force, or through fear of disrupting a relationship in which there is economic dependency. Ideology makes it appear that subordinates have no reason to be angry. In the case of women, anger is seen as incompatible with women's identity, and also with their role as carers and nurturers. As a result, women's anger becomes transformed into depression, confusion and indirection, or eventually may emerge in exaggerated form, inviting the label of 'overreacting' or 'hysterical'.

In the course of her analysis Miller (1986; 1991b) also identifies psychological themes related to domination. In many ways dominants are the mirror image of subordinates. They regard themselves as superior, and as being strong and emotionally independent. They wish to be visible, and to be seen as successfully pursuing goals judged to be important. Their emphasis is on doing, rather than on giving, and on direct action rather than on indirect action. Like subordinates, they have difficulty developing a realistic self-perception both because of cultural stereotypes and because they are denied realistic feedback about themselves and their emotional needs, or even about the consequences of their actions. Dominants have a fear of admitting weakness and vulnerability. They are encouraged from early life to be active and rational. This tends to block inclinations towards cooperation, and to encourage competition.

Miller argues that these patterns create difficulties for intimate relationships between dominants and subordinates: 'What is immediately apparent is that mutually enhancing interaction is not probable between unequals' (1986, p. 12). Indeed the experience of disconnection, with its accompanying anxiety, isolation and depression is more probable in relationships between unequals (Miller and Stiver, 1997). Both have unrealistic self-concepts, different emotional orientations, and different patterns of interests and modes of action. Men, who are usually in a dominant position, hope that their needs will be met without needing to acknowledge them; women, who are usually in a subordinate position, have difficulty acknowledging their own needs. Thus there is little scope for open expression and negotiation of emotional needs. Even at the sexual level, the differing emphases of men and women mean that sex tends to involve doing for men, while it involves giving for women.

Charlotte Davis Kasl

Charlotte Davis Kasl is a white North American psychologist and researcher working in the field of addiction, codependency (or internalized oppression syndrome, as she would prefer to call it) and child abuse (Kasl, 1989; 1992; 1998). Her theoretical analysis is based on her practice as well as on extensive surveys and interviews with women from a variety of settings. What is distinctive about her work is her explicit linking of addiction to domination–subordination, patriarchy and capitalism, and her elucidation of some of the processes whereby these macro systems have an impact on psychological functioning.

The following quote summarizes Kasl's position (Kasl, 1992, p. 53):

> Patriarchy, hierarchy, and capitalism create, encourage, maintain and perpetuate addiction and dependency. Patriarchy and hierarchy are based on domination and subordination, which result in fear. This fear is expressed by the dominators through control and violence, and in the subordinated people through passivity and repression of anger. The external conflict of hierarchy between dominants and subordinates becomes internalized in individuals, creating personal inner chaos, anxiety, and duality. To quell the inner conflict, people resort to addictive substances and behaviors.

Kasl (1992) argues that the constant fear created in hierarchies can lead to a kind of dissociation similar to that found in child abuse cases. Dissociation involves disconnecting or detaching from a set of experiences or feelings, especially related to fear or terror. The hierarchical mechanism of fragmentation, where people are isolated from each other, and different areas of life and experience are separated or compartmentalized, also produces dissociation. Hierarchies also emphasize conformity and stifle critical thinking. Both dissociation and conformity are incompatible with the questioning and compassion which are essential for spiritual development. The development of spirituality is thus blocked, creating a spiritual vacuum which fosters addiction.

The dynamics of hierarchies – 'manipulation, violence, exclusion from decision-making groups, and economic deprivation' (Kasl, 1992, p. 56) – also create a variety of negative emotions which further feed the addiction process. These include exhaustion and shame, as well as fear, self-hatred, apathy, hopelessness, despair and pain. A fundamental emotion for women, and other subordinates, is shame. Shame is instilled especially through the dynamic of inferiority–superiority and through 'blaming the victim', where subordinate groups are made to feel inferior, defective and blameworthy. At a physical level, people suffer exhaustion and depletion as they use stimulants and anti-depressants to push themselves beyond the natural limits set by the body. Exhaustion becomes a chronic condition of everyday life.

Like Miller (1986), Kasl (1992) suggests that both dominants and subordinates suffer restrictions of self, as they are overdeveloped in certain areas and underdeveloped in others. Dominants suppress sensitivity and love, become trapped in competitive behaviour and relationships, and constantly fear loss of status. They are highly developed in the use of power and rationality. Subordinates lack self-understanding because they are so focused on dominants, and are both deprived of power and inhibited in their use of power. They are highly developed in empathy and cooperation. These imbalances create the basis for relationships based on dependency.

Many of the psychological patterns associated with subordination coincide with the concept of codependency, a term of which Kasl, like many others, is highly critical. Kasl (1992) argues that the term is itself oppressive, blaming minorities and women for traits that they have been moulded to develop. Kasl (1992) coins the phrase 'internalized oppression syndrome' to replace the term 'codependency', arguing that the patterns labelled codependency are nothing less than internalized oppression. These patterns include unawareness or neglect of personal needs and compulsive focusing on others, inability to express anger or emotional needs, feelings of powerlessness, dependency and lack of self-worth. The fundamental dynamic is a denial of the self and attunement to dominants, resulting in an inner duality or conflict: 'the constant struggle between speaking out or being silent winds like a thread through the fabric of one's existence' (p. 280). At its core is intense psychological dependency, an inability to believe that one can survive on one's own, which Kasl believes is the experience of many, if not most, women, and which is instilled through patriarchal conditioning.

All of these psychological processes – negative emotions, dissociation, imbalances in psychological development and blocks to spiritual growth – are likely to lead to addiction, the compulsive use of mind-altering substances or behaviours. Addiction itself is a form of duality or split, experienced as an inner conflict between the desire not to use and the compulsive urge to use, and this duality in turn feeds the addictive process. For Kasl (1992), addiction is ultimately an outcome of hierarchical social organization, and its elimination requires political and social change, as well as empowerment at the personal level.

Judith Herman

The themes of dissociation, and of tension between speaking out and remaining silent, also occur in Judith Herman's comprehensive synthesis of research and theory on trauma and recovery (Herman, 1981; 1997). Drawing on a wide range of research on war trauma, hostages and women who have been raped and battered, as well as on her clinical practice and experience with victims of violence, Herman, a white North American psychiatrist, identifies patterns which are common reactions to different types of trauma, and outlines the processes involved in recovery from trauma. Elements of the traumatic situation which are also present in systems of domination include the experience of violence, and the fear of violence and also isolation, powerlessness and enforced dependency. Additionally, like dominants, the perpetrator of trauma is motivated to deny the trauma, either through secrecy and silence, or through discrediting the victim: 'to this end he marshals an impressive array of arguments, from the most blatant denial to the most sophisticated and elegant rationalization' (Herman, 1997, p. 8). These dynamics are part of 'the central dialectic of psychological trauma', namely 'The conflict between the will to deny horrible events and the will to proclaim them aloud' (Herman, 1997, p. 1). Denial may be perpetrated by communities and societies – Herman notes that both war veterans and rape victims very often find that the communities and societies to which they return have an interest in denying the extent of their trauma.

Inner tension also arises from reactions to trauma, which include hyperarousal, intrusion and constriction. Hyperarousal or hypervigilance is a form of chronic autonomic nervous system arousal also found under conditions of chronic stress, and associated with irritability, sleep disturbances and startle reactions. Intrusion is the experience of memories intruding on consciousness, while constriction keeps memories out of consciousness. These two processes are in tension with each other, and there is often oscillation between the two. The victim of trauma 'finds herself caught between the extremes of amnesia or of reliving the trauma' (Herman, 1997, p. 47), which creates further inner tension and sense of helplessness and unpredictability.

Trauma has pervasive effects on all aspects of psychological functioning: it creates emotions of terror, despair and shame; it undermines self-worth and dehumanizes the victim; it isolates the victim and separates or disconnects her from close ties, and from community. A fundamental outcome of trauma is disconnection, because trauma undermines the sense of trust in the world, and damages 'the systems of attachment and meaning that link the individual and community' (Herman, 1997, p. 51). This in turn damages the individual's basic sense of self, which is formed in relation to others, and creates shame and doubt. The regulation of intimacy is undermined, as

> Trauma impels people both to withdraw from close relationships and to seek them desperately. The profound disruption in basic trust, the common feelings of shame, guilt and inferiority, and the need to avoid reminders of the trauma that might be found in social life, all foster withdrawal from close relationships (Herman, 1997, p. 56).

The reactions of those with whom the survivor has close relationships are therefore crucial in the immediate and long-term aftermath of trauma. The community more generally can have a profound impact, through denial or through acknowledging the trauma, and community is essential for recovery.

bell hooks

bell hooks has written extensively and radically about racism and black liberation, and has been at the forefront of black critiques of white feminism (hooks, 1984; 1991; 1993; 2002b). In her book *Sisters of the Yam: Black Women and Self-Recovery*, she writes that while the emphasis must be on political change, her involvement in feminist and black liberation movements convinced her of the importance of mental health or 'psychic well-being' (hooks, 1993, p. 15) for effective political action: 'when wounded individuals come together in groups to make change our collective struggle is often undermined by all that has not been dealt with emotionally' (hooks, 1993, p. 5). While acknowledging the strengths of black culture, she notes that the hatred and negativity of images and stereotypes of blacks in culture generally, and the ways in which black culture has adapted to this situation produce patterns which are damaging psychologically (hooks, 2002b). For example, racist culture criticizes and dismisses black achievements and cultural practices; these patterns are reproduced in black parenting practices, in an effort to insulate black children against the inevitable harshness of a racist world.

In *Sisters of the Yam* in particular, hooks writes of racism as a system of domination, focusing especially on violence, economic discrimination and racism in culture, and emphasizing 'the interconnectedness of systems of domination, of racism and sexism' (hooks, 1993, p. 3). In addition, she writes that 'a culture of domination is necessarily a culture where lying is an acceptable social norm' (1993, p. 20). Active deception, withholding of information, hiding behind deceptive appearances – various practices of dissimulation – were an essential part of black culture under slavery. In contemporary underprivileged groups, deception is also used to cover up 'realities that are regarded as shameful' (hooks, 1993, p. 24), or to ensure access to government resources. For those with a chronic experience of powerlessness, the ability to withhold or disclose information provides a fleeting sense of power and control. Thus dissimulation serves complex political and psychological purposes. Yet dissimulation undermines relationships, creates stress and prevents clear political analysis and action.

In a further analysis of negative patterns which have developed in black culture in response to the assaults of a racist culture, hooks (1993) suggests that a pattern of being harshly critical with each other developed, both because it reflected the negative views of the dominant culture, and because it was an 'attempt to second-guess what the critical white world might say to disparage, ridicule or mock' (p. 34). In an effort to prepare children for the harshness of white culture, black parents adopted harsh parenting practices, criticizing their children and warning them against expecting too much. hooks (1993) writes that 'The vast majority of black people, particularly those of us from non-privileged class backgrounds, have developed survival strategies based on imagining the worst and planning how to cope with it' (p. 62). Thus negative thinking becomes an ingrained pattern and mutual criticism the accepted norm. hooks links these patterns to tendencies to push beyond limits and to develop addictions.

The harshness of the white culture is also accompanied by an unwillingness to appear weak, with an emphasis on stoicism in the face of adversity and difficulty admitting problems or seeking help and sympathy. hooks (1993) asks 'where are the spaces in our lives where we are able to acknowledge our pain and express grief?' (p. 104). Survival for blacks was often linked to the capacity to repress feelings, including feelings of love (hooks, 1993 p. 131):

> Our collective difficulties with the art and act of loving began in the context of slavery. It should not shock us that a people who were forced to witness their young being sold away; their loved ones, companions, and comrades beaten beyond all recognition; a people who knew unrelenting poverty, deprivation, loss, unending grief, and the forced separation of family and kin; would emerge from the context of slavery wary of this thing called love.

This overlooking of emotional needs extends to the world of work, where there is an emphasis on working for material survival rather than out of a vocation. Again there is a need to challenge socialization: 'Many of us must work hard to unlearn the socialization that teaches us that we should just be lucky to get any old job. We can begin to think about our work lives in terms of vocation and calling' (1993, p. 47).

hooks (1993) devotes considerable attention to the images of beauty to which black women are subjected, with their emphasis on modelling white standards rather than valuing and loving blackness. She writes that 'personal power really begins with care of the self' (1993, p. 89), and in particular of the body. She argues that internalized racism, or self-hatred, has been heightened by racial integration and by constant exposure to white-dominated TV and mass media. For black women, the mere act of refusing to straighten their hair is an assertion of defiance of white cultural norms, yet it is likely to be greeted with derision by other blacks, and particularly by black men (hooks, 2002b).

In almost every area of functioning, hooks (1993) sees the need for black women to question and break away from the forms and patterns shaped by the dominant culture, and construct new ways of being that are life-affirming and self-loving. In the area of eroticism and sexuality, hooks writes that the use of black women in pornography and prostitution and the permeation of heterosexuality by violence and abuse means that 'the realm of black heterosexual sexual expression is rarely a place where black females learn to glory in our erotic power' (1993, p. 119). She speculates further that the general harshness of black childrearing, with its emphasis on emotional toughness, may create needs based on physical and emotional deprivation which are inappropriately acted out in the realm of sexuality. Citing Audre Lorde (1984), she urges a re-visioning of the erotic as 'an assertion of the life force of women' (hooks, 1993, p. 113). The experience of a life-affirming sexuality and eroticism will involve a reclaiming of the body, of communication, of bi-sexuality and lesbianism, even of spirituality and connection with the universe. Indeed hooks places the cultivation of spirituality at the centre of the process of self-recovery.

Cathleen O'Neill

In presenting her interviews with women living in poverty, Cathleen O'Neill, an Irish community activist, presents rare experientially based insights into the psychological dimensions of poverty (O'Neill, 1992). Poverty has much in common with racism at the material level – it creates social conditions of deprivation and marginalization where the constant day-to-day tasks of physical survival take precedence. In her discussion of a community 'fractured by poverty and unemployment' (1992, p. x), O'Neill begins with the physical environment: 'the landscape they confront daily is grim, spare and bare' (1992, p. 11). Houses are small and badly designed, making socializing and studying for exams very difficult, while those living in flats have a host of problems with space and security. There is a lack of playing spaces or recreational facilities, poor public transport and few other amenities.

Lack of space and privacy are accompanied by lack of time, which is spent negotiating with various state agencies, queuing for hospital and other health services, shopping for the best bargains, rationing out food and fuel supplies, juggling payment of various bills and overseeing childcare. The delicate financial balancing act is constantly threatened by the unexpected – a sickness, for example – and by events such as Christmas, marriages, births, deaths and the religious ritual of First Holy Communion. Yet such rituals are crucial for the maintenance of family and community, to assert the capacity to exchange gifts, to celebrate and take pride.

Poverty involves 'living with strain and anxiety every day' (O'Neill, 1992, p. 32), 'saying "No" to your children so often that you become worried when they stop asking' (1992, p. 32), 'dragging yourself up from your toes regularly, putting on a happy face to stop your husband and family from sinking into despair' (1992, p. 32). The family and the community are constantly faced with fragmentation as individuals move on to better areas, or in search of jobs. There is constant insecurity both because of the temporary and unstable nature of whatever work is available, and because of the constant turnover in family and neighbourhood composition. Feelings of hopelessness – 'growing up with no hope of better things to come' (1992, p. 55) – become pervasive, leading to depression and drug usage.

O'Neill writes that 'repeated application, negotiation and supplication to social welfare authorities has become a regular feature of life' (1992, p. 58). This undermines self-worth, and creates a double dependency for women. They are dependent on the state for income, and since social welfare money is often paid to the husband as head of household, they are dependent on his signature and/or generosity for access to financial resources. Feelings of humiliation, debasement, anger and frustration are generated by practices such as severely restricting hours of opening, repetitive filling out of forms and interviews requiring personal details, cases being passed from one officer to the next and repeated and unexplained refusals and delays.

Problems with physical and mental health are often outcomes of the material deprivation, constant anxiety and tension, and feelings of hopelessness and worthlessness: 'Ill health, depression, stress and the past and present use of tranquillizers were the common denominators' (O'Neill, 1992, p. 77). There is little time, motivation, or resources for preventative health care, and the health services are almost exclusively oriented towards dealing with illness, with few resources for health education or counselling. Use of tranquillizers and sleeping pills is widespread, with consequent dangers of addiction and worsening social conditions as inability to cope increases.

The education system itself is a source of humiliation, with many women reporting that they felt that teachers 'look down on them' (O'Neill, 1992, p. 96). Difficulties with the cost of education, with competition, with the irrelevance of the curriculum, with finding the motivation and the means to succeed were constantly reiterated, along with the recognition of the importance of education for advancement. Thus both the health and educational systems are more likely to be sources of humiliation and frustration than of support and advancement. The constant stress creates problems not just for health, but also for interpersonal relationships, with marriage and families breaking up, or being forced to break up in the search for employment. Yet community, and particularly neighbourliness, are of crucial importance in living under deprived conditions. Neighbours share and exchange resources and provide emotional and practical support. O'Neill (1992) writes of the extraordinary generosity and solidarity among neighbours, who share whatever financial resources they have, pass on clothing and other resources, and take over in times of crisis. Community is maintained by strong traditions, and by participation in the community associations. Obviously structural changes in the distribution of wealth are the ultimate means for alleviating poverty, but additionally, for O'Neill, the building up of community associations and the provision of health and education are crucial to an improvement in living conditions.

Suzanne Pharr

Suzanne Pharr was one of the first to write on homophobia as a form of internalized oppression and on the damage to interpersonal relationships and to the lesbian community of interpersonal patterns which have developed in response to domination (Pharr, 1988). The words 'homophobia' and 'heterosexism' have been coined to refer to prejudice, hatred and discrimination directed towards lesbians and gay men, along with the assumptions about heterosexuality as natural and superior. Both of these have been discussed by feminist writers who have written critically of the construction of heterosexuality, particularly the ways in which heterosexuality is permeated by violence and domination, and of the damages wrought by homophobia and heterosexism on all expressions of sexuality. Indeed the damage to sexuality and to sexual relationships has been touched upon to various degrees by all of the authors discussed in this chapter. Here the focus is on the impact of homophobia as experienced by lesbians.

Pharr is an American lesbian political activist whose experience with battered women and with lesbians provided her with insights into the psychological aspects of oppression, and more specifically, lesbian oppression (Pharr, 1988). Placing homophobia in the context of patriarchy, she links it to violence, economic control and the construction of gender roles. Linking internalized oppression to social conditions, she records the experiences of oppression, especially of social exclusion, recounted by lesbians: violence and harassment, exclusion from clubs, organizations and friendship circles, loss of custody of children, rejection by family and friends, loss of jobs and restricted opportunities for employment, failure to complete educational and training programmes because of harassment, lack of attention to health care or inadequate health care. A fundamental feature of lesbian existence is invisibility – lesbians are a hidden population, whose stories and lives are absent from mainstream culture and mass media, and, where they are present, their stories are most often ones of loneliness and despair. Negative stereotypes of lesbians as deviant, mentally ill, perverted and disordered are internalized to create feelings of self-hatred, shame and isolation (Pharr, 1988).

Out of fear of discrimination and rejection, most lesbians keep their sexual orientation hidden for at least some period of their lives. Pharr writes of the divisions and of the alienation both in relation to the world and to the self that this produces: 'I acted out of my sexual identity and had a social life that was woman-centered but I lived externally in and lied to a man-centered world' (1988, p. xiii). All of her relationships were permeated by this double life, which necessitated constant vigilance, and constant dissimulation, resulting in the undermining of the sense of integrity. While coming out or disclosing her sexual orientation alleviated the sense of an undermined and split identity, it in turn created a constant tension between the desire to disclose and challenge the assumption of heterosexuality and the desire to avoid the negative consequences of coming out. Thus homophobia leads to the constant restriction of self-expression and behaviour out of fear of rejection and/or discrimination, with accompanying dissimulation and tension or duality between speaking out and remaining silent.

Pharr (1988) points out that not only does homophobia act as a mechanism for controlling sexuality, it also creates divisions among women. Fear of being labelled lesbian or of actually being lesbian leads to the censoring of any behaviours that might be associated with lesbianism, to the exclusion of lesbians from groups and political activism, and to fear of close relationships or physical affection between women. This creates further isolation for lesbians, and lesbian friendships and relationships are expected to be a major source of love and support, but also bear the burden of being the only source: 'Having no real safety in other places, we give our relationships a sanctity and importance that is larger than life' (1988, p. 75). For lesbians themselves, the tendency to direct anger and despair towards each other further increases feelings of isolation and despair, and also creates difficulties for group or political organizing: 'Suffering the pain and damage of a world that despises us, we transform our pain into anger and turn it against one another' (1988, p. 56). For Pharr, community-building is the most effective way to combat the damage of homophobia.

This review of selected feminist writers provides further elaboration of both the social conditions associated with oppression and the psychological patterns which may develop under these conditions. Frequent references were made to the patterns discussed in the previous chapter – violence, lack of power, economic deprivation, control of sexuality, demeaning cultural patterns and the breaking up or fragmentation of families, communities and cultures. Experiences of humiliation, economic insecurity and dependency, negative stereotypes, social exclusion, isolation and restriction were common, with damaging effects both for individual psychological functioning and for interpersonal relationships and community. Possibilities for counterbalancing these damaging effects, particularly through building on the strengths gained from resistance, were acknowledged by most of these writers, and these possibilities will be reviewed in Chapter 4.

Colonialism

In turning to writings on colonialism, it will be apparent that there are many themes which parallel those in feminist writings. At the personal level, patterns of dualities of identity, ambivalence, negative and conflicting emotions and vulnerability to mental illness are common. At the interpersonal level, lateral or horizontal violence recurs as a theme. There is particular emphasis on the impact of violence and hatred, and the restrictions on community and political activism by the colonized. There is also considerable reference to the interconnections between the colonized and the colonizer at the psychological level. This last theme allows for further insights to be gained into the psychological aspects of colonizing, or of domination. The writers on colonialism reviewed below have also discussed processes involved in decolonization, which will be viewed in the next chapter on liberation.

The first psychological analysis of colonialism, written by the French psychoanalyst Mannoni, was originally published in 1950. Mannoni argued that the European 'inferiority complex' created a need to dominate, whilst the African 'dependency complex' led to a need to be dominated (Mannoni, 1962). Mannoni's work has been dismissed for a variety of reasons, most obviously his reduction of economic, political and cultural forces to psychological patterns. Other problems include racism, ethnocentrism, internal contradictions and his methodology, which relied on the analysis of myths and dreams. Most obviously, it failed to distinguish the effects of colonialism from its antecedents. However, Mannoni's analysis laid the basis for the insight that colonialism shapes psychological patterns in the colonizer and in the colonized, and that some of these patterns may be complementary.

The writers to be reviewed in this section are selected from a variety of cultural settings, again allowing for common themes and connections to emerge. They include first of all Fanon (1967a; 1967b) and Memmi (1967; 1968), whose writings about French colonization in Algeria and Tunisia respectively have been widely regarded for decades. These are followed by the Indian writer Nandy (1983) discussing British colonization in India and by Irish psychologists Kenny (1985) and Ruth (1988), who draw on the Irish experience of colonization by the British. Next are Native American psychologists Duran and Duran (1995) writing in the North American context. Finally, although not strictly an analysis of colonialism, the work of the South American writer Freire (1970) will be included, primarily because of his insights into liberation, which will be discussed in Chapter 4. Again works by these authors have been selected on the basis that they make explicit links between psychological patterns and oppressive social conditions. It should be noted here that few of these authors attend to gender in their writings, often using the universal 'he', and, for the most part, write of colonized and colonizer with little reference to variations based on class, sexual orientation or other social categories.

Frantz Fanon

The colonial experience of Frantz Fanon involved French colonization of the Caribbean island of Martinique, where he was born, and of Algeria, where he practised as a psychiatrist and fought in the Algerian war of independence. The French style of colonization was to completely replace the indigenous culture with French culture, claim the natives as French citizens and foster divisions between the various African and Caribbean natives around class and degrees of negrohood versus whiteness (Bulhan, 1985). Fanon's family belonged to the emerging black middle class, and their assimilation into French culture included, for example, rejection of the local dialect. Fanon joined the French army to fight against Germany and later travelled to France to study medicine. Both experiences exposed the racism of French culture. Later, in Algeria as a psychiatrist and revolutionary he witnessed and experienced the military and police violence which were central to colonial domination (Bulhan, 1985).

The theme of violence became central to Fanon's (1967a; 1967b) writings, and is also the source of major criticisms of his work (Bulhan, 1985). His view was that colonial domination was maintained through systematic and institutionalized violence. He further argued that violence necessitates and creates a Manichaean psychology, a psychological worldview where the world is divided into 'us' and 'them', 'good' and 'bad' and 'white' and 'black'. This is the basis for racist ideology, created and reflected in institutionalized racism which sustains the belief in white superiority and black inferiority. The hatred, brutality and dehumanization associated with violence and with racism permeate the psyches, everyday relationships and cultural practices of the colonized, and are manifest in a state of permanent tension. The constant bombardment of racist hatred and violence in a situation where there is total prohibition on reacting to the aggressor creates either extreme psychological repression with accompanying psychopathology, or outbreaks of violence directed towards each other. In this context the slightest insult from another native becomes an occasion for a violent reaction, for as Fanon writes: 'the last resort of the native is to defend his personality *vis-à-vis* his brother' (1967a, p. 54). Fanon argues that anger is an inevitable response of the colonized, but this is directed towards each other: 'The colonized man will first manifest this aggressiveness which has been deposited in his bones against his own people' (1967a, p. 40).

The first essay in *Black Skin, White Masks* (1967a) contains a number of themes which recur in Fanon's writings. He begins by noting a basic 'self-division' (1967a, p. 17) in the black man whereby he behaves differently with black men and with white men. The black man is faced with the unremitting message of the white man's superiority and the black man's inferiority, inducing a desire in the black man to be white, to be accepted. The desire is pursued through assimilation, including adopting the linguistic and cultural practices of the colonizers. Indeed, the black man's status is directly linked to the degree of assimilation. The black man has essentially two frames of reference, that of the black man and that of the white man; this creates a split in identity.

The desire to be white is associated with a denial and even a hatred of blackness, which is fed by negative stereotypes of blacks as dirty, lazy, emotional, savage, dull. Fanon (1967a) describes a range of feelings in response to such stereotypes – a devaluation of self, a lack of confidence, a basic insecurity, feelings of worthlessness, shame and self-contempt and anger at being black. Alienation is an inevitable outcome of these conditions. Alienation permeates the colonized psyche, as the colonized are alienated from their own culture, history, language, identity and labour. The colonized are also filled with ambivalence about their own identity, and their mixture of attraction and revulsion for the colonizer.

Ambivalence towards the colonizers is highlighted in Fanon's (1967a) discussion of interracial heterosexual relationships – between the woman of colour and the white man, and man of colour and the white woman. Here the search for recognition motivates a desire for a white lover, even though feelings of inferiority prevent authentic love. Ambivalence is unavoidable in this situation: the white man or woman is invested with attractiveness and potency, yet the man or woman of colour knows that they will always be regarded as inferior in the eyes of a white partner. Conflict is created between black men and women, who resent each other's preference for the white.

Difficulties with identity arise from the inferior status of blacks, and from the dual frame of reference noted above. Fanon (1967b) argues that this dual frame of reference produces a constant preoccupation with comparison:

> The Antilleans have no inherent values of their own, they are always contingent on the presence of the Other. The question is always whether he is less intelligent than I, blacker than I, less respectable than I. Every position of one's own, every effort at security is based on relations of dependence, with the diminution of the other (1967b, p. 211).

There is a reluctance to grant recognition to other blacks, whose only function is to afford recognition.

Fanon notes that while the black man is enslaved by his inferiority, the white man is enslaved by his superiority. Both end up with characteristics which Fanon associates with neuroticism. The claims of superiority by the colonizers are associated with self-delusion and self-adulation, a form of narcissism and self-aggrandisement. On the other hand, the colonized Negro is emotional and insecure: 'Affect is exacerbated in 'the Negro', he is full of rage because he feels small, he suffers from an inadequacy in all human communication, and all these factors chain him with an unbearable insularity' (1967a, p. 50). He writes that 'In the man of colour, there is a constant effort to run away from his own individuality, to annihilate his own presence' (1967a, p. 60). For Fanon, high levels of criminality and mental illness are the outcome of the social and psychological pressures of colonialism. Symptoms regarded as psychopathological – obsessions, inhibitions, anxieties, withdrawal – are clearly internal manifestations of social conditions.

Albert Memmi

Albert Memmi grew up as a Jew in Tunisia, which was then colonized by the French, and published *The Colonizer and the Colonized* in 1957. The experience of being Jewish in Tunisia provided Memmi with a sense of identification with both the colonized Tunisians and the colonizing French, since many Jews in Tunisia, which was primarily Muslim, attempted to assimilate as French. 'For better or worse, the Jew found himself one small notch above the Moslem on the pyramid which is the basis of all colonial societies' (Memmi, 1967, p. xiv). Memmi's attunement to both sides heightened his awareness of the destructive effects of colonialism for both the colonizer and the colonized: 'For if colonization destroys the colonized, it also rots the colonizer' (1967, p. xvii). Colonized and colonizer are trapped: 'the bond between colonizer and colonized is thus destructive and creative. It destroys and re-creates the two partners of colonization into colonizer and colonized. One is disfigured into an oppressor... the other into an oppressed creature' (1967, p. 89).

Memmi's description of the colonized starts with the example of laziness, a trait commonly attributed to the colonized. He writes 'Nothing could better justify the colonizer's privileged position than his industry, and nothing could better justify the colonized's destitution than indolence' (1967, p. 79). This label serves the double function of diminishing the colonized while elevating the colonizer and providing justification for economic inequalities. It is an easy move from this to a view of the colonized as generally deficient and in need of protection. The list of characteristics which Memmi sees being assigned to the colonized includes poor, lazy, stupid, backward, evil, brutish, cowardly, indulgent, uncivilized, unreliable, irresponsible, extravagant, unpredictable, mysterious, impulsive and undisciplined. These are, of course, stereotypes of inferiority in contrast to which the colonizer is intelligent, brave, civilized and responsible. This labelling process not only involves stereotyping but also depersonalization – the colonized are treated as an undifferentiated mass, 'an anonymous collectivity' (1967, p. 85). Furthermore, their behaviour is attributed to these characteristics rather than to social conditions or to specific personal circumstances. The end point of this process is objectification and dehumanization, which facilitate the brutal treatment of the colonized by the colonizer.

Memmi argues that because of the superior power of the colonizer and the degrading conditions of the colonized, these stereotypes cannot be dismissed by the colonized. Rather, 'this mythical and degrading portrait ends up being accepted and lived with to a certain extent by the colonized' (1967, p. 87). Furthermore, the situations into which the colonized are placed actually tend to produce behaviours and characteristics which reinforce these stereotypes. The military control of the colonized, and their removal from history, from community and from political power, erase a sense of responsibility, hope or courage.

The only sphere of action available to the colonized is their own local community or family, and it is in this sphere that rebellion, anger and resentment must be acted out. The scope for social mobility or social change is rigidly constrained, stifling vigour and initiative. Stagnation and inertia follow as the colonized are cut off from the past, alienated from the present, and deprived of a future.

For the colonizer, guilt and ambivalence are the prevailing emotions, and this is so whether the colonizer adopts a critical position towards the colonial regime, or completely upholds it. The former, referred to by Memmi as the benevolent colonizers, find themselves outsiders in relation to both the colonizers and the colonized. They are regarded as traitors by the colonizers, while the prejudices and racism inherent in the colonial situation deprive them of a sense of belonging with the natives even if they become revolutionaries, a situation which itself is fraught with ambivalence. Indeed, Memmi describes the position of the benevolent colonizer as one of 'solitude, bewilderment and ineffectiveness' (1967, p. 43).

Memmi's (1967) portrayal of 'the colonizer who accepts' – the colonialist – emphasizes the ambivalence of the colonizers' situation, and the rationalizations and justifications associated with it. The colonialist is blind to injustice, poverty and suffering. He believes absolutely in the excellence of the system, and justifies everything. He justifies his title and position by developing 'inordinate self-confidence' (1967, p. 102). A process of self-selection results in a colonial class marked by mediocrity and conservatism which is disguised by cultivating a sense of superiority and entitlement, and a glorification of power, especially the power of the home country. This assertion of superiority is fuelled by the illegitimacy of their situation.

The fundamental illegitimacy of the colonizers' position produces what Memmi (1967) calls the Nero Complex, an obsession with denying the extent of usurpation, and establishing legitimacy. This is done primarily by relentless demonstrations of the colonizer's merits and the colonized's flaws. This assault on the colonized creates guilt which fuels further denigration of the colonized, ultimately turning into the urge to destroy the colonized. Yet this dynamic cannot be brought to its ultimate conclusion because of the dependency of the colonizer on the colonized. Trapped by this dynamic, the colonizer becomes conservative, even fascist, justifying discrimination and violence against the colonized. Guilt and denial become inevitable. Rationalization and self-justification can be invoked at will. Extreme rigidity results from fear of changing the 'superior' colonial institutions.

Ashis Nandy

Writing in the post-colonial Indian context, Ashis Nandy (1983) sees colonialism as involving a complex relationship between colonizer and colonized which dehumanizes and objectifies both. Nandy pays particular attention to the processes whereby both groups become polarized, and especially, to how polarization is linked to the construction of gender. He argues that both the colonizers and the colonized become invested in models of masculinity which are divested of femininity, with masculinity then becoming polarized into two models: one, suitable for the lower classes, based on sexual prowess, the other, suitable for the ruling class, based on abstinence and self-control. This is accompanied by a denigration of the feminine. The feminine, traditionally associated in Indian society with power, maternity and protective magic, becomes passive and weak. The colonized and the colonized country become associated with a particular version of femininity – irrational, magical, intuitive, infantile, weak, soft, devious. The colonizer becomes associated with masculinity – 'aggression, achievement, control, competition and power' (1983, p. 9). Indian traditions of androgynous masculinity and of powerful femininity are erased, and problems for both national identity and for gender identity are created.

A fundamental asymmetry of the situation of colonization for Nandy is that the colonized have internalized the colonizers' culture, not vice versa. A splitting of self is inevitable – one part acknowledged and accepted, the other rejected. The colonized survive by 'overstressing those aspects of the self which they share with the powerful, and by protecting in the corner of their heart a secret defiance' (1983, p. 100), a defiance based on cunning and passivity. Thus in their reaction to the colonial situation, the colonized often reinforce colonial stereotypes of themselves.

In looking at the impact of colonialism on the colonizers, Nandy focused on British society, where he identified 'cultural pathologies' (1983, p. 35) associated with colonialism. Here there is a valuing of hypermasculinity, aggression and rationality, and a devaluing of femininity, emotion and compassion. Nandy cites E.M. Forster's concept of the 'undeveloped heart' to capture the outcome of this process – a split between affect and cognition, and a public domain which emphasizes violence and survival of the fittest. The belief in the superior development of the colonizers encourages them 'to impute to themselves magical feelings of omnipotence and permanence' (1983, p. 35) leading to over self-confidence and hypermasculinity, 'a life long fear of and respect for violence' (1983, p. 70), a refusal to look within, an avoidance of all deep conflicts, and a rejection of weakness and vulnerability.

Vincent Kenny

Writing in an Irish context from a constructivist perspective, Vincent Kenny draws on the ideas of Gregory Bateson and George Kelly in particular to elaborate ideas about 'The Post-Colonial Personality' (Kenny, 1985). By 'personality' he means 'forms of role-taking and construal options' (1985, p. 70). Focusing on the complementary nature of dominance and submission, he argues that various patterns of constriction develop in subordinates. By constriction he means: 'To constrict or draw in the outer boundaries of our perceptual field, which means limiting our interests, taking a near-sighted view of the world, dealing with only one issue at a time, and essentially moving in smaller and smaller circles which leads to a relatively repetitive mental process' (1985, p. 71). Kenny identifies two categories of constriction, namely social withdrawal and personal withdrawal, and describes examples of each.

Social withdrawal, which involves withdrawing from the environment and going 'underground' at the sociological level, has three forms. The first form is 'elaboration of secret worlds...which remain hidden from the external dominant reality' (Kenny, 1985, p. 71). These micro worlds may be formalized as secret societies, or secrecy may be enforced through custom and ritual. The second pattern is 'superficial compliance', where there is pressure on the one hand to be seen by the oppressor to comply with the oppressor, and on the other hand to be seen by the oppressed group to present a united front of resistance to the oppressor. The third pattern is 'indirect communication', where there is evasion, deceit and manipulation. While this serves the positive function of depriving the dominants of information and insight, it works against the subordinates by preventing clear communication with each other about either positive or negative feelings. A related pattern is 'avoidance of self-revelation', where subordinates reveal as little as possible about their own inner feelings, motives and needs.

Personal withdrawal involves 'increasing withdrawal into the self', and a turning away from reality. An example of this is 'elaboration of the inner world...of fantasy, magical thinking, superstition, creativity, aesthetics, poetry, music, etc.' (1985, p. 74). This is accompanied by decreasing attention to external reality, including other people. Personal withdrawal can also lead to helplessness and passivity, with components of 'despair, dependency, self-abnegation, withdrawal, shame, guilt, loss of pride, loss of confidence, sense of worthlessness, etc.' (1985, p. 75).

Finally, there is 'elaboration of the negative self', where individuals develop increasing levels of self-hatred and anger directed towards themselves.

An overall effect of constriction is several patterns of splitting, both within the self, and between the self and external reality (Kenny, 1985). Individuals become increasingly withdrawn from reality, and see themselves as unable to play a constructive role. They assign complete responsibility to the oppressor, while becoming increasingly absorbed in a fantasy world. Problems in relationships arise because of poor communication, lack of self-disclosure, and failure to understand the inner world of others. Passive aggression develops, where subordinates become more resistant when subject to pressure, sabotage plans without being obvious and undermine people by backbiting and gossip. Irresponsibility increases as the boundary between fantasy and reality becomes obscure, and external reality becomes increasingly 'unreal'. Isolation, unexpressed and repressed emotions, disintegration and madness are the end result.

Sean Ruth

Based on his involvement in industrial and educational settings, and drawing on the theory of re-evaluation counselling (Jackins, 1977), Irish psychologist Sean Ruth provides an analysis of psychological aspects of oppression which echo some of the themes discussed above (Ruth, 1988; 2006). He writes that 'the key to the maintenance of oppression...is what we can call internalized oppression or internalized control. This is where people come to believe in their own inferiority and their power-lessness to change things' (1988, p. 435). Ruth links low self-esteem, sense of inferiority and shame in the oppressed with 'mistrust in their own thinking and intelligence' (1988, p. 436), with the result that the oppressed tend to pay less attention and respect to each other and to their own thinking, and give more weight to the views of outsiders, particularly the dominant group. Mistrust in turn leads to divisiveness within the group: 'We come to be ashamed of one another, to mistreat one another, to be very critical of one another, to be unable to unite in a common cause, to feel hopeless about one another, and so on' (1988, p. 436).

Ruth identifies three other features of internalized oppression which centre around power and authority. Under situations of oppression, the oppressed 'learn to behave in ways that do not provoke retaliation or invite attention' (1988, p. 437), leading to lack of assertiveness. The oppressed have ambivalent attitudes towards their own leaders: 'On the one hand we come to have unrealistically high expectations of leaders, and, on the other hand, we fail to adequately support them' (1988, p. 436). And the oppressed also have an ambivalent attitude towards other oppressed peoples, often being willing to participate in the oppression of others: 'They may seek relief from the oppression by oppressing some other groups rather than trying to change the system' (1988, p. 437). Ruth developed this analysis further through a focus on leadership in a work that will be discussed more fully in Chapter 8 (Ruth, 2006).

Eduardo Duran and Bonnie Duran

In presenting a Native American post-colonial psychology in a North American context, Duran and Duran (1995) write that the concepts of soul, psyche, myth, dream and culture are central to Native Americans. Native American society was based on a worldview and cosmology that was very different from that of Western societies. It was highly structured with clearly defined roles and functions, initiation rituals, and a holistic spirituality. Its experience of colonization included military defeat and slaughter, dispossession, cultural erasure and enforced assimilation. Duran and Duran use the phrase 'soul wound' to refer to the psychological, social and spiritual damage which colonization created. The concept of soul wound captures the damage to the central core of being which they believe is caused by the trauma and displacement of colonization. It is both an individual concept and a collective one. It operates through myth and dream, which must become the vehicles for its healing.

Duran and Duran adapt the concept of post-traumatic stress disorder (PTSD) to the Native American situation, using the phrase 'intergenerational PTSD' to capture the way in which the traumas of colonization are passed on through generations. Loss and separation with accompanying grief are reactions to dispossession, slaughter and enforced relocation. Emotional reactions are polarized along gender lines. For men, Duran and Duran suggest that the process of identification with the aggressor may be particularly likely where there is the loss of the warrior role, motivated by the desire to gain the aggressor's power. In the absence of protective roles, aggression becomes channelled into violence against other Native Americans. Feelings of pride and rage traditionally channelled into protecting the tribe are displaced by shame, helplessness and hopelessness. Women, on the other hand, carry the burden of grief partly because they are more likely to accept the reality of colonization and bear the losses associated with it. In both cases, suppression of emotion is associated with either stoicism or problems with alcohol.

Paulo Freire

Paulo Freire, writing on the basis of his experience with the poor in Brazil, writes both of the overwhelming nature of oppression, and of practices which will facilitate the development of critical thinking and the capacity to take action (Freire, 1993). Like the preceding writers, Freire recognizes the complementary relationship of oppressor and oppressed. He defines oppression as 'Any situation in which "A" objectively exploits "B" or hinders his and her pursuit of self-affirmation as a responsible person' (p. 37). Both the act of oppressing and of being oppressed hinder self-affirmation – 'Once a situation of violence and oppression has been established, it engenders an entire way of life and behavior for those caught up in it – oppressors and oppressed alike. Both are submerged in this situation, and both bear the marks of oppression' (1993, p. 40). The oppressors develop a focus on possessing and controlling, leading to dehumanization and objectification of the oppressed, which in turn generates more violence and even sadism.

Like Fanon (1967a), Freire writes of the ambivalent attraction that the oppressed feel for the oppressors, of horizontal violence, and of a split or dual consciousness in the oppressed: 'The concrete situation of oppression...dualizes the I of the oppressed, thereby making the oppressed person ambiguous, emotionally unstable, and fearful of freedom' (1993, p. 154). The worldview of the oppressed includes viewing themselves as ignorant, unproductive and lazy, and the oppressor as all powerful and invulnerable. They depend on the oppressor, and therefore become dependent. Freire writes of alienation, of the loss of sense of hope or of the future: 'The individual is divided between an identical past and present and a future without hope. He or she is a person who does not perceive himself or herself as becoming; hence cannot have a future to be built in unity with others' (1993, p. 154).

One of Freire's (1993) major concerns is with the 'submerged' state of consciousness characteristic of the oppressed, a state which is created and maintained especially through control of education, and in particular through what he calls the 'banking model' of education. Here there is a clear distinction between the expert teacher who determines the curriculum and who 'deposits' knowledge into the students, who themselves are cast as ignorant and compliant objects in the educational process. This model of education can operate as a form of propaganda through the content of the curriculum, but also acts to control consciousness through suppressing the capacity of learners to be active agents critically evaluating their situation.

In a situation of submersion the individual is unable to stand back from the situation and critically evaluate either the situation or their own perceptions, feelings and actions in the situation. Confusions and contradictions, created by ideology and education, prevail, and there is a lack of a sense of the historical and changing nature of the situation. The situation is seen as overwhelming and unchanging, as 'a closed world from which there is no exit' (Freire, 1993, p. 31). When individuals are submerged in reality, they are primarily feeling their situation, and are unable to identify the causes of their feelings, leading to feelings of resignation and fatalism rather than hope.

An overview of psychological oppression

Although the authors reviewed above obviously shared a common interest in oppression and in psychological patterns associated with oppression, they wrote from diverse social contexts and personal experiences. What emerges is a broad, in-depth and evocative portrayal of psychological experiences of oppression, with both considerable range and remarkable convergences in the patterns identified. Many of these are congruent with research findings on oppressed, minority and marginalized groups (McAuliffe, 2008). However, empirical research has barely addressed, and indeed may have great difficulty addressing, many of the patterns identified: for example, duality of consciousness, horizontal hostility, patterns of dissimulation and loss of history. Yet these patterns recur not only in the authors reviewed above, but in a host of authors who have written of oppression from personal experience or from a theoretical analysis, and they are also pervasive in the literature and culture of oppressed people (Ashcroft et al., 2006).

It must be emphasized again that the aim here was to review writings on the damaging effects of oppression; these must be seen in the broader context of psychological development generally, and of the strengths which develop in situations of oppression. As Chapter 4 will show many of the writers reviewed above have written of the courage, perseverance, creativity and generosity of women, people of colour and others who have been subject to oppression. Furthermore, each individual negotiates personhood in relation to a range of social forces. Writing of racism in the British context, Amina Mama (1995, pp. 111–12) reminds us that

> racism can be seen as texturing subjectivity rather than determining black social and emotional life. Put another way, race is only ever one among many dimensions of subjectivity and it never constitutes the totality of an individual's internal life. Even where racial contradictions feature a great deal in people's history and experience, the fact they are responded to by personal change means that they are not an omnipresent force acting on passive victims.

This must be tempered by the reminder that there are social conditions which are virtually omnipresent – conditions of extreme poverty, ghettoization or warfare – which place intense pressure on individual psychology.

Overall, a number of themes recur which are familiar – lack of self-worth, suppression and displacement of anger, vulnerability to psychological distress – but which are elaborated from a number of different angles. The aim here is to present an overview of psychological oppression based on a synthesis of the writings reviewed above. It must firstly be acknowledged that oppression has an impact on the physical domain. There are frequent references to exhaustion and ill health brought about by the continuous tension and physical deprivation associated with oppression, and this will obviously interact with psychological functioning. Secondly, two strong themes emerge which have an impact on all of the above areas, and will therefore be discussed first. These themes are duality of consciousness and restriction/constriction.

A number of different dimensions of dual or double consciousness are identified. First, there is the familiar insight that those in positions of subordination have access both to their own consciousness and culture, and also to dominant consciousness and culture. Duality in the form of tension emerges through the gap between the inner person which is constructed and the outer images and norms. Duality also emerges in the 'dialectic of trauma', in the conflict between naming experience and reality – speaking out – and keeping silent. Another source of duality or tension which is particularly obvious in the writings on colonialism lies in the ambivalent relationships between colonizers and colonized, which contains both love and hate, admiration and contempt, attraction and repulsion. Relationships between those who are oppressed may also be a source of tension, as they become the focus both of solidarity and support and of displaced anger.

The theme of restriction is evident in a number of areas, with psychological constriction often presented as a reflection of restricted social conditions. The colonial worldview is characterized by a restrictive duality, the 'Manichaean' worldview of colonialism which polarizes everything into 'good' and 'bad', 'black' and 'white', 'us' versus 'them'. The need to focus on dominants provides subordinates with a restricted view of their own capacities and needs. Trauma and fear of trauma or assault is another source of restriction. Where there is an emphasis on material survival, attention is confined to this pressing need. Where there is isolation, emotional needs are confined to particular relationships. Through mystification, cultural erasure and loss of history, the worldview of oppression tends to be ahistorical, with reality seen as unchanging. Possible spheres of activity are restricted, so that the oppressed end up being focused on their own specific conditions in isolation from a broader social and historical analysis.

There is a general emphasis on loss and restriction of identity related especially to the erasure of history and culture, and on the restrictions of worldview discussed above. Lack of self-worth, feelings of inferiority, self-doubt and even self-hatred emerge repeatedly as responses to the myths of inferiority and expressions of contempt and hatred directed at subordinates. A variety of negative emotions are described, including fear, terror, anxiety, insecurity, humiliation, shame, guilt, confusion, despair and hopelessness, powerlessness, frustration, grief, isolation and loneliness. Anger is particularly problematic. Firstly there are difficulties experiencing anger directly, as the worldview perpetrated in systems of domination tends to obscure both the reasons for anger and the targets of anger. The expression of anger is often met with retaliation, with the result that anger can be directed at peers rather than at those in positions of domination.

Interpersonal relationships are characterized by a mixture of solidarity and support on the one hand, and by anger and manipulation on the other. The emphasis on attunement to others creates sensitivity and empathy, and interdependency creates close bonds based on shared experiences of oppression. However, there are difficulties with direct expression of emotional needs, and particularly with the experience of anger. Anger becomes directed towards peers in a pattern referred to as horizontal hostility or lateral violence, and this is fuelled by a lack of self-worth and other negative emotions. Patterns of criticism and dissimulation create further difficulties with communication and expression of emotional needs. Sexual relationships are permeated by these difficulties and by the power dynamics of domination–subordination.

The possibilities for direct action are clearly undermined by the experience of oppression. Direct action is prevented by fear of visibility and of retaliation, by lack of clear analysis, and by restrictions on the spheres of activity available to the oppressed. Lack of power, and discomfort with exercising power, further inhibit the capacity for direct action. Leadership is undermined by horizontal hostility and fear and distrust of authority. Vulnerability to psychological distress and madness is clearly increased by these damaging patterns, as well as by the external stresses created by oppression. Depression and drug usage, including alcohol, are linked to lack of self-worth, self-hatred and hopelessness. Constant vigilance, fear, distrust and suspicion can undermine psychological health and predispose to more severe forms of madness. Suppression of spirituality, or blocks to the development of spirituality, deprive the oppressed of the support and sustenance provided by spirituality.

The following chapter will discuss processes which can help to counterbalance these damaging effects, but it is already evident that the most fundamental antidote to these damaging effects is in the cultivation of strong and sustaining bonds through groups and communities, thus building on the strengths gained from oppression, which include empathy, the capacity for cooperation, perseverance and determination. Liberation from the damaging effects of oppression cannot occur in isolation, although individual or personal change is obviously necessary, but can only be gained and sustained through interaction with others, and through engagement in social transformation. This requires analysis of the dynamics of oppression, which itself is best obtained through dialogue and interaction with others.

It is also possible here to discuss patterns relating to being a member of the dominant or oppressor group as identified by some of the writers reviewed above, in particular Miller (1986; 1991b), Memmi (1967) and Nandy (1983), and also by Ruth's later work (Ruth, 2006). Like the oppressed, oppressors have difficulty developing an accurate self-concept, in this case because of myths of superiority, and because they lack direct feedback about themselves. Their position of power and control leads to feelings of aggrandisement and even delusions of grandeur, as well as high levels of self-confidence. At the emotional level, oppressors have difficulty admitting emotional needs and vulnerabilities, and tend to suppress feelings of sensitivity and love. The capacity to foster growth and development is underdeveloped in favour of an emphasis on taking action. Repressed guilt and the need to justify the oppressive situation can lead to dehumanization or lack of compassion, which may be fuelled by hostility and challenges to the status quo by the oppressed. Fear of loss of status and the need to defend the status quo can lead to rigidity and inability to admit mistakes. Oppressors experience tension between colluding with the status quo or aligning themselves against it. Relationships with subordinates lack authenticity, while those with oppressors are marked by competition. Overall, oppressors may also experience a sense of alienation from themselves, from each other, and from the status quo, especially if they doubt the legitimacy of the oppressive situation.

These observations would support the view that authentic relationships between dominants and subordinates are difficult and challenging. Heterosexual relationships are permeated by interdependency as well as by difficulties in communicating and satisfying needs. The polarization of masculinity and femininity, the objectification of women, and the dynamics of power and violence between men and women create further difficulties. Gender dynamics thus maintain a central role in oppression.

If these psychological patterns are related to social conditions, then it follows that they can only change if the social context changes. However, it is also clear that these patterns, however underdeveloped or overdeveloped in a particular individual or group, and however tempered by other qualities, create obstacles to taking action. They prevent a clear analysis from being formed, create self-doubt, generate inhibiting feelings and block the capacity for direct action. This creates a cycle of oppression, whereby conditions of oppression are associated with psychological patterns which undermine the capacity to resist domination. Furthermore, there are enormous barriers created in systems of domination to efforts to change the status quo. It is necessary both to develop practices which will counteract them within the limits of oppressive conditions, as well as to develop practices which will aid in taking action to bring about change. The following chapter will review themes and practices which writers on oppression and liberation have described, while later chapters will elaborate on the practices identified.

4
Breaking Out: The Cycle of Liberation

Obstacles to bringing about change in oppressive situations are created by the material and political conditions of oppression, by the mystification brought about under oppression, and by the psychological and interpersonal difficulties associated with oppression. It is difficult to develop a clear analysis of the situation, and it is difficult to marshal the psychological resources required to take effective action for change. A psychology of liberation, or a liberation psychology, aims to facilitate social change by aiding in the development of a clear analysis, confronting the psychological difficulties associated with oppression and enhancing the capacities for organizing and taking action.

Although the focus of the previous chapter was on psychological aspects of oppression, many of the writers reviewed there made either passing references to or theorized explicitly about processes and practices which could aid in liberation. Almost all of the writers, for example, made reference to the importance of self-definition as a response to the cultural definitions imposed in situations of oppression, and almost all made reference to the necessity of community, or of obtaining support from peers, in this process. This chapter will highlight the themes of liberation in the writers discussed in Chapter 3, and will additionally review the writings of American radical feminists Daly (1978; 1984; 2005) and Starhawk (1987; 2005), and the El Salvadoran writer Ignacio Martín-Baró (1994), who have written extensively on liberation.

Feminist writers

The feminist writers under consideration vary considerably in their emphasis, with some, for example O'Neill (1992) and Pharr (1988), oriented primarily towards oppression, while others, such as hooks

(1993; 2002b), have clearly developed insights into processes which can transform damaging psychological patterns. They also differ in their approach – Maracle (1996), for example, focuses primarily on her personal and political journey, Kasl (1992; 1997) and Herman (1997) theorize on the basis of theory, research and clinical experience in the area of addiction and trauma, respectively, while hooks (1993) combines her personal and political experience with her involvement in self-recovery groups for black women.

Some writers – Miller (1986) and Herman (1997) – focus on the self and the individual level of analysis, although they acknowledge the importance of interpersonal relationships and of community. The remaining writers – Maracle (1996), Kasl (1992; 1997), hooks (1993), O'Neill (1992) and Pharr (1988) – place considerable emphasis on community, both in the sense of re-establishing a historical sense of community and tradition, and of building a community which can sustain resistance and action for change. There is a clear acknowledgement by these authors of the need to change social conditions. Indeed all of them share an explicit focus on social conditions in their analysis of oppression. However, there is relatively little direct discussion by these authors of the capacities involved in taking action to bring about change.

Maracle (1996) provides the most direct reference to political activism when she writes that awareness of and belief in resistance are a vital source of strength. Whether resistance takes the form of political lobbying, defiance, community-building or cultural resistance, it is essential to continue to resist, to fight, to assert the reality of domination and the wish for self-determination. She argues that a sense of history is essential:

> Before I can understand what independence is, I must break the chains that imprison me in the present, impede my understanding of the past, and blind me to the future. Without a firm understanding of what our history was before the settlers came to this land, I cannot understand how we are to regain our birthright as caretakers of the land and continue our history into the future (1996, p. 40).

Maracle also sees strength, independence, self-determination and love as key elements of liberation. Maracle (1996) writes that her own life experience has taught her the power of love as a vital source for survival and hope: 'In the early years of my political activism the passion expressed itself as a virulent hatred for the system which destroyed our lives, our families; today the passion expresses itself as deep caring' (p. 3). The events of her life 'moved me to see that through all the hurt and the anger written into the lives of Native people, great love has survived' (p. 5).

For Miller (1986) the path to liberation lies primarily in a fundamental revaluing of the role of growth and development, and of the capacities for nurturance, empathy and vulnerability which accompany the fostering of growth and development. Miller and her colleagues (Miller and Stiver, 1997; Jordan 2004) argue that the capacities for empathy, cooperation and connectedness which are essential for fostering growth and development have been devalued and labelled as weaknesses – emotionality, sensitivity, dependency – contributing to women's lack of self-worth. These capacities for relating to others should be seen as strengths, and as essential for full personhood.

Miller (1991a) sees authenticity as a key goal of women's transformation, requiring the development of a new sense of personhood. For subordinates used to being defined by others, liberation must therefore involve attaining self-definition. This requires creativity, the creativity required to create a new sense of personhood, vision and an inner sense of what is worthy. Developing an authentic personal vision requires challenging the status quo, the standard dominant definitions of womanhood and of personhood, and stepping outside prescribed roles.

For liberation there will also be a need for reconceptualizing power and self-determination. Miller (1986; 1991c) points out that women have not been used to wielding power, and are therefore not practised in the conventions which men learn from childhood. Confronting power issues, she believes, will involve changing old concepts of power which view power as 'all or none', or as a win–lose situation. Old definitions of power have often involved 'the ability to advance oneself and simultaneously, to control, limit, and if possible, destroy the power of others' (1986, p. 116). Miller defines power as 'the capacity to implement' (1986, p. 116). Women must overcome their fears about power, and their belief that doing something 'just for me' has no point, or indeed is shameful.

Handling conflict with each other – about power, about women's roles, about class and race – and with men is another essential part of change identified by Miller. As in the case of power, women do not have traditions of handling conflict, or of being open about conflict. As women speak more openly and assert themselves, they are likely to run into conflict with each other. Differences between women will create conflict, which Miller suggests may be alleviated by developing an analysis of the system as a source of difficulties – 'a system which sees difference as deficiency' (1986, p. 138). Transformation will require making connections and gaining support from other women (Miller, 1986, p. 132):

> There will inevitably be conflict with one's own old level of consciousness – in the broadest sense. In the midst of such a process, we have an absolute need for other people... Further, as one attempts to develop in opposition to the prevailing framework of the dominant culture, it is difficult to be certain that one is perceiving things clearly. It is not easy to believe one is right, and more basically, that one has rights. For all this, a community of like-minded people is essential.

For men, the tasks of liberation are different. Men need to 'reclaim the very parts of their own experience that they have delegated to women' (Miller, 1986, p. 47). This means acknowledging vulnerability and weakness, and cultivating the capacities to foster growth and development, and, indeed, assigning greater values to these capacities. Society has held up 'narrow and ultimately destructive goals for the dominant group and attempts to deny them vast areas of life' (1986, p. 47). Men must expand their emotional repertoire and develop their capacities for cooperation and nurturance. Miller suggests that if women stop fulfilling men's emotional needs, and being the carriers for vulnerability and connectedness, men 'will be forced to confront the ways in which their social forms do not adequately deal with these necessities. They will have to go about finding their own newer and better ways' (1986, p. 47).

Kasl's (1992; 1997) writings are primarily oriented towards addiction and internalized oppression syndrome. Much of her work is devoted to a critique of 12–step programmes which she believes are unsuitable for women and minorities because of their emphasis on powerlessness and deficiencies of character. For Kasl, transformation of addictive and other patterns requires understanding the link between these patterns and hierarchical social organization – indeed failure to see this connection perpetuates self-blame and feelings of helplessness. The cornerstone of transformation for Kasl is the development of spirituality. She presents a developmental model of 'faithing', the mature stages of which are questioning the given order, developing an integrated and internalized belief system, and experiencing a compassionate connection with other people. Taking steps to be economically independent, however difficult in the face of discrimination, is an important part of overcoming dependency. Other processes include acknowledging and expressing feelings of shame and guilt, finding a voice for self-expression, identifying personal strengths, and changing destructive relational patterns. These processes are more easily experienced in group settings. Groups repair the fragmentation brought about by hierarchical organization, and help to sustain the processes involved in growth and development. Building communities based on shared values, solidarity and support are a further element in liberation for Kasl (1997).

Herman (1997) outlines three stages in recovery from trauma which can provide the basis for more general insights into transforming damaging psychological patterns. In her analysis, trauma, or experiences of terror, helplessness and isolation, undermine the sense of self and self-worth, the sense of trust or meaning in the world, and the feeling of connection with others and with community: 'The core experiences of psychological trauma are disempowerment and disconnection from others. Recovery, therefore, is based upon the empowerment of the survivor and the creation of new connections. Recovery can take place only within the context of relationships; it cannot occur in isolation' (1997, p. 133). Furthermore, the survivor 'must be the author and arbiter of her own recovery' (1997, p. 133). In her discussion of recovery, Herman focuses on a healing therapeutic relationship, and on therapeutic groups, but the elements she identifies have wider relevance.

The three key elements of recovery for Herman (1997) are: the establishment of safety; remembrance and mourning; and reconnection with ordinary life. The establishment of safety is a prerequisite for the essential task of fully remembering and naming the trauma, which in turn lays the basis for reconnecting with others and re-establishing trust and meaning in life. A key element in the establishment of safety is the restoring of a sense of control, and for Herman, this must start with the body, gradually moving outward to control of the environment. Working with safe and supportive relationships, usually involving those with whom the survivor already has supportive bonds, must also occur. Abusive relationships must be terminated if the next step in recovery is to occur. Herman assumes that such a safe environment can be found in therapy; other examples of safe environments include shelters for battered women, rape crisis centres and particular kinds of women's groups.

Remembrance is a process of bringing the traumatic experience fully into memory and creating a coherent narrative out of what initially are usually fragmented and disorganized images, sensations and feelings. This must be accompanied by full expression of the feelings associated with the trauma and its aftermath, and an exploration of the meaning of the trauma and the reactions to it. Remembrance will usually involve a fundamental re-evaluation of important relationships and a reconsideration of basic beliefs about justice, guilt and responsibility. Herman links the construction and telling of the narrative of trauma with the political act of witnessing and providing testimony. It is only when the story is heard and believed that mourning can occur, as mourning requires the courage to acknowledge all of the losses brought about by trauma. Mourning involves not just grief, loss and despair, but also rage, or more specifically, a shift from 'helpless fury' to 'righteous indignation' (1997, p. 189). This is often accompanied by desire for revenge or compensation, but in Herman's view these are futile, as neither is likely to occur. Remembrance and mourning are never complete, but when the story has been told and there are glimpses of 'hope and energy for engagement with life' (1997, p. 195), it is possible to move on to the next stage, that of reconnection.

The tasks of reconnection involve not only building new relationships with others, but also a reconstruction of the self, and the development of a new and sustaining belief system or 'sustaining faith' (Herman, 1997, p. 196). Herman suggests that physical challenges through self-defence, sport, or outdoor activities, which involve a confrontation with fear and an assertion of strength, can be a starting point for the reconstruction of self. Overcoming pressures to respond in traditional 'feminine' ways to social situations through submissiveness, obeying rules and observing silence, which actually place women at risk of violence and exploitation, also build up awareness and strength: 'For some survivors, it is a completely novel experience to be the maker of rules rather than the one who automatically obeys them' (1997, p. 201). Drawing upon aspects of self which were valued before the trauma, acceptance of new aspects that arose from the trauma, and developing new fantasies involving desire and initiative rather than re-enactment of trauma help to reconstruct the self.

The final steps in recovery are reconnecting with others and, sometimes, finding a 'survivor mission', that is some form of social action which helps to give meaning to the traumatic event, sustain the new beliefs which the survivor has developed, and forge a sense of alliance with others. Reconnecting is most effective in a group context, and Herman's (1997) discussion here also focuses only on therapy groups. She identifies the characteristics of groups oriented towards each of the three stages of recovery. Groups with the goal of safety can be highly structured, goal oriented and flexible, with clear non-exploitative leadership and a cognitive rather than an emotional orientation. Members do not necessarily reveal a lot about each other or confront each other;

the emphasis is task or problem oriented. Short-term stress management groups and educational groups may conform to this model. Groups for remembrance and mourning obviously place more emphasis on feelings, and must be carefully selected and highly structured, with a clear focus on sharing experiences, and a definite time limit. Bonds form between group members and develop and change over time, and therefore clear boundaries are required. Groups for reconnection can take a variety of forms, and do not need to be trauma focused. Indeed joining political or educational groups with an emphasis on making new and broader connections can facilitate relinquishing the survivor identity and developing a sense of commonality with the difficulties of different social conditions. This sense of commonality, for Herman, means that recovery has been accomplished.

The wide-ranging discussion of the damages associated with racism offered by hooks (1993; 2002b) also contains a number of insights into counteracting these patterns. At a fundamental level, there is a need to confront the many ways in which socialization has instilled self-hatred, unrealistic standards, negative emotional patterns and expectations, and alienation from culture and spirituality, and to construct new patterns which are self-affirming, loving and life-affirming. This includes developing a positive, black-centred body image and revisioning sexuality, as already mentioned in the previous chapter. hooks argues in favour of positive thinking, mutual affirmation, love and forgiveness to counteract criticality and negative thinking, and in favour of speaking honestly, writing of 'the personal power and dignity that comes from being honest' (1993, p. 29).

Learning to love blackness requires constant vigilance against the racism of the dominant culture, a rejection of white standards, and an active embracing of blackness. Spirituality and the building of self-esteem are key elements in liberation. This last requires the creation of positive images of blackness, and black-centred artistic products. Interviewing black-identified women, hooks writes that 'They all talk about going through a stage where they had to unlearn old negative ways of thinking about themselves and learn how to be positive. They talk about surrounding themselves both with friends and comrades who affirm their looks, but also with pictures and other representations' (hooks, 1993, p. 93).

hooks (1993) emphasizes the importance of community and of spirituality in supporting these processes: 'Throughout our history in this country, black women have relied on spirituality to sustain us, to renew our hope, to strengthen our faith' (1993, p. 184) and writes that 'Much that is beautiful, magical and unique in black culture has come from the experience of communal black life' (1993, p. 152). Traditions of community, of spirituality and also of political resistance must be used along with personal development: 'No level of individual self-actualization alone can sustain the marginalized and oppressed. We must be linked to collective struggle, to communities of resistance that move outward, into the world' (1993, p. 162).

For O'Neill (1992) the most fundamental requirement for psychological transformation is economic security and the opportunity for productive labour, which, she argues, can only be attained through political change. Her account also emphasizes the importance of community, with its traditions of providing practical and emotional support, filling in in times of crisis, developing rituals which create social cohesion and offering a cultural context for self-expression. She also argues that the formation of politically oriented community associations can be a further step in political development, furthering the capacity to engage with structures of power.

Pharr (1988, p. 66) writes that lesbians provide a model of how to survive in the face of oppression through the building of community and culture:

> Despite the harsh damaging effects of homophobia, we have created a magnificent lesbian culture of books and music and crafts and film and painting and newspapers and periodicals. We have created social communities in cities, lesbian land communities in rural areas, and retirement communities for older lesbians. With little support except from other lesbians, we have created lesbian counselling centers, support groups for chemically dependent lesbians, coffee houses, lesbian retreats and art festivals and music festivals, healing centers, outdoors clubs, support groups for lesbian survivors of battering, rape and incest, rituals for our passages and our spirituality support groups for lesbian mothers, lesbians of color, differently abled lesbians, Jewish lesbians. The list goes on and on.

Mary Daly

The work of Mary Daly, a white North American radical feminist philosopher, provides ample analysis of the workings of patriarchy, emphasizing particularly violence, control of culture and fragmentation. Violent practices range from witchburning and genital mutilation to sexual assault and verbal abuse. In the realm of culture, mythology and culture are used to mystify and obscure; language erases agency and limits thinking; religion, psychiatry and psychology distort and control. Women are split from nature and from each other, and women's psyches are imbued with 'ghostly false images of ourselves which have been deeply embedded in our imagination and which respond like unnatural reflexes to the spookers' unnatural stimuli' (1978, p. 409). Women's passions are perverted and dulled into 'plastic passions' and 'potted passions' whose cause or object is hidden and which therefore remain fixed and floating in their psyches. Women's urge to transcendence is blocked by the distorted images of the male god. In short, patriarchy is damaging to all aspects of women's psyches – the self, awareness, emotions, relationships and spirituality. Fundamental to Daly's analysis is the view that women are disconnected from their 'Original Self', or the Self that is connected with nature and with transcendence.

Liberation must involve undoing the 'mindbindings' and 'psychic numbing' to which women are subjected, reconnecting with 'Original Self' and creating new consciousness. Daly presents liberation as an active process with each woman operating as an active agent in solidarity with other women, bringing a visionary consciousness to bear on political action. Awareness of oppression must be maintained through continuing education and naming of oppressions. The full horrors of oppression must be faced, and the emotions which this arouses acknowledged. Efforts must be made to shield the psyche from the messages of oppression, and the psyche must be nourished through creativity, and by positive language, metaphors, images, myths and stories. Divisions between women must be overcome and new contexts created. Political action must be informed by a constructive vision as well as by the desire for retribution. The following discussion will focus on seven elements of Daly's analysis of liberation namely demystification, the Courage to See, anger/rage, separatism, Evoking the Archimage, Telic Focusing and sisterhood.

Demystification is a central element in coming to awareness of patriarchal oppression. Demystification involves recognizing the lies and distortions which block a clear analysis. For example, Daly sees the classic myths of Western patriarchy as 'something like distorting lenses. We can correctly perceive patriarchal myths as reversals and as pale derivatives of more ancient, more translucent myth from gynocentric civilization' (1978, p. 47). Demystification involves not just seeing through the distortions of myths, but exposing the lies and deceptions which are part of everyday life, of mass media, academia and the professions. Creative use of myth and media is therefore a tool for liberation.

A fundamental insight of Daly's is that it takes courage to maintain a clear sense of patriarchal oppression. 'To see the extent of patriarchal oppression means that everything has to change.' Four blocks to seeing are: (1) trivialization, the argument that 'women's issues' are not important; (2) universalization, the argument that it's not just a women's problem, but a human problem; (3) particularization, a focus on details which obscure the overall argument; (4) spiritualization, a refusal to look at material reality. A tactic frequently used in myth, mass media and language is erasure of responsibility, where the real agents of oppression are denied or obscured, for example through the use of the passive voice, or through naming only the victim. The 'Courage to See' has to be maintained in the face of continuing efforts to mystify, and continuing assaults on mind and spirit.

Demystification and raising awareness usually lead to anger or rage. As Daly writes: 'Anger is unpotted and transformed into Rage/Fury when the vast network that constitutes the context of our oppression is recognized' (1984, p. 258). Blocks to anger or rage are created by the patriarchal tactics of erasure of responsibility, use of the passive voice, tokenism and blaming the victim. All of these have the effect of obscuring who the agents or the beneficiaries of oppression are, making it difficult to identify the cause or the object of anger. This results in such 'plastic passions' as hostility and resentment, which have no clear object. Naming the agents of oppression can unleash anger and rage, which in turn can move women to action.

Separatism, or separating from patriarchy, is a key strategy for transformation, since, as discussed above, Daly (1984) sees patriarchy as a state of possession, where women's psyches are assaulted by false images and symbols. Yet the act of separation itself requires courage, since it involves turning away from familiar although damaging cultural practices and facing into unexplored territory. Separatism is often interpreted to mean physical separation from men. Daly emphasizes what may be called 'psychic separatism' (Crone, 1988), a separation from the numerous messages in patriarchal culture which activate the 'ghostly false images' referred to above, and which block a clear view of patriarchal oppression. For Daly, separatism is both a turning away from oppressive forces, and a turning towards women, involving creating a context which can evoke the powers of women through, for example, woman-identified writings, images of women's power, and positive connections with other women.

Evoking the Archimage, or imagining goddess and woman-centred images and powers, is another process in psychic liberation for women.

This requires developing connections with other women, with a woman-centred past and future, with female power and energy. The Archimage is a reversal of the archetypical or stereotypical representations of women as impotent objects. Evoking the Archimage is a process of reconnecting with memories of female potency, or a process of Re-membering: 'healing the dismembered Self – the Goddess within women' (Daly, 1984, p. 87). This is an undoing of the erasure of woman-centred traditions and mythologies, uncovering and rereading myths of ancient goddesses which often contain the most powerful and inspiring descriptions and images of female energy and power. The active seeking of positive images, myths and herstories of female power is essential to undo the psychic damage of oppression.

If oppression is marked by being cut off or disconnected from sources of psychic power, liberation involves reconnecting with these sources, and creativity plays a central role in reconnecting. For Daly, a fundamental part of oppression is a disconnection from the Final Cause or source of transcendence – 'the centralizing force/focus within the Self and within all being' (1993, p. 155). 'Telic Focusing' is the phrase used by Daly to refer to reconnecting with this centralizing force/focus, with the centre of the psyche. Getting in touch with creative powers is a key element in Telic Focusing. The creative process, whether it involves talking, travelling, writing or painting is characterized by the way that it originates with the self and requires a focusing within.

Obviously, for Daly psychic liberation is not a solitary process, but one which must occur through connecting with other women, and through creating a context, a woman-centred space. It is essential to build bonds and develop a sense of solidarity with others who are oppressed/possessed, rather than being cut off from each other and isolated from traditions and herstories of resistance. Again this has to be an active process of reaching out over the barriers and divisions which have been created by patriarchal tactics of divide and conquer: 'Overcoming the disconnect within and among women is profoundly related to the project of healing the fragmentation (environmental, social, political) inflicted on all inhabitants of this planet' (Daly, 2005, p. 2). Daly suggests that solidarity and connectedness can be gained not just by bonding with other women, but also with foresisters, women from the past who have resisted and created, again emphasizing the importance of uncovering the past, and creating a woman-centred 'herstory'. The processes of liberation described by Daly can be seen as a developmental process, as a movement from the initial steps of raising consciousness or awareness (demystification and the Courage to See) through anger/rage, separatism, Evoking the Archimage or powers of women, developing creativity and cultivating sisterhood. Ultimately, for Daly as for other writers, liberation cannot be a solitary journey, nor can it be an internal journey. It must involve manifesting potency in the world, taking action to eliminate atrocities, taking action to create new structures. In Daly's terms, it may be seen as a spiralling process. As she points out, each movement or moment creates momentum for the next: 'One Moment leads to an Other. This is because it has consequences in the world and thus Moves a woman to take the Leap to the next moment' (Daly, 1993, p. 5).

Starhawk

Starhawk is a white North American psychotherapist, witch and activist who identifies estrangement from nature and from spirituality as a fundamental feature of patriarchy. In her work she has combined ritualistic practices from the traditions of Wiccan or witchcraft with political activism to offer a new model of empowerment. In her book *Truth or Dare* (1987), she writes of the need for a liberation psychology which will emphasize the collective and the communal as well as the personal, and recognize the interconnectedness of the personal and the political: 'Unless we change the structures of the culture, we will mirror them again and again; we will be caught in a constant battle to avoid being moulded again into an image of domination' (1987, p. 71). A liberation psychology must be understandable, and therefore requires a new language, and must be based on a sense of connectedness between intellect and feeling, between body and spirit, between humans and nature.

Starhawk's interest is in exploring the ways in which dominator patterns disrupt group and community processes, and in developing new group structures which can counteract this and create mutual empowerment. She distinguishes three types of power. In a society based on domination and estrangement, power is exercised as 'power over', as controlling and often violent, as authority eliciting obedience and submissiveness. In hierarchical situations it is almost impossible not to exercise power in this manner. Such power relies on external structures for its effectiveness, and motivates through fear. A second type of power is 'power from within', which is based on a sense of connection with the self, with other human beings, and with nature and the environment: 'We can feel that power in acts of creation and connection, in planting, building, writing, cleaning, healing, soothing, playing, singing, making love' (Starhawk, 1987, p. 10). It is motivated by the desire for and the sense of connectedness. It is related to the third kind of power,

'power-with', which is afforded individuals on the basis of respect and listening, on being in tune with the needs of a group and acting as a facilitator and on life experience and wisdom. These last two kinds of power rely on relationships and structures of equality.

The fundamental aim of a group structure is to create an environment in which the will of the group can be focused to produce action, which for Starhawk (1987) is the exercise of magic. At the individual level, this will involve confronting what Starhawk calls the 'self-hater', the internalized voices of fear and criticism which emphasize control and obedience, and produce patterns such as withdrawal and manipulation which undermine group effectiveness. At the group level, the first step, reiterating Herman (1997), is the creation of safety and of clear boundaries. For Starhawk a group will function most effectively when solidarity is forged through action for social change, and this in turn will increase feelings of safety and trust. All of these must be actively maintained by consciously responding to changes such as someone entering or leaving the group, and by regular monitoring of group dynamics, especially those around power.

Starhawk's (1987) solution to many of the dilemmas which arise in groups, such as dilemmas of inclusion–exclusion, decision-making and power struggles, is to use storytelling, mythmaking and rituals to identify the dilemmas, and work with them in non-linear ways which invoke intuition and connectedness rather than rationality and estrangement. Concepts such as 'the Censor' and 'the Star' identify typical roles adopted by individuals in groups which block cohesion, while processes such as brainstorming, storytelling and passing a wand or rattle facilitate the handling of conflict and movement towards decision-making. Forming and developing sustainable groups which will engage in 'resistance and renewal' are essential steps towards liberation:

> First we can create structures of support, situations that by their inherent structure and function unravel the self-hater's bindings and embody a different reality rooted in freedom. Nourished by that support, using the tool of ritual and the consciousness-changing skills of magic, we can take action in many ways to resist domination, to stop war, to envision and create ways of living that renew and sustain the richness and diversity of life (Starhawk, 1987, p. 313).

When these groups form bonds with each other and develop solidarity, community will emerge. This will require engagement with differences in privilege and culture. Starhawk suggests that designing concrete actions, for example, around housing and street safety, which will create a sense of community, while also developing a larger strategy for economic and political change, will forge solidarity and political effectiveness.

In developing her activism, Starhawk combines anti-capitalist activism with the development of spirituality. Arguing that capitalism, with its exploitation of natural resources, is based on a disconnection from nature and a denial of consciousness in nature, she emphasizes the vital role of reclaiming connection with nature and with spirituality through concrete actions such as developing sustainable agricultural methods as well as through rituals that connect with the consciousness of the universe. These connections evoke compassion and love, the psychic resources for resistance and activism: 'They are the emotions that mobilize us as human beings' (Starhawk, 2005, p. 32). Starhawk promotes actions such as making consumer choices based on sustainability, or developing sustainable communities, and has been involved in sustainable peace camps at several G8 summits.

Just as their discussion of oppression contained both common themes and more specific concerns, so the discussion of liberation in the writers reviewed so far highlighted some core processes and practices which could be linked to liberation, and also reflected the particular interests of the different writers. Between them they consider a wide range of topics – sense of self or self-definition, socialization and cultural norms, creativity, spirituality, community, sense of history, power and conflict, connections with others. The importance of supportive relationships with others in the process of transformation was a central theme, as was the role of culture and community. The value, indeed the necessity of engaging in transformative action was recognized, and in some instances specific practices were identified which will be explored more fully in the following chapters.

Writings on decolonization

Many of the writers on colonialism reviewed in the previous chapter also discussed processes of decolonization, or the process of breaking free of colonization. Mirroring the discussion by feminist writers, there is considerable emphasis on self-definition in writings on decolonization. Additionally, these writers share a concern with the continuing influence of colonizers in the post-colonial situation, an influence which arises out of the complementary relationship between the colonizer and colonized discussed in the previous chapter. Both are focused on each other even at the psychological level, and this mutual focus, as well as economic, cultural and other interdependencies, can be a block to self-determination for the colonized, and to psychological transformation generally. Thus many writers, particularly Fanon (1967b) and Memmi (1967), emphasize the need for a decisive break between the colonized and the colonizers so that new patterns can be established.

Fanon's discussion of decolonization in *The Wretched of the Earth* (1967b) begins with violence; indeed his advocacy of violence has been a source of considerable controversy. His ideas on violence are presented here to highlight his emphasis on active agency in the process of decolonization. He argues that violence serves the function of unifying the natives, overcoming the fragmentation of colonization. It also serves to break internalized fears and inhibitions instilled by the colonial regime: 'It frees the native from his inferiority complex, and from his despair and inaction; it makes him fearless and restores his self-respect' (1967b, p. 74). It is a vehicle of political education through action: 'Violence alone, violence committed by the people, violence organized and educated by its leaders, makes it possible for the masses to understand social truths and gives the key to them' (1967a, p. 147).

Decolonization comes about because it is willed: 'The extraordinary importance of this change is that it is willed, called for, demanded' (Fanon, 1967b, p. 28). It must involve 'decisive rejection' of colonial, i.e. Western values (1967b, p 33), including colonized intellectuals, and blacks who are 'whiter than whites' (1967b, p. 115). For Fanon, decolonization will be incomplete without radical political and social change, nothing less than the complete restructuring of the social order, whereby 'the last shall be first' (1967b, p. 43). Psychologically, the damage to identity and to self must be repaired through the reclaiming or recreation of black history and culture, an exploration of potentials which have been forbidden under colonialism. Fanon argues that while decolonization must be brought about through the agency of the colonized, it will only be complete when the colonizers afford recognition to the colonized. This will involve direct confrontation with the colonizer, an assertion of difference and a demand for recognition.

Memmi (1967), like Fanon, believes that revolt is the only way out of the colonial situation: 'His condition is absolute and cries for an absolute solution; a break and not a compromise' (1967, p. 128). Everything from small-scale revolts such as boycotts to explosive outbursts can play a role in this rupturing of the colonial relationship. This is important because decolonization involves a conflict between rejection and emulation of the colonizer. Given the relentless exposure to the superiority of the colonizer, the first temptation is to emulate the model offered by the colonizer. This involves not only acceptance of the colonizer, but a rejection of the culture and practices of the colonized. Ironically, it is the barrier of racism, erected by the colonizer, which prevents complete emulation. The opposite pattern of rejection and hatred of the colonizer, 'self-assertion, born out of protest' (1967, p. 139), is incomplete, as it reproduces colonial patterns of racism and zenophobia, and is still determined by the colonizer. Ultimately 'The colonized's liberation must be carried out through a recovery of self and of autonomous dignity' (1967, p. 128).

Kenny (1985) argues that to obtain liberation from the patterns of constriction associated with submissiveness it is ultimately necessary to move towards a relationship of symmetry rather than complementarity with the oppressor, and this involves both parties – oppressor and oppressed – moving towards a new relationship. Applying the parent–child analogy to that of oppressor–oppressed, Kenny (1985, p. 78) writes that the problem is first to help 'the hitherto dominant parent to acknowledge and accept the fact of its decline in terms of potency' and secondly to encourage the child 'to take full responsibility for itself and cease the easy option of endlessly blaming its parent for its traumas and its relative inaction'. Indeed he suggests that parenting styles reflect patterns of dominance and submissiveness, and that changing parenting styles to emphasize independence and pride can play a role in liberation. At a broader level, Kenny suggests that in the absence of movement on the part of the oppressor, triangulation, where a third party is brought into the oppressor–oppressed dyad, may be used as a strategy for change. Developing relationships with other groups, or becoming part of a superordinate group, are examples of triangulation.

Ruth (1988; 2006) identifies stages in the liberation process which are marked by changes in the relationship between the oppressed and the oppressor. The first step in the liberation process is 'when a group first becomes aware that what it took for granted as the way things had to be, or thought of as natural, is in fact a reflection of a system-based process of prejudice and discrimination' (Ruth, 2006, p. 213). The first part of the process of liberation for the oppressed, then, is an analysis of the situation of oppression, and of their relationship to the oppressor. Ruth observes that there may be a polarization within the oppressed group at this point which can become entrenched. One group may demand, sometimes violently, an acknowledgement of their anger and grief at their mistreatment. The other group may seek to appease, acting to demonstrate their 'reasonableness' by downplaying their oppression, diluting their demands, and possibly allying with the oppressors to suppress other viewpoints. Such a polarization within the oppressed group is obviously exacerbated by the 'divide and conquer' strategy of oppressors, by divisions within the oppressed group, and by their own ambivalence towards each other and towards their leaders.

The next stage in liberation involves shifting the emphasis away from the oppressor and the situation of oppression, and developing pride and self-respect based on their own independent evaluation, rather than on the opinions of others. This is a change both in self-concept and identity, and in the relationship with the oppressor. The oppressed group no longer accepts stereotypes of inferiority or acts in subservient ways. This challenges the self-concept of the oppressor, which is often based on comparisons with the oppressed, and on a sense of superiority. It thus puts pressure on the oppressor group to examine themselves and their relationship with the oppressed group. Indeed Ruth argues that liberation cannot proceed any further without changes in the dominant group.

Another step in liberation occurs when all groups acknowledge that oppression arises from a system in which all groups are conditioned or socialized to act out their role as oppressor or oppressed. Furthermore, the oppression of one group is interlinked with the oppression of other groups. Ruth (2006) argues that it is more effective to develop an understanding of how systems of oppression operate and aim to change these dynamics than to attack the agents of oppression, since they have been conditioned by a system of oppression to act in an oppressive manner. Liberation will only be attained when all of the groups who are involved in oppression recognize the interconnections of different oppressions and participate in the liberation process.

Paulo Freire

Freire's (1993) fundamental assumption is that liberation requires praxis – both a reflection on reality and action to change reality. Furthermore, reflection and action – praxis – must originate with the oppressed people themselves. It cannot be handed to them either by their own leaders for liberation, or by members of the oppressor group who might see themselves as allies and liberators of the oppressed. Freire writes that 'Manipulation, sloganizing, "depositing", regimentation, and prescription cannot be components of revolutionary praxis, precisely because they are components of the praxis of domination' (1993, p. 107). The oppressed must apprehend reality in their own way, and must themselves become actors in a process Freire calls 'conscientizacao' or 'conscientization'.

Awareness and action feed each other:

> It is only when the oppressed find the oppressor out and become
> involved in the organized struggle for their liberation that they begin
> to believe in themselves. This discovery cannot be purely intellectual
> but must involve action; nor can it be limited to mere activism, but
> must include serious reflection: only then will it be a praxis (Freire,
> 1993, p. 47).

The process is dynamic and changing over time. As the oppressed
become aware of their situation of oppression (what Freire calls the
'limit-situation') and take action to change, this action increases and
expands their awareness, which in turn leads to more action.

Liberation is a process of discovery through posing problems and
engaging in dialogue so that the oppressed can view their situation as a
problem which challenges rather than as unchanging and fixed: 'It is not
the limit-situations in and of themselves which create a climate of hopelessness, but rather how they are perceived by women and men at a given
historical moment: whether they appear as fetters or as insurmountable
barriers' (Freire, 1993, p. 80). Once people perceive that there are possibilities for changing their situation, hope arises: 'As critical perception
is embodied in action, a climate of hope and confidence develops which
leads men to attempt to overcome the limit-situations. This objective can
be achieved only through action upon the concrete, historical reality in
which limit-situations historically are found' (1993, p. 80).

Once the oppressed engage in dialogue, perceptions change, and
they begin to undo the blinkers of banking education, 'they begin to
direct their observations towards previously inconspicuous phenomena' (Freire, 1993, p. 63). Each transformative act uncovers further
themes which open up new possibilities for limit acts or transforming
responses. Freire uses the phrase 'untested feasibility' to refer to formerly
unseen possibilities for transformative action which become apparent
as perceptions change through dialogue. This process involves uncovering themes which can be concealed by limit-situations; such conceal-
ment inhibits authentic transformative action. Themes may be broadly
common in a particular epoch, such as domination, more specific to
a region, such as underdevelopment, or very localized to a sub-group.
Ultimately, liberation will require an analysis of the totality of oppression with all of its interrelationships; however, it may begin with a focus
on a particular dimension of oppression. As each individual's unique
perspective emerges in an exploration of their own specific situation,

contradictions become apparent. These become a focus for further dialogue and stimulate the exploration of hitherto unperceived possibilities or untested feasibilities. The role of leadership is to facilitate the posing of problems and the engagement in dialogue and action.

It is important for the oppressed to start with particular specific concrete situations, and build from there, through dialogue and action, to a broader analysis. Ultimately the aim is to achieve social justice, and to become fully human. This requires becoming a subject who acts on and transforms the world, and who can be productive and make a contribution to society. The opportunity for productive labour plays a crucial role in this. Acknowledging the importance of labour, Freire (1993) ends with an analysis of how a demand may initially take the form of a search for work or for higher pay. Through the process of facilitated dialogue and action, this can be expanded to an understanding of how labour 'constitutes part of the human person' (1993, p. 164), and that one must be 'owner of one's own labor' (1993, p. 164) and on to an analysis of the exploitation of labour and of economic inequality.

Ignacio Martín-Baró

Writing as a Jesuit in El Salvador, Ignacio Martín-Baró (1994) sought to develop a liberation psychology modelled on liberation theology: that is, a psychology which could facilitate liberatory movements through enabling people to critically reflect upon their situation. While aware of the many damaging effects of the war situation in El Salvador, Martín-Baró, who was executed by the El Salvadoran army, was also struck by the strengths exhibited by people under severe oppression, in particular 'commitment, solidarity, hope, courage, collective virtues' (1994, p. 31). As a psychologist, he argues that psychological understanding can only come about by acknowledging the social conditions in which people live their lives. Martín-Baró writes that the reality of social conditions for the majority of people in El Salvador is one of warfare, poverty and class domination, accompanied by control of discourse and propaganda, which means that for the vast majority of people their own lived experience is at odds with the reality presented to them. He discusses many of the oppressive psychological patterns which have already been reviewed in Chapter 3 – fear, restriction, alienation, submissiveness, dependence and fatalism. Conditions of warfare erode social relations and produce inevitable polarization and dissociation: 'both polarization and dissociation crack the foundation of coexistence and induce an exhausting climate of socio-emotional tension' (1994, p. 113).

A key task for a liberation psychology, according to Martín-Baró, is 'in training and socialization so that people's desires truly conform to their needs' (1994, p. 121). This requires a fundamental reassessment of needs and desires, because, in the course of socialization, people's needs and desires are shaped by the dominant social order:

> A successful political socialization from the point of view of the established system would be one in which the individual's thoughts, values, and abilities are congruent with those of the political system – with the interests of the dominant classes and the hierarchy of values the system implicitly or explicitly defends (1994, pp. 76–7).

Thus those needs which are outside the interests of the ruling class are more difficult to identify, but also 'contain the potential for rebellion and political subversion' (1994, p. 73).

Another task for a liberation psychology is a process of 'de-ideologization', or development of critical consciousness. One element in de-ideologization is providing information which challenges the dominant view and reinforces what the people know to be true: 'What this involves is introducing into the ambience of the collective consciousness elements and schemata that can help dismantle the dominant ideological discourse and set in motion other dynamics of a process of de-alienation' (Martín-Baró, 1994, p. 188). A concrete example of this which Martín-Baró cites is his own use of public opinion polls. He argues that properly conducted public opinion polls are a tool of social psychology which can play a role in de-ideologization by allowing people to agree with views that go against the 'official' line, and by giving these views scientific credibility.

A third element in a liberation psychology is 'the recovery of historical memory' (Martín-Baró, 1994, p. 30). This both challenges the prevailing propaganda which presents reality as 'natural and ahistorical' and fosters identity and sense of community:

> Only insofar as people and groups become aware of their historical roots, especially those events and conditions which have shaped their situation, can they gain the perspective they need to take the measure of their own identity. Knowing who you are means knowing where you come from and on whom you depend. There is no true self-knowledge that is not acknowledgement of one's origins, one's community identity, and one's history (1994, p. 218).

Finally, a fourth task in which psychologists can play a role is that of 'utilizing the people's virtues' (Martín-Baró, 1994, p. 31). Martín-Baró writes of the tremendous qualities which the people in El Salvador exhibit under appalling circumstances: 'their uncompromising solidarity with the suffering, their ability to deliver and to sacrifice for the collective good, their tremendous faith in the human capacity to change the world, their hope for a tomorrow that keeps being violently denied to them' (1994, p. 31). Faced with the everyday situation of war and oppression, people may discover inner resources they may have been unaware of, and ask fundamental questions about values and goals. The cataclysm can offer 'the opportunity to break the chains of their submissive alienation, of their existential fatalism and dependence' (1994, p. 31), characteristics which Martín-Baró firmly links to the nature of the social conditions in which people find themselves.

Psychological analysis of liberation: The cycle of liberation

The writings reviewed in this chapter emphasize even more clearly a fundamental point which became clear in the previous chapter, namely that liberation must be an interactional process: that is, one which occurs in interaction with others. It can only be undertaken and sustained in the context of supportive relationships, and it requires groups which are formed for specific reasons, communities which build on traditions and provide connection and ritual, and a culture which gives positive expression to the identity and history of the oppressed group. It is therefore difficult to discuss any of the processes involved in liberation as if they were individual or solitary ones. However, for the purposes of analysis I have classified the processes identified into three categories, namely a personal, an interpersonal and a political category. The personal category refers primarily to processes such as building self-esteem and expressing emotions, which, while clearly interactional, refer to changes within the person or to do with the self. The interpersonal category involves processes in relationships with others, such as communication and support, groups and communities. The political category refers to processes directly involved in taking action for change, ranging from speaking out to political advocacy. The categories overlap and feed each other, forming a cyclical process where change in each area reinforces changes in the other areas, forming a cycle of liberation. There are some processes, such as analysis, which are relevant to each category. Here they will be briefly described, while the following three chapters will elaborate on each level.

It should be noted here that while the discussion focuses on changes associated with oppression, there is also need for changes on the part of those in positions of domination, as Miller's (1986) analysis and the discussions of decolonization emphasize. Denial of vulnerability and restrictions on emotions are among the psychological patterns associated with domination. Miller (1986) argues that these must be transformed through acknowledging a wider variety of emotions, and cultivating cooperation and nurturance. Discussions of decoloniza-tion emphasize the complementarity between the colonized and the colonizer, suggesting that there will be a limit to the degree of change possible in the colonized unless there is also change in the colonizers (Memmi, 1967; Kenny, 1985; Ruth, 2006). Indeed, many of the processes identified below are relevant to those in dominant positions.

A fundamental point, expressed most forcefully by Freire (1993), but also by Herman (1997), is that individuals must themselves be the agents of their own change. Herman (1997) writes of the need of survivors to be in control, to regain their sense of autonomy, to trust that their own insights and intuitions are correct. Freire (1993) argues that any pro-gramme which prescribes or manipulates is itself reproducing the prac-tices of domination. Individuals must be engaged on the basis of their own experience and, through a process of dialogue and action, develop their own analysis. It is only through active engagement that empower-ment can be attained. Unfortunately, the experience of oppression itself undermines both a sense of agency and a belief in the possibility for change. Thus one of the tasks of a liberation psychology is to convince of the possibility for change, to persuade people that they can become agents in their own transformation, and that they can play a role in social and political change.

Another insight is that liberation requires understanding and analysis of the source and nature of oppression. Daly (1978) in particular writes of the role of mystification both in covering the existence of oppres-sion and in obscuring emotional responses to oppression. Analysis is also necessary for action, and at the same time, as Freire (1993) notes, it is developed through action. Consciousness-raising, conscientiza-tion or the development of critical consciousness are phrases used to refer to the process of developing awareness of the social condi-tions impacting on experience. Analysis is important for naming the agents of oppression, but also for understanding the systemic nature of oppression, both of which are necessary for personal and politi-cal change, and for transforming relationships between the oppressed and oppressors.

An insight common to many of the writers reviewed is that liberation requires not just analysis of oppression, but also a vision of new ways. The visions outlined involve the personal level, where, for example, Miller (1986) and Freire (1993) write of being fully human, or of new visions for humanity which emphasize love and the central value of fostering growth and development. They also involve the interpersonal level, emphasizing the power of love, solidarity, empowering group processes and communities which foster creativity and spirituality. At the political level, visions of freedom from domination, of justice and economic equality, of sustainable environmental policies and of respect for difference and diversity, recur. Vision, then, is important for all three levels of change.

Finally it is important to bear in mind that the psychological processes being discussed are essentially developmental: that is, they involve change over time which may occur in small incremental steps, and some changes cannot occur until other changes are in place. Herman's (1997) analysis of recovery illustrates this point: she writes that the experience of safety must precede remembrance and mourning, which in turn precede reconnection. Similarly, Freire (1993) emphasizes the necessity for the oppressed to start with their own 'limit-situation', take small steps for change, further develop their analysis which in turn broadens their view of the situation and enables them to take larger steps. A developmental view does not necessarily involve identifying stages, each of which must occur in sequence: rather it involves the acknowledgement that processes take time, that they feed each other, and that it is likely that some steps may precede others. Liberation may be viewed as a cycle, involving personal change, such as building self-confidence, facilitating interpersonal change, such as providing support, which in turn empowers people to take action. Taking action itself feeds self-confidence and fosters solidarity which facilitates further action. It may be seen as a spiralling process in that changes may be small to begin with, but may get bigger and more dramatic with time.

Bearing these points in mind, I will firstly consider processes which involve change at the *personal* level, specifically changes which involve the self and identity, emotions, sexuality, creativity and spirituality. They are considered areas of personal change because, although they involve interaction, education and action, they are primarily concerned with the way in which the individual thinks and feels, and especially with self-concept, feelings of self-worth, and self-expression. The main aim of change at this level is to counteract the damages associated with oppression, to build strengths, and to provide a foundation for building solidarity with others, creating community and taking action.

In the area of self and identity, there is a need firstly to challenge the false views of self and identity presented to the oppressed by the ideologies of oppression. A number of writers refer to the need to challenge false stereotypes, to question norms and expectations, to defy or resist convention, whether this be in areas to do with being a woman, with being black or native, or more specifically, with just following rules. In challenging the status quo and in rejecting conventional discourse, there is a need not to shift to the other polarity, and embrace the model of the dominator, a theme which particularly recurs in writings on colonialism. It is important therefore to develop a vision which will prevent merely choosing between a dominator or a subordinate model. This vision could involve valuing strengths, as Miller (1986) has argued, or reclaiming or developing new cultural and political forms, as Starhawk (1987; 2005) suggests.

The development of self and identity, like the other processes to be discussed here, is an active process which the individual can consciously facilitate by engaging in particular activities, whether alone or in groups. Identifying strong role models, and finding strong and positive images, whether from history or through creativity, are among the practices which help to build a strong sense of self and identity. Many of the writers reviewed above highlight the importance of drawing on the history of resistance, acknowledging the ways in which oppressed groups have always resisted, and valuing the ingenuity and perseverance of that history. A sense of history is also important to undo the erasure of the oppressor culture, to give a sense of time and place, and to highlight the culture and achievements of the oppressed group.

In the area of emotions, there is first of all a need to acknowledge and express the many negative emotions that accompany oppression, especially the emotions of shame, guilt, grief and anger. These are emotions which are difficult to acknowledge, or which are repressed or misdirected. In particular, mystification tends to create difficulties in identifying these emotions, in being aware of their causes, and in expressing them. Analysis and expression of emotion are interconnected, a point highlighted by Herman's (1997) analysis of recovery, where she writes of the necessity to develop a full and clear narrative of abuse and to express the feelings that have been repressed or unexpressed. The implication of this, and this is also supported by Daly's (1984) analysis, is that until the agents of oppression are clearly identified, and their actions named and acknowledged, there will be difficulty acknowledging the negative feelings that accompany oppression, and, in particular, with expressing and directing anger. A further example of the interconnections between analysis and emotions lies in Martín-Baró's (1994) exploration of political socialization, where he suggests that it is vital to examine needs, such as consumer needs, which have been moulded by the political system to preserve the status quo.

Three areas which have received particular mention by a number of writers are those of sexuality, creativity and spirituality. All of these involve connectedness both with self and with others, and are therefore damaged both by the difficulties with self-knowledge and by the negative patterns in interpersonal relationships. All of them are socially constructed in ways which distort or undermine their development. Sexuality is distorted through the power imbalances, stereotypes and gender polarities inherent in domination. Creativity is blocked through lack of self-worth, and by the erasure of culture and community. Spirituality is undermined by fear and isolation. Exploration of sexuality, the cultivation of creativity and the development of spirituality are part of the psychological processes which strengthen the self, enhance interpersonal connectedness, provide sustenance and hope for political action, and create vision and community.

A final area which will be considered at the personal level is the need to be a productive member of society through labour. This obviously requires structural opportunities for engaging in productive labour, but at the personal level it is also possible through analysis to develop an understanding of the ways in which labour contributes to society. This is particularly important in the area of women's unpaid labour, for which there is little acknowledgement or recognition, but can also be relevant in the area of unskilled and low-paid labour, where analysis can illuminate the way in which this labour is essential for social functioning.

At the *interpersonal* level, it is clear that negative patterns which develop as a response to oppression are damaging to interpersonal relationships, and that the continued enactment of these patterns helps to sustain a system of domination by undermining solidarity and cohesiveness among the oppressed. A number of writers, Miller (1986) and hooks (2002a) particularly, emphasize the need for honest and affirming interactions, and also of discovering ways of handling conflict and difference among subordinates. There is a need for a re-evaluation of the tendency to give to others, to be supportive and nurturing, so that individuals can set limits, especially in situations of oppression where considerable demands are placed on relationships.

The group situation is obviously an interpersonal context where many of the processes of liberation occur. At a fundamental level, groups break the isolation associated with oppression. They provide support for questioning and developing analysis, a place to explore and express emotions around oppression, and the basis for taking action. Without the support of other individuals, those who are questioning or developing new ways are under constant pressure from the dominant discourse, and receive little support for defiance or development of new ways of thinking and acting. Other functions which groups serve include the provision of support and the development of solidarity.

It is clear that groups serve a number of different functions, but that their effectiveness is threatened in quite a few ways. Considerable challenges are posed: in particular, the enactment of negative patterns referred to above, as well as patterns of domination such as power struggles, suppression of conflict and denial of difference. Groups can be mired in difficulties with subordinate patterns, and as these are challenged, switch to dominator patterns. Clearly there is a need for new group structures and imaginative methods to break out of this polarization. Flexibility is needed, as Herman's (1997) analysis suggests that groups will serve different functions at different points in the liberation cycle, and that different structures will be needed to fulfil these different functions.

Individuals and groups are embedded in communities, and the cultivation of community and of a sense of community is a further essential task at the interpersonal level. This requires overcoming the erasure of history and culture, and the fragmentation that is a feature of oppression. hooks (1993) and O'Neill (1992) suggest that building on the community traditions that are already in place, which include providing material support, fostering cultural expression, creating rituals and social occasions, and participating in decision-making, can facilitate the process of community-building.

At the *political* level, taking action is a necessary part of the cycle of liberation both because it is vital to counterbalance some of the psychological damage associated with oppression, and because it is necessary to change social conditions. Taking action to bring about change is linked to the personal and interpersonal changes discussed so far in the cycle of liberation. Action also requires analysis both of oppression and of the kinds of actions that are possible, since analysis and action, as Freire (1993) and others point out, are in a dialectic process with each other. Action to bring about change counteracts the alienation and powerlessness that is experienced under oppression and is essential for a sense of agency, which is the opposite of alienation and powerlessness. hooks (1993) and Maracle (1996) suggest that historical traditions of resistance as well as the activities of contemporary political movements can provide inspiration and models for engaging in action to bring about change.

The three levels of change – the personal, the interpersonal and the political – will be elaborated more fully in the following chapters. They have been identified separately from each other for the purpose of analysis, although it has already been acknowledged that they overlap and interconnect with each other. The three levels feed each other to form a cycle of liberation, as described above. Taking action disrupts oppression, because it challenges the alienation and isolation associated with oppression. It can also bring about changes in social conditions and therefore change psychological patterns. Developing analysis which makes the links between psychological patterns and sociological patterns is involved at each level. Analysis informs the reconstruction of self and the expression of emotions, it highlights the nature of interpersonal difficulties and identifies practices to counteract these, and it underlies the capacity to explore options for action and to take action. Analysis and action are thus key elements in liberation.

5
The Personal Level: Building Strengths

Liberation at the personal level will involve counteracting the damaging psychological effects of oppression and building psychological strengths. Oppression was seen in Chapter 3 to undermine self-worth, create negative and confusing emotions, distort sexuality, and block the development of creativity and spirituality. Obviously any one of these patterns, however experienced at individual or group level, would create psychological difficulties. Liberating practices identified in Chapter 4 involved working individually, in groups and in communities to address these difficulties. Analysis plays a vital role because oppressive systems often mystify the nature of oppression, and attempt to convince the oppressed that their oppression is natural or inevitable, and may even be good for them. This combination of mystification and psychological damage creates a self-perpetuating system, or a cycle of oppression, as without a clear analysis it is difficult to identify the source of psychological difficulties, and difficult to identify practices which could aid in counteracting or transforming these difficulties.

It must be reiterated again that, although the processes discussed in this chapter are labelled personal because they refer to changes that occur primarily within the individual, these processes all occur in interaction either with other individuals or with discourses of various kinds. Indeed, it became clear from interviews with women, which were undertaken for the purposes of furthering the analysis, that women themselves very quickly identified the need to be with like-minded individuals, to join a group or to get support in some way from others as they underwent processes which involved challenging the status quo and seeking change of some kind. They articulated their desire for 'personal development' both as a need to be supported by others and as a need to take time for themselves, build up strengths and self-esteem, and through education and other endeavours further their own development.

The underlying processes of liberation discussed in this chapter are identified as *building strengths*. Analysis is central to this process, and the development of awareness is seen as key in the process of building strengths. The chapter draws on the theoretical analyses of the previous chapters, and on interviews with 16 women who had been involved in the women's movement for a number of years. The purpose of the interviews was to gain insights into the processes whereby women developed awareness and became involved in varieties of political activism. The chapter will also make reference to focus group discussions which were undertaken with four women's groups in education and community development settings with the aim of discussing women's involvement in political action. These group discussions will be discussed more fully in Chapter 7, but references to personal change which are relevant to this chapter will be presented.

Of the 16 women interviewed, 11 had children, and it became clear that for these women, their experience in the home as full-time mothers, while rewarding in many ways, left them lacking in confidence about their capacity to speak out or contribute in a group or public setting. Ten of these women spoke of their need to build up confidence and develop themselves, while all five of those women without children also expressed this need. The areas which they specifically mentioned were the need to build up confidence and self-esteem, which motivated them to take assertiveness training courses, to explore their sexuality, and to try out their capacities for creativity. Another area which was mentioned repeatedly by women who had been full-time in the home, and which also emerged in group discussions, was the need to value fully women's unpaid labour. Women make repeated reference to their anger at the ignoring and undervaluing of their contribution to society, and of the fact that work which was not paid for was unrecognized and undervalued. This clearly connects to the importance of being able to engage in productive labour and to feel that one is making a contribution to society. It is also related to the need for economic independence.

The interviews and group discussions thus identified developing self-confidence and self-worth, exploring sexuality and creativity, and valuing unpaid labour as practices which could build strengths. These practices recurred in the discussions of liberation reviewed in Chapter 4. This chapter will also explore four more areas which the theoretical analysis of Chapter 4 identified: namely, the need to develop a sense of history, to identify role-models, to find positive images, and to cultivate spirituality. To assess the relevance of all of these practices, a short open-ended questionnaire was administered to 68 women who had taken courses in women's studies. All of these processes were judged to be highly valuable and practical, and comments indicated that a link was clearly seen between these practices and structures of oppression.

A theme which emerges from the interviews is that developing awareness and building strength reinforce each other. As awareness of injustice and oppression grows, women are less likely to blame themselves and more able to identify the social causes of their emotions and experiences. This helps them to feel more justified in seeking change and in developing their analysis. As their confidence and esteem build up both through personal development courses and through their involvement in groups, they become better able to articulate their analysis, stronger and clearer in their arguments, and more consistently able to identify ways in which oppression undermines them at a personal level. This in turn strengthens their capacity to take actions to counteract such undermining, and to build up areas which will further increase their confidence and capacity for self-expression.

Developing awareness

Interviews with women began with the question of when they first became aware of political issues. The most commonly occurring response was to recall an early experience of injustice, most often in relation to themselves or their family situation. For example, one woman recalled visiting a hospital emergency ward with her mother, becoming aware that they were not treating her with the same respect that they were treating other patients, and realizing that this was because of her mother's poverty. Another recalled her feelings in relation to the abuse which her father enacted against her mother. Another recalled being picked out at school and being aware of favouritism on the part of a teacher. These early experiences created an awareness that things were 'not fair', and gave them a suspicion that what they were hearing was not the full story:

> I knew that there were an awful lot of things that were never spoken about. A lot more was going on than anyone ever said, but I really didn't know what to do. Every now and again I'd see my mother pressing her lips or just refusing to go along with something. One time I said to her that it wasn't fair, and she said things were always like that. But I decided I'd try and make things better when I had

children. I began to look really suspiciously at people in authority, realized that half the time they didn't mean a word they said.

A second experience was that of violence and harassment. None of the women interviewed indicated that they had had personal experience of violence, although two had witnessed violence in their family of origin. However, three of the women mentioned knowing someone who was in a violent relationship. Seven women in total mentioned violence and sexual harassment, either because they had witnessed it or were angered by their own experience of harassment:

> watching my mother, I knew as soon as I had the chance I was going to do something.

> I realized how much I had to tolerate from men, and I was just fed up with it. All the times I dreaded walking by a group of men…the looks and the jokes…that you couldn't go anywhere on your own.…I realized that I was constantly down on myself…felt bad about myself.

A third experience mentioned in interviews was the occurrence of some specific political event which seemed to act as a 'last straw', provoking a sense of outrage or injustice. A dramatic example of this in the Irish context which was mentioned frequently was the so-called X case. In this case, a 14-year old girl who was pregnant as a result of being raped by a neighbour was prevented from leaving the country to have an abortion. Over the years on which women were reflecting there were a number of such dramatic 'single-issue' cases which evoked very strong reactions:

> when I heard about the X case I just blew my top. I just felt this is too much. I looked at my own daughter, who was 12 at the time, and thought, this could happen to her. I listened to all the talk, and felt really angry at all these men. They're the ones who make the rules, and half the time they don't know what they're talking about. I didn't care that I had no experience. Surely there was something I'd be able to do.

A number of women described reaching a point where they were looking for something new, something to get out of the house and expand their horizons. This most often resulted in either taking a course in personal development, or an education course. This in turn led to greater political awareness, and to a desire to become involved in activism or community development:

> I was sitting at home thinking that it was time to get involved in something. My children were older, I wanted to be out and doing something. When I heard about the women's group I decided to see what it was about.

Other factors that were mentioned in interviews included developing awareness through reading, and from this seeking out a political cause or group in which to get involved, or being asked by someone to join a group, especially in a local context. Initial awareness thus arose from a variety of sources.

Awareness was almost always accompanied by a desire to join a group or seek out experiences and resources that would help them to develop their analysis further. Most of the women interviewed either joined a local women's group or took a women's studies course, and in these contexts they realized that the more developed their analysis was, the better they felt about themselves and the more able they were to stand up for themselves.

> I found taking the course in women's studies was a great experience. It helped me to realize that the problem is not always me. The odds and structures are against me. ... It isn't women's hormones or their nature that makes us behave like this, it's the way society makes us.

> It's important to see the reality of any situation before you can change it. Even though a lot of the stuff is depressing at first, it makes you realize what you're up against, it makes you more determined to stick with it. ... It makes you realize why a lot of women don't seem to want change.

> discussions with other women really helped me to understand things better. ... I just felt that I knew more, and that made me more confident. ... I was able to stick up for myself, get my arguments down.

> In the study group it was great to hear other women agreeing with you ... it definitely helped me to communicate better ... I was able to see connections between different things. ... seeing connections between my experience and what they were saying.

In these quotes a variety of processes are described. There is a recognition of the link between psychological experience and society, and between one's own personal experience and the experiences of others, which is the core of consciousness-raising. It was clear from interviews that experiences in groups facilitated making this connection, and helped overcome isolation and the feeling that women often expressed that they are the 'only ones'.

Education plays a key role in raising awareness, and that what is needed is education which facilitates making critical connections between the personal and political. This is of course one of the aims of women's studies courses and critical education generally (Connolly, 1997; Gilligan and Zappone, 2008; Ryan, 2001). However, what may also be needed more explicitly in this context is a more direct personal challenging of socialization and of cultural norms in areas such as needs and emotions, as suggested by hooks (1993) and Miller (1986), both of whom emphasize the internalization of cultural norms. Martín-Baró (1994) also suggests that critical analysis of the ways that needs are socialized to serve economic and political interests can be part of consciousness-raising. The need for a critical analysis of psychological and behavioural patterns as well as of society is also highlighted by a danger identified by many writers on oppression and liberation, namely that the oppressed, in breaking out of oppressive psychological and behavioural patterns, may adopt patterns associated with domination.

Daly's (2005) approach emphasizes that the process of analysis requires courage, a point which is alluded to in the above quote in which women's reluctance to change is mentioned. Although this quote illustrates a common experience in women's studies classes, namely a sense of being overwhelmed by the extent of oppression, it also states an important point in the context of critical education, namely that awareness is preferable to lack of awareness. It takes courage, as Daly points out, to name oppression, and, as the above quote illustrates, naming oppression itself can create courage. Thus awareness is linked to the development of confidence, courage and the capacity to challenge the status quo.

Self-confidence and self-worth

A common experience upon joining a group was that of feeling overwhelmed, of not being able to speak out, or becoming aware of lack of confidence. While groups themselves sometimes provided the necessary support, most women felt the need to engage in some form of personal development, with assertiveness being the most commonly mentioned. The need for personal development in order to build up confidence and self-esteem was mentioned by all but one of the interviewees.

> I really needed to build up my confidence. I felt really frustrated sitting at meetings and not being able to say anything. I felt everyone was better than me, I was afraid they'd laugh at me. They all seemed to know everything. A few times when I tried to say something I just couldn't get the words out, I just couldn't make my point.... Doing an assertiveness course helped me to learn to speak up in groups, get my point across, not be intimidated.

Women expressed a need to have time out for themselves, when they could focus on their own development in a structured way:

> even though the women in the group really encouraged me, I really felt overwhelmed by all the things that had to be done, and I was afraid to take things on.... I took a personal development course, it was the first time I thought much about myself.

The interest in assertiveness training manifested in the interviews is reflected in the widespread practice at the time among local women's groups in Ireland and elsewhere to organize assertiveness training for their group, and to seek other areas of personal development. Assertiveness training, leadership skills and health were key areas of interest to women's groups (Mulvey, 1994). These aim to build up confidence and self-esteem and facilitate women's active involvement in bringing about longer term social change. Health care is seen as vital for women's development, especially in areas of social deprivation where stress and lack of resources place a constant strain on both physical and mental health.

Thus a major focus of many individual women and of women's groups was involvement in courses which aimed to build up self-confidence and self-esteem, many of which fall under the heading of 'personal development'. However, personal development courses have been criticized for their failure to take account of social conditions. Critics argue that personal development without a social analysis can serve to perpetuate a 'blame the victim' ideology. Such courses place the focus on shortcomings in women's own personalities and behaviour patterns, and cultivate the belief that difficulties in living will be solved through personal change (Rapping, 1996; Ryan, 2001).

The point was already made that in breaking out of subordinate modes of behaviour, oppressed groups and individuals may embrace dominator modes of behaviour. This would seem to be clearly relevant in the context of personal development, and especially of assertiveness training. Not only is there a need to retain a political analysis which acknowledges the limits to assertiveness, but there is also a need for a critical analysis of the values and modes of behaviour engendered by assertiveness training. Writers on liberation reviewed in Chapter 4, particularly hooks (1993) and Martín-Baró (1994), called for a self-determination which is based on the values and lived experience of the oppressed, which often emphasize negotiation, solidarity and cooperation rather than individualized goal seeking. References were made to a variety of practices which could facilitate this, including developing a sense of history (Maracle, 1996) and identifying positive role models and images (hooks, 2002b) which will be discussed more fully below.

The development of self-confidence and a sense of self-worth as a countermeasure to the sense of inferiority and lack of self-worth associated with oppression was repeatedly discussed by writers on liberation. Assertiveness may also be relevant to Miller's (1986) discussion of the importance of overcoming blocks to direct action on one's own behalf, which is one of the central goals of assertiveness training. It may be seen as an important step in the process of becoming an agent with a sense of entitlement, a process which is fundamental in breaking out of oppression. Many of those who referred to personal development courses saw them as first steps in the process of becoming more involved in political activism.

Positive role models and images

The importance of role models lies both in providing women with the confidence and the courage to engage in action for change, and in giving voice to the concerns of women. Many of the women interviewed made references to specific women whom they admired or were inspired by. They were familiar with many names from the Irish women's liberation movement, and from Irish history more generally. Historical figures can increase women's confidence in their capacity to bring about change and provide models from history of women who have participated in social change. However, even feminist scholarship on the lives of women who are considered to be significant historical figures tends to be confined to exceptional women, who by virtue of their class and other circumstances had considerable freedom and were able to devote resources to their political activities (Lerner, 1993; Mac Curtain, 2008). Women who are prominent public figures can be a source of role models for women, as shown by the impact of figures such as the former President of Ireland, Mary Robinson, who continues to be an important source of encouragement and inspiration for women and who was frequently mentioned by the women who were interviewed. It is not so much Robinson's public achievements as her personal integrity and her courage in speaking on behalf of women as a feminist that inspires women. Writing of her presidency at the time, Coulter (1993, p. 1) notes:

> While no-one can deny her outstanding record as a lawyer and champion of women through the avenue of the courts, or her role in sponsoring liberal legislation on issues like contraception, it is clear that this is not what she means to many of the thousands who work to transform their villages, towns and neighbourhoods in anticipation of her visits, who flock to hear her speak, who seek the sanctification of her presence at cultural and community events.... This unprecedented popularity of a political figure has much to do with Robinson's personal qualities – her evident honesty and integrity.

Coulter further argues that Robinson gives recognition to 'another kind of politics marginalized and driven underground by the institutional politics in operation since the foundation of the state' (p. 2). Thus it is the personal qualities and the particular nature of her politics which enabled former President Mary Robinson to be a source of inspiration and encouragement for women.

There is also a need for accessible role models which emerged particularly in group discussions with women, where many women expressed a sense of admiration and respect for public figures, but felt very clearly that they could not enter the public arena and speak or act in a like manner themselves. While they felt respect and admiration for such figures, they also sought figures from their own lives with whom they could identify. In particular women who assumed leadership roles in community development or political groups, and who were seen to sustain commitment over time were identified. A difficulty that arises here comes from the patterns of horizontal hostility and distrust of leadership outlined in Chapter 3. Some women felt a mixture of admiration and resentment for such figures. Other possible role models were women who were seen to cope with difficult circumstances or overcome personal problems with difficult marriages or addictions. Thus role models were identified either because of political skills and courage or because of capacities to bring about change in their personal lives.

Fictional characters can also provide role models, as much feminist writing indicates. hooks (2002b) in particular emphasizes the importance of characters in black fiction as sources of inspiration and models of strength, compassion and agency. Lesbian literature and culture has been enormously important for many lesbians in providing models and visions for lesbian existence. Literature, art, film and culture generally obviously play an essential role in liberation, and also as vehicles for breaking out of oppression, for freeing the imagination and discovering new ways of being.

While images do not receive as much attention as role models in psychological theory, it is clear from the writings on oppression and liberation that negative visual images play an important role in undermining feelings of self-worth. Again hooks (1994; 2002b) in particular, writing about black women, devoted attention in her books to negative images of women in culture, media and film, and wrote of the need 'to create images – representations of their world that were pleasing to the sensibilities and to the eye' (hooks, 1994, p. 82). The creation of such images has clearly been a focus for many women artists and for the women's movement generally. Gadon, for example, provides a compendium of positive images of women both by contemporary women artists and from goddess iconography, arguing that 'Affirmation of the female body as a source of pleasure and power is a major goal of the Women's Movement' (Gadon, 1989, p. 285). She writes that 'The image is the key to our transformation of culture. The change cannot come about without the reinforcement of new icons and symbols of female power' (p. 370). Strong and positive visual images of women have been produced by a host of contemporary women artists in Ireland and elsewhere, images which emphasize the beauty of women's bodies, including genitals, challenge the weakness, passivity and thinness of popular cultural images, depict women at work, taking strong and assertive stances, in religious and warrior roles, nurturing, enraged and creative.

Gadon (1989) links the creation of images not only with positive esteem and body image, but also with spiritual transformation. Certainly the images and symbols of ancient goddess culture provide some of the most contrasting images to contemporary cultural representations, and have been a source of inspiration to contemporary women artists. These ancient female representations are imbued with power and dynamism which is very difficult to attain in contemporary culture, representing, as Gimbutas points out, life-giving, transformative and also powerfully destructive forces. It is noteworthy that ancient images and icons often involve female forms of a very large size, which itself is a striking contrast to contemporary images (Gimbutas, 1991; Noble, 2003).

Sexuality

Sexuality was one of the most frequently mentioned areas of development pursued by the women interviewed. This interest in exploring sexuality followed particular experiences of violence and harassment which were mentioned in the course of the interview, or was linked to objections to the way in which women were represented in media and advertising:

> I really found it hard to feel comfortable in myself, with the way I looked and felt about my body.

> I realised that I was fed up with what I was seeing on TV, and also with how women are treated. I hadn't really seen how weak and passive women are portrayed until I took the women and media course.

The desire to explore sexuality was not always motivated by an analysis of oppression. In some cases, it was offered as a possibility in a group or educational setting, and women just thought that it would be an interesting and relevant course to take. Where gains from the course were mentioned, the most common theme was the realization of how much disapproval there was for women to experience sexual pleasure:

> I realized that I spent most of my time worrying about how he was feeling, and that I hadn't really paid attention to what I wanted, or even thought much about how I felt.

> There was much more to sex than I realized...we had really only been doing the one thing, which was fine, but really there's a lot more to it.

These quotes illustrate the relatively narrow construction of sexuality which is linked to the mechanism of sexual exploitation and also draw attention to body image and its link to media representations of women, which have been the focus of a considerable amount of feminist analysis. Representations of women's bodies and the relentless pressures from the beauty and diet industries play a key role in maintaining women's low sense of self-worth and contribute to patterns of depression and eating distresses in women (Orbach, 2009). Orbach argues that body anxiety continues to be a central problem for women.

Domination–subordination clearly has an impact on sexuality and sexual relationships, as the writers reviewed in Chapter 3 indicated. However, many courses in sexuality attend primarily to personal experience, at least in the Irish context. They focus on providing concrete information about women's sexual anatomy and means to pleasure, and on exploring sexuality in the context of assertiveness, emphasizing women's right to sexual pleasure and also to refuse sexual demands. This is obviously important in the context of subordination, but in the context of liberation there is also a need for a critical analysis of the social construction of sexuality. Early feminist writers have provided critical analyses of the way in which sexuality has been constructed as a particularly narrow form of heterosexuality (Rich, 1980; Raymond, 1986).

Feminist explorations of heterosexuality have highlighted the challenges of negotiating authentic heterosexual relationships in the context of institutionalized male domination (hooks, 2002a; Rowland, 1996; Wilkinson and Kitzinger, 1993). Explorations of lesbian sexuality involve both acknowledgement of its positioning in a hetero-patriarchal society and a celebration of its possibilities (Diamond, 2008; Penelope and Wolf, 1990; Rich, 1980). There have also been challenges to the dichotomizing of sexuality into 'heterosexual' or 'homosexual', and calls to broaden views of sexuality from a woman-centred perspective – 'to discover the erotic in female terms: as that which is unconfined to any single part of the body or solely to the body itself' (Rich, 1980, p. 53).

Lorde links the erotic to women's power, writing that 'the erotic offers a well of replenishing and provocative force to the woman who does not fear its revelation, nor succumbs to the belief that sensation is enough' (1984, p. 54). This highlights another political dimension to sexuality, namely the importance of sexuality as a source of energy and well-being, a dimension which was also recognized particularly by Maracle (1996) and hooks (1993). Control and suppression of sexuality thus has a fundamental impact on psychological functioning. The capacity for authentic experiences of sexuality and of sexual relationships, and the need to explore new models of sexuality are clearly important elements in the liberation process.

Creativity

Creativity was another area that featured in the interviews that were conducted – 6 of the 16 women had taken courses in creativity of some kind. What was striking in the comments about creativity was how often women said that they had done it 'just for themselves', rather than out of a political analysis or some feeling of a lack or deficit:

> To take time to create is selfish, women need to be selfish. They have been self-sacrificing for too long.

> taking a writing course was the first time I did something 'just for me'. I had to take time out to practice, shut myself away from everyone. There was no reason, I wasn't particularly learning a skill that could get me a job.... I found it really great just to sit down and try and express myself.

This last quote highlights the function of creativity from a liberation psychology perspective. As Daly's (1984) analysis suggests, it is a means towards focusing inwardly and connecting with self, and for counteracting the disconnections that are associated with oppression. Creativity in this context does not mean the production of works of art or literature which are judged to be creative by others, but rather involves activities which provide a vehicle for self-expression, or for finding a voice.

From a liberation perspective, one essential function of creativity is that of reconnection, but the conditions required for creativity are antithetical to oppression. At a material level, creativity requires time, place and resources, all of which are problematic in women's lives. Psychologically, creativity requires a focusing within, and an openness or freedom from blocks to self-expression Other qualities which Miller (1986) associates with creativity are a sense of identity, and of autonomy, power, abundance, strength and compassion. Miller writes that creativity draws on these capacities, and cultivating creativity can build them, again highlighting the value of creativity for transforming psychological patterns associated with oppression.

Further functions of creativity which reflect the themes of writers on liberation are highlighted in Crone's (2004) analysis of theatre and creative drama as a means towards developing confidence, self-expression and political awareness in women's groups. Drawing on Boal's (1993) analysis, Crone highlights how drama can be used with women to explore and develop an analysis of issues that are relevant in their lives. Drama helps to encourage self-expression, explore conflicts and develop insights into transformation and new possibilities. In working together, women develop a sense of camaraderie which facilitates group organization and activism. This highlights the value of creative activity in creating collective and community understanding, a point which will be discussed further in later chapters.

Spirituality

Spirituality did not feature strongly in research interviews as a positive force. However, religion, and particularly the Catholic Church, featured strongly as a negative experience of oppression. Feminist writings in this area have obviously provided a critical analysis of institutionalized religion, criticisms which are captured by the well-known quote of Daly's (1973, p. 41): 'if god is male then the male is god'. Daly, and others, argue that conceptualizing the urge to transcendence or the focus of spirituality as masculine creates a block to women's spiritual development. In response to this, some feminists focused on developing conceptualizations of goddess, which were criticized as lacking in a fundamental re-analysis of spirituality (Daly, 2005). Feminist explorations of spirituality have developed a variety of ways of conceptualizing spirituality and its relationships to nature, the environment and community (Starhawk, 2004; Zappone, 1991).

The destruction of spirituality or the blocking of spiritual development recurred as a theme in writings on oppression and liberation reviewed in Chapters 3 and 4. These writings also acknowledged spirituality as a powerful sustaining force in the struggle to survive under oppression, in the effort to transform the damage of oppression, and in the construction of new culture and new ways of being (Daly 1978; 2005; hooks, 1993; Kasl, 1992; Maracle, 1996; Starhawk, 1987; 2005). Spirituality is used here in its broadest sense to refer to a sense of union or harmony with a greater or universal force. hooks refers to concepts such as life-affirming spirituality, connection with the earth, divine spirits and higher powers, which those who have rejected traditional religions have developed (hooks, 1993).

A central feature of liberation for Daly is 'recovering the Archimage' (see Chapter 4), an undoing of the erasure of women and women's powers from mythology and religion, and a reconnection with a sense of women's 'Elemental' powers, that is, powers which are 'in harmony with the Wild in nature and the Self' (Daly, 1984, p. 7). In this context, goddess mythology can be an evocative source of inspiration in relation to female energy and power (Noble, 2003). For example, Skadi, Scandinavian Goddess of the North Wind, is a skilled and powerful communicator; Pele, Polynesian Fire Goddess, evokes female energies of fiery liquid; Kuan Yin, Chinese Earth Goddess, evokes compassion and magical powers; Boann, Irish Water Goddess, recalls the flow of life and death.

Starhawk (2005) presents the view that pagan or Wiccan spirituality can provide a complete alternative to institutionalized religion. She writes that Wiccan spirituality places immanence at its centre, in

contrast to institutionalized religions. She describes rituals and practices for drawing on nature, on elemental powers, and on psychic
capacities, and advocates the use of ritual in everyday life and in political activism. Drawing on new paradigm thinking about consciousness, energy and form, she argues that the frame with which we view
the world has a profound impact on how we create the world, personally, ecologically and politically (Starhawk, 2005). Both Wiccan and
shamanic (Matthews, 2002) approaches share a positive emphasis on
directly connecting with greater consciousness as a form of spirituality
and also as part of the process of transformation at personal, community and transpersonal levels.

This highlights one of the important functions of spirituality from a
liberation psychology perspective, in addition to its role as a source of
hope and sustenance, which is that of recreating the sense of connection
which is damaged by the fragmentation and dissociation of oppressive
social conditions. Zappone (1991) captures the many dimensions of this
by identifying 'hope for wholeness' as central to feminist spiritualities.
'This "hope for wholeness" includes several components: that the broken selves of women (and men) may be healed through the process of
self-determination; that separation due to racism, classism, poverty, sexism, and heterosexism may be transformed into a freedom to seek mutual
relationships; that polluting and exploiting of the natural world may be
stopped through humanity's recognition that it is part of and not separate
from nature' (p. 2). Intellectual questioning, spiritual practices, the development of rituals, symbols and images, and the creation of relationships
and communities are among the processes which feminists have identified and undertaken as part of spiritual development (Zappone, 1991).
In the Irish context, women have sought inspiration from mythological
sources, from the archaeological legacies referred to above, from the landscape, from spiritualists and psychics, and from Celtic, pagan, shamanic
and Wiccan traditions, either alongside of or instead of institutionalized
religions.

Valuing women's unpaid labour

The lack of value afforded to women's work in the home as mothers and
home-makers and their contribution to society emerges repeatedly as
a source of low self-worth and of anger for women. It is an area where
the discrepancy between public discourse and women's own experience is most at odds. In particular, women were aware of public discourses which place great value on women's role as mothers – in the

Irish context, for example, the Constitution contains an article which acknowledges the important contribution made by women through their work in the home. Yet what women experienced was a loss of status and respect on becoming mothers, a denigration and neglect of their skills as mothers, and a complete lack of acknowledgement of their contribution as carers. What emerged in interviews is the view that if work is not paid for it has no value, and while there has been considerable controversy and discussion about whether women should receive direct payment for their work in the home, it is clear that the absence of payment is symbolic of the lack of value afforded this work:

Work that isn't paid for has no value.

In our society, your value depends on how much you get paid.

While women are aware of the value of their unpaid labour and of their contributions as childrearers, it is more difficult to articulate the vital contribution to society which this makes, partly because it has been relatively ignored by economists and sociologists (Delphy and Leonard, 1992; Lynch, 2007). Feminists have firstly documented the amount of productive labour engaged in by women in household production and household management, emphasizing the time, skills, and economic contribution of such labour. A second area which feminists have analysed is women's role in caring, both in terms of the hours and type of labour involved, and in terms of the economic contribution that this labour makes. A third area which has been acknowledged is the role of women in maintaining kinship ties through keeping contact, organizing family events and other rituals which observe kin transitions. Fourthly the contribution that women make to the maintenance of community and the interpersonal fabric of society has been elaborated (Delphy and Leonard, 1992; Lynch, Baker and Lyons, 2009).

In the course of this work feminists have exposed the limitations of traditional economic and sociological concepts which do not provide frameworks in which to acknowledge or conceptualize these contributions. Irish sociologists Lynch and McLaughlin use the phrase 'love labour' to refer to the work of caring for and catering for emotional needs, writing that 'what is required is a radical review of the relationship between caring, love labour, and so-called productive work' (1995, p. 251). Love labour does not simply involve 'emotional care', but also refers to the building of bonds, including bonds of solidarity. Lynch, Baker and Lyons (2009) emphasize that like other so-called productive work, love labour takes time, mental energy, skills and resources and detail the vital importance of love and care to human and social development.

Childrearing, love labour and caring labour are all examples of relational work that women do which forms an essential cornerstone of society. This work not only provides care, it takes care of emotional needs and fosters growth and development on a one-to-one basis. Through the networking, kin maintenance and fostering of solidarity, women weave a web of interpersonal relationships which underpin the social structures which have been the focus of sociological analysis. This is a web of interpersonal relations which exists both within and outside social structures, and which contributes to the creation of society and to social cohesiveness.

Sense of history

Sense of history emerged from the theoretical analysis of the previous two chapters for a variety of reasons. Control of culture involved the erasure of subordinates from history, leaving subordinates with a lack of awareness of their own lives, their contribution to culture and society, and their accomplishments and achievements. A sense of identity and of pride is thus undermined, and the oppressed are deprived of a sense of their own situation as historically constructed and as changing over time. A sense of history is essential both for a strong sense of self and identity, and for an analysis of the nature of oppression and of social change.

While developing a sense of history did not emerge in the interviews conducted for this analysis, it has long been an area of much attention in women's studies, in black liberation movements and in decolonization movements (Freire, 1993; hooks, 1993; Maracle 1996; Martín-Baró, 1994). Lerner (1986) has provided a number of arguments for the importance of sense of history, based on her observation of 'the profound changes in consciousness which students of Women's History experience' (p. 3), writing that 'Women's history is indispensable and essential to the emancipation of women' (p. 3). She argues that 'The contradiction between women's centrality and active role in creating society and their marginality in the meaning-giving process of interpretation and explanation has been a dynamic force, causing women to struggle against their condition' (p. 5).

For Lerner, the writing of women into history acknowledges that 'Men are not the center of the world, but men and women are' (p. 13). The erasure of women from history established men as the norm, and gave them the power to define meaning, and indeed to define what is political. With no historical knowledge, women lack the authority and historical traditions that men took for granted; the few women who were acknowledged in mainstream histories reinforces the view that only exceptional women made a contribution; whole areas of existence such as the family, childrearing and community life were ignored or judged to be unimportant; 'human development' was seen as spurred by men's initiative and creativity.

Two important contributions from a feminist perspective are, firstly, the role of history in identifying patriarchy as a historical system: that is, one which has evolved over time; and, secondly, affirming women's involvement in resistance to oppression. In the Irish context the work of Mary Condren is notable for her analysis of Celtic mythology and the historical development of patriarchy from pre-Celtic times to the establishment of Christianity and English colonization (Condren, 2002). Condren firstly identifies themes in Celtic mythology which link it to ancient Near Eastern goddess-mother mythologies. She writes

> Even before the serpent symbol arrived in Ireland, the essence of goddess religions was to be found. Just as in the Sumerian religion we saw that the idea of divinity could not be represented by any one divine image, so too in Ireland there were many gods and goddesses, all with their own particular functions to fulfill (p. 25).

She evokes a pre-patriarchal matri-centred society in which 'there was an essential wonder to life and an awareness that all things were connected' (p. 25), in which 'the source of life was so integrally associated with women' (p. 26). Celtic mythology abounds with female goddesses – of sovereignty, of death, of healing – who undergo magical transformations and who confer power on the male warriors who are the main protagonists of the recorded mythology. It is clear from myths, laws and other sources that Celtic society had a consciousness of divinity, of nature, of healing and of spirituality which was quite different from modern consciousness.

Condren's interpretation of Celtic mythology is supported by the rich abundance of archaeological remains from pre-Celtic times in Ireland, dating back to around 3,500 BC, which includes the well-known Winter Solstice oriented mound at Newgrange and a large number of other stone structures. Archaeologist Marija Gimbutas, who has extensively researched archaeological evidence from this era from all over Europe, argues that during the era between around 10,000 BC and 3,500, civilization in Europe was peaceful, egalitarian, goddess and nature-centred, and places the artwork and archaeological findings from Ireland firmly in this context (Gimbutas, 1991; 1999; Moane, 1997; Stout 2003). The value of these historical analyses lies not only in showing the historical development of patriarchy, as Lerner's (1986) analysis in Chapter 2 has shown for Mesopotamia, but also in challenging one of the fundamental myths of patriarchy, namely that male domination is natural and inevitable.

The historical resistance of women to patriarchal oppression, colonial domination and other forms of exploitation has been thoroughly documented by feminists (Jayawardena, 1986; McAllister, 1988; 1991; Ward, 1983), and will be discussed more fully in Chapter 7. There has been a wide range of explorations of this theme in the Irish context, ranging from historiography to social and political history (McAuliffe, O'Donnell and Lane, 2009; MacCurtain, 2008; Valiulis and O'Dowd, 1997; Ward, 1995). Here the involvement of women in a range of activities and movements over hundreds of years is documented. Examples include women's involvements in wars, land movements, religious changes, development of agriculture and industry, labour movements, poverty, prostitution, legislative changes, and a host of other local and national activities. What emerges from much of this writing is not only the active role played by women in many areas of social and political life, but also the efforts to confine women to the home and to erase their contribution.

In one analysis that links the women's movement to colonial history, Coulter (1993) discusses women's political organizing during a particularly conservative time in Irish history, between the foundation of the state and the 1960s. She argues that despite the vital role that women played in the political and armed movement for independence in the early twentieth century in Ireland, the newly emerging state moved to confine women to the home legally and socially. She writes that like many other post-colonial countries, women 'found themselves excluded from political life in the new state, which usually established its own specific form of patriarchy, combining the institutional patriarchy of the former regime with all the most conservative elements of local religious and cultural traditions' (p. 3). Yet she argues that despite this exclusion from the structures of the state, women adopted 'new strategies more appropriate for the time they were living in. Their old talents for organization around questions of immediate interest to women, children and the poor came to the fore, though in a more muted way than in the early years of the century' (p. 28). Women organized the Irish Housewives

Association and the Irish Countrywomen's Association, both of which developed programmes to support women in the home and also to support local and national initiatives on family-related issues (Tweedy, 1992). While their agenda was criticized for its conservatism with the rise of the modern women's liberation movement, Coulter argues that they were important outlets for women's organizational skills in a particularly conservative climate, and provided a vital basis of support for the emerging women's movement (Connolly, 2003).

Personal processes and liberation

The practices discussed in this chapter were based primarily on theoretical analysis of oppression and liberation, on interviews with women, and on the experiences of women involved in the Irish Women's Movement. They focused on the personal level of building strengths, and this included physical strengths – through, for example, health care – as well as psychological strengths. They addressed primarily the areas of self, identity and self-expression, aiming to counteract the damages associated with oppression, and also to build positive strengths. Practices such as developing a sense of history, identifying positive role-models and images, valuing unpaid labour and cultivating sexuality, creativity and spirituality involved protecting the psyche against the undermining associated with patterns such as economic exploitation, cultural control and fragmentation described in Chapter 2. They also involved nurturing the psyche with positive and self-enhancing messages and opportunities for self-expression which link the individual with the past and with community and culture.

The processes discussed in this chapter were directed at the personal level of building strengths and developing awareness, but obviously they also feed the interpersonal and political processes of liberation. While they are best pursued in an interpersonal context, it is also the case that many of them can be undertaken on a private and individual basis as well, for example through education and cultural pursuits. This analysis shows that individuals can actively seek out experiences which can build personal strengths and develop awareness, either privately or in group, community and cultural settings. Engaging in such processes without interpersonal support and without changing social conditions, however, will be of limited value in the face of the pressures created by social conditions associated with oppression. Hence developing practices at the interpersonal and the political levels are also essential for personal change.

6
The Interpersonal Level: Making Connections

Interpersonal relations, whether dyadic, group or community, are vehicles through which oppression is enacted and through which psychological transformations are facilitated; they are of vital importance in taking action to bring about social change. Under oppression, interpersonal relations may be fragmented and fraught with horizontal hostility, and at the same time they are the mainstay of survival, growth and development, resistance and transformation. While there are many barriers to effective political action, it is certainly the case that interpersonal conflict and destructive group dynamics play their role in undermining effective action. Conversely, supportive and empowering interpersonal, group and community structures are cornerstones of activism. From a psychological perspective, the interpersonal level refers to relationships between people at the three levels of one-to-one or social relations, groups and community. The key process at the interpersonal level is overcoming the fragmentation and isolation that arises under oppression through making connections with others, and particularly through developing a sense of solidarity and of belonging to a community or collective. In this chapter women's writings and experiences will be drawn on to elucidate the practices through which connections can be supportive and empowering, and a sense of community can be created.

The concept of empowerment has gained widespread currency in feminist writings, in community development and in political activism. Definitions of empowerment historically emphasized increasing the capacity to bring about change and refer to changes in psychological capacities and skills rather than to the actual power available in situations. For this reason the concept was criticized by Kitzinger and Perkins (1993), who argue that the word empowerment locates power inside the individual and therefore ignores the social reality of powerlessness. They cite a variety of self-help and psychotherapeutic writings which speak of power as if it were an inner resource which merely needed to be developed, writing that 'at its most extreme, psychology claims that we have total power over our own lives, because we create our own reality' (Kitzinger and Perkins, 1993, p. 41).

These conceptions of power are clearly victim-blaming, as Kitzinger and Perkins point out. The concept of empowerment is open to such interpretations, but is more often used in a political context to refer to experiences of personal development, education, and group and community activism which increase women's awareness, confidence and skills, and which help women to be more effective at using whatever power is available (Parsons, O'Connor and Conlon, 2003). This usage reflects an acknowledgement that both individual women and women's groups experience difficulty with the exercise of power, and express the need for training and skills in the exercise of power. The emphasis in the word empowerment is therefore on the effective use of power, rather than on power itself as a personal resource.

The word empowerment is not only used widely in the women's movement and in women's groups, but has also been an important concept in the area of community development. Here there has been considerable development in the understanding of what kinds of processes, experiences and structures enhance the opportunities for individuals to get involved in groups and communities, to actively participate, to gain a sense of confidence, and to acquire skills and other capacities which will enable them to participate more fully in society and take action to bring about change (Murray and Rogers, 2009). The concepts and practices which feminists have developed in this context will add to the insights of the writers reviewed in the previous chapters.

Social relationships

Social relationships involve one-to-one interactions and relationships between individuals. In this context feminists have written of the challenge to confront the negative patterns which have developed in response to domination, and also of the strength, love and solidarity that are possible between women (O'Connor, 2002; Orbach and Eichenbaum, 1987). Writers reviewed in Chapters 3 and 4 acknowledge the impact of oppression and domination on social relationships. In also acknowledging relationships as a source of strength, they call for new ways of relating. They see women's friendships and women's connections with each other are a vital source of both joy and love despite the difficulties created by oppressive conditions (Daly, 2005; hooks, 1993; 2002a; Maracle, 1996; Miller, 1986; Pharr, 1988).

Maracle (1996) and hooks (2002a) in particular emphasize the importance of love and compassion in relationships which are formed under conditions of oppression, where on the one hand so much reliance is placed on friendships and relationships, and on the other hand patterns of dissimulation and of horizontal hostility are acted out. hooks writes of the need to forgive rather than to blame: 'Our capacity to forgive always allows us to be in touch with our own agency' (p. 167), while Maracle wishes women to be seen as 'powerful sensuous beings in need of compassion and tenderness' (p. 22). Maracle calls for an acknowledgement of love as a central value, writing that 'nowhere in the white male conception of history has love been a motive for getting things done' (p. 23).

hooks writes that women's search for love is vitally important, part of the journey of overcoming the isolation and blows to self-esteem that are part of female socialization. Like Miller (1986), she discusses women's tendency to set aside their needs and focus on others, thus inhibiting their capacity to know their own needs and therefore to communicate with others. She addresses the ways in which heterosexuality is constructed to place relationships with men as primary, arguing that this has deprived women of the deep bonds of love and friendship that they can form with each other. Arguing that self-love is the key to loving others, she advocates the cultivation of self-esteem and sustaining bonds with other women (hooks, 2002a). Feminists have also written of the need to enact patterns of affirmation, support and love based on new values and visions that challenge the ethics of care and focus on giving that is associated with being a woman (Gilligan, 1982; 1994).

An example of this is the discussion by Sarah Hoagland, who explicitly links such ethics with domination. Hoagland writes of the need to challenge ethical values which emphasize self-sacrifice and taking care of others. Hoagland argues that such an ethics is part of a dominator culture, requiring the sacrifice of one for the sake of the other. An ethics which emphasizes altruism and self-sacrifice is permeated by a belief in winner and loser, and the superiority of the giver is asserted against the inferiority of the one in need of help. Hoagland suggests that what is needed is a new understanding of self-interest and of differences, and an analysis which acknowledges the limits to choice created by social conditions. This involves challenging the value placed on such self-sacrificing concepts as unconditional love, emotional disclosure, caring, support and vulnerability. Hoagland proposes 'an ethics which recognizes separation or withdrawal at any level as a moral option' (Hoagland, 1988, p. 297), an ethics which would revision concepts such as nurturing and caring as genuine choices rather than moral/emotional imperatives.

Such an ethics, according to Hoagland, would require firstly self-understanding, so that interpersonal relationships are based not on the demands made but upon a realistic assessment of what is possible within the boundaries of personal resources. It also requires some degree of autonomy, so that help and support are provided from a position of what Hoagland calls 'enabling' (p. 267) rather than either overinvolvement or detachment. A clear analysis is essential for such an ethics, as it involves recognition of the demands and choices which are present in a situation and an ability to act within these limitations as well as to think creatively about further options. Hoagland also calls for greater integration of 'dreaming, psychic faculty, intuition, humor and imagination' (p. 267) into relationships. Thus she presents a challenge to the focus on others which is a pattern associated with oppression, and also seeks to develop a wide range of psychological capacities in a relational context.

In her analysis of female friendship, Janice Raymond also describes many of the psychological patterns discussed in Chapter 3 as barriers to female friendship (Raymond, 1986). She emphasizes that the construction of relations between men and women – 'hetero-reality' (p. 9) – places an imperative on women to attend to men: 'the norms of hetero-reality have intended woman for man and not man for woman' (1986, p. 10). Like Hoagland, she critically discusses 'therapism' – an endless focus on feelings about the relationship – and 'the tyranny of tolerance' – the incapacity or unwillingness to make moral judgements about others' behaviours. For Raymond, it is as important for women to fight for female friendship as it is to fight for political or economic rights, in part because female friendship provides the ground for political and other struggles. Raymond does not subscribe to the view that all relationships between women can be ones of friendship, but seeks, through an examination of female friendship, to elucidate emotions and values which can serve as ideals and which can counteract the disillusionments brought about by disappointment, hostility and betrayal.

At a concrete level the concept of support has already emerged in interviews and discussions with women from the previous chapter, where frequent references were made to encouragement and positive feedback received from others. Support also features prominently in women's accounts of their experiences in groups and communities, as a word which captures the positive ways in which women encourage each other, provide each other with practical and material assistance, affirm each other's opinions and worldviews, and provide recognition for achievements and aspirations. Support does not necessarily require a close relationship or feelings of love or affection, but rather a willingness to provide encouragement and assistance. It is thus often seen as embedded in a social network, and as a concrete manifestation of social connections. Although the focus of this chapter is on face to face relationships, social relations can also of course involve electronic social networking which offers a variety of new methods for making connections.

Group structures and processes

While feminist writings on dyadic relationships have been largely idealistic, writings on group structures and processes have been more practically oriented, drawing on the experiences of women in groups as they have tried to develop structures and processes which are supportive and empowering. Many of these groups have been formed in community contexts for purposes ranging from personal development through a large range of education and training courses to community and political initiatives. In this discussion the emphasis is on group structures and processes rather than on the wide variety of activities undertaken by women's groups. The structures of such groups vary from small-scale collectives with an emphasis on consensus to large organizations with officers and representatives. These structures may develop out of pragmatism or out of strategic or principled commitment to particular group structures.

Some of the elements of group structures and processes judged to be important for support and empowerment, and which facilitate the goals of making connections and creating a sense of community were identified by Herman (1997) and by Starhawk (1987) in the previous chapter. While Herman's discussion focuses on trauma, her insights may be used to gain understanding of breaking out of oppression. From Herman's (1997) discussion it can be concluded that effective group structures are related to the aims of the women joining the groups. In particular, at an initial stage, where a woman may be coming to awareness and lacks confidence and skills, a group which emphasizes safety may be most effective. Herman suggests that this will require clear structures and goals and an educational focus. The emphasis should be on information sharing, and on providing a 'cognitive framework' for understanding rather than on in-depth exploration of feelings about the situation. These groups can have open structures and membership, with a great deal of flexibility about individual participation in the group.

It was suggested in the previous chapter that analysis is an important element in breaking out of the often confusing and conflicting emotional states associated with oppression. This may correspond to the 'remembrance and mourning stage' identified by Herman (1997), where there is an acknowledgement of the full extent of oppression, and of the emotional reactions to this. The development of a narrative which is advocated at this stage by Herman may take the form of a narrative identifying links between personal experience and oppressive social conditions. Herman's account suggests that the need here is for a cohesive group in which there are clear boundaries, and a reasonably constant membership with a willingness to acknowledge the extent of oppression so that solidarity can develop.

Creating connections may correspond to Herman's (1997) reconnection stage, where the emphasis is on building strengths and developing a sense of belonging to community which can give sense to the experience of oppression and provide a positive focus for action. Groups can be more loosely structured as the psychological capacities to be more action oriented are already in place. They may have open membership, and be goal oriented or action oriented. Conflict and diversity can be more easily tolerated, and individual needs can be second to the activities of the group.

This analysis is not to suggest that women's groups should become therapeutic, but rather that women at different stages in personal and political development will have different needs. The aim, for example, at the second stage above is not to engage in therapeutic exploration of feelings, but to acknowledge and express emotional responses to oppression such as anger. When women at different points in development are in the same group, there may be a clash, providing a source of conflict within the group. It may be valuable to acknowledge this in developing group structures, and in particular, in making decisions about openness, group aims and leadership roles.

The main point of Starhawk's discussion is the need to develop group processes which can counteract the destructive patterns engendered by domination–subordination and facilitate the focusing of the group's energy into taking action (1987). For Starhawk it is important firstly to acknowledge that individuals come into groups with internalized 'power-over' or dominator patterns. Secondly, she notes that conflict is inevitable in groups, and it is particularly likely at times of transition or when there is a lack of clarity about the group's goals. Conflict must be acknowledged, as 'Hidden conflict creates an atmosphere ruled by the Censor, in which more and more cannot be said and no-one can feel truly safe' (Starhawk, 1987, p. 261). Starhawk emphasizes the hidden or subterranean dimensions of groups, where the destructive dynamics associated with domination–subordination are likely to be played out, and agendas are hidden. Her methods involve identifying the different roles, such as the censor, which are played out in groups, and the tasks which must be performed, such as setting boundaries.

A basic principle for groups to be empowering is that each individual is able to speak and be heard, itself a principle that counteracts hierarchical structures where a few people do the talking. Decision-making by consensus is another important principle, one which involves a commitment to taking the concerns of each group member and constructing a plan which will creatively encompass each of them. A third principle is active acknowledgement and acceptance of diversity, which Starhawk sees as counteracting the divisions created in a dominator system.

Based on her experience in non-hierarchical groups, Starhawk identifies the need for explicit attention to be paid to group dynamics and group energy through the assignment of roles, which include facilitator (task-oriented), peacemaker (calming function), vibeswatcher (tension awareness), priest/priestess (energy channelling), mediator (conflict resolution), and co-ordinator (communicator). Group dynamics and patterns can be disrupted constructively through shifting around these roles so that individuals are obliged to disrupt their own personal pattern of group involvement (e.g. being a star or a clown) and also to pay attention to group patterns.

An account which clearly aims to integrate psychological processes and structural inequalities in groupwork is provided by Butler and Wintram (1991). Their account is still widely cited as it provides a rare analysis of the interconnections between psychological patterns and group structures, and is thus particularly relevant to the present discussion. They describe of some of the psychological processes which they observed occurring in women's groups on the basis of their experience as social workers, and on specific experiences with two community-based women's groups which existed over three years with a changing membership. Placing women's experiences in the context of oppression, they write that 'Fear, isolation and loneliness lay at the root of the experiences of many of the women with whom we were involved over the years' (p. 2), stating that 'One of the central tenets of this chapter is that women's groups provide a basis for overcoming some of the psychological obstacles produced by occupying subordinate positions' (p. 5). The feminist groupwork which they describe incorporates a number of psychological techniques, as well as a focus on bringing about changes in personal and community life. Butler and Wintram's aims included building self-confidence and self-esteem, breaking isolation, helping women to make links between their personal or private difficulties and structures of oppression, and supporting women in making good decisions and implementing changes in their lives. They suggest that groups of between 8 and 12 women are suitable if trust, intimacy and self-revelation are to develop, and that groups should remain closed for a period of time and open up on a regular basis. Even with a very open structure, group recruitment and membership, they argue, is almost always 'a value-laden exercise' (p. 33). Members of the groups with whom they worked were drawn from populations in contact with social services, and were all working class with considerable experiences of deprivation and stress which included violence, poverty, multiple caring responsibilities and lack of education. This meant that there was already a basis for commonality in women's experiences of oppression which Butler and Wintram believe was sufficient to ensure both diversity and cohesiveness in the group. The emphasis was on group ownership by the members, with social workers playing a facilitative role. Women 'shared control of planning, co-ordination and facilitation of group sessions' (p. 41). While there was a clear programme for the group, there was also an attempt to keep structures flexible, and undertake a variety of activities which included role plays, physical exercises, fantasy and creativity, discussions and trips. These activities drew on a range of skills, offered a variety of means for self-expression, and helped to draw connections between experiences within the group and those in the external world. A balance was sought between activities which emphasized personal development and those which provided social analysis.

One of the processes which Butler and Wintram (1991) describe is the attempts by women 'to move from this isolation from each other to the identification of a group consciousness, that sense of belonging which leads to concerted action' (p. 73). Two practices which facilitated this were firstly the identification of structural relationships within the group, and secondly an analysis of interaction patterns in the group. Structural analysis involves explicitly addressing differences in status and identity in order to highlight stereotypic assumptions. Rather than ignoring differences which arise from status differentials, Butler and Wintram confront them directly and use them to further their aims, writing that 'Sisterhood does not mean obscuring the fact that women have different and unequal material circumstances' (p. 75). The analysis of interaction patterns, or patterns of interruption, turn-taking and group participation, highlighted how power and status differences which undermined equality were established. The awareness of group dynamics which arose from these practices provided a mirror for women's reflection on how status and power differentials are played out both at the macro level of society generally, and at the micro level of the group.

Obviously these processes require considerable facilitation and group skills. Processes which Butler and Wintram (1991) identify as essential are identifying with the group, development of trust, positive reciprocity, open self-disclosure, positive feedback and mutuality. These are facilitated by paying considerable attention to interaction patterns, for which all members of the group take responsibility. Inevitably in this situation, conflicts will arise as individuals challenge each other's behaviours and values. Indeed Butler and Wintram argue that conflict is a necessary part of the development of group cohesion, as rather than suppressing differences, they are brought out and addressed. As members recognize the benefits to be gained from group participation, such as confidence, self-awareness, friendship and solidarity, group cohesion and commitment increase. In their groups, Butler and Wintram observed a conflict between what they call 'The Caring Self' (1991, p. 105), with an emphasis on attunement to and care of others, and 'The Agential Self' (p. 107), the capacity to act on one's own behalf, a conflict which was identified in some of the writings on oppression reviewed in Chapter 3. The former, although an important part of women's psychology, is devalued, while the latter is submerged. The group provided a context in which conflict and ambivalence about the Agential Self could be explored, and aspects of it developed and acted out. Conflicts between caring and agency could also be addressed. This exploration highlighted paradoxes and contradictions between social roles and the ideologies which are attached to them. For example, while caring is supposedly a valued role, carers are often ignored in discussions of health policy and in the provision of support services. Connections and disconnections between personal experience and the social construction of women's roles could be identified through this exploration. Other areas were explored in a similar manner – that is, through practices which combined personal exploration with social analysis in a group context characterized by trust, cohesiveness and openness about difference. These areas included mental health, sexuality, anger and identity. In each case, the group experience enabled women to place their personal experience into a comparative context, explore various experiences of contradiction and conflict, and make connections to social structures and ideology. The group provided a buffer between women and the oppressive messages from society, providing them with 'windows into the self' (Butler and Wintram, 1991, p. 102) which facilitated self-determination.

As women's awareness of the connection between self and society developed, the challenge arose of translating these insights into personal and social transformation. Butler and Wintram (1991) describe a number of ways in which their groups supported the enactment of change. These included providing a context for testing out new ideas, behaviours and attitudes, helping women to resolve contradictions and failures in their efforts to change, supporting women in confronting partners, families and bureaucracies, and helping women to handle their frustrations in the face of failures to bring about change. Butler and Wintram report that almost all of the women in their groups made changes in their everyday lives and put more care and thoughtfulness into their female friendships.

In the Irish context Prendiville (1995) provides an account of feminist group facilitation which became a leading work for community support groups in Ireland. Facilitation 'enables or empowers people to carry out a task or perform an action' (p. 4), allowing group participants to 'value their own expertise and skills' (p. 5). There is an emphasis both on achieving a task and on the process, so that 'group members work together towards a defined end/goal and, at the same time, focus on how they are cooperating to ensure the development and support of each other within the group and throughout the process' (p. 5). A high value is placed both on equality, with group members being valued equally and encouraged to participate, and on agency, where 'people should be actively involved in determining their own lives'. Prendiville notes that psychological needs for safety, belonging, esteem, acceptance and achievement must be met in a context of trust, safety, inclusion and encouragement, while at the same time the goals or tasks of the group must be accomplished. Clearly, the discussion of facilitation outlined here articulates with some of the psychological processes associated with liberation.

An important task for facilitation, according to Prendiville (1995), is the general encouragement of equality of participation, which requires a recognition of 'the institutional and personal barriers to genuine participation' (p. 42). This may involve decisions at the outset about membership of the group designed to ensure that all who are in the group are able to participate. Barriers to participation include social, material and attitudinal factors which prevent access to the group, as well as internal dynamics such as lack of trust or communication, and unresolved conflict. Inequalities which derive from difference are given particular attention by Prendiville. Differences based on class, age, gender, sexual orientation, ethnic and racial backgrounds, and disabilities, create inequalities in group participation and decision-making which must be addressed, often explicitly, through challenging stereotypes, monitoring of tasks and responsibilities, sensitivity to different ways of handling conflict, and modelling of inclusive verbal and non-verbal behaviour.

Prendiville (1995) describes a variety of techniques which encourage participation and the development of skills in groups, and which reflect Starhawk's emphasis on engaging not just with cognitive and rational processes, but also with intuition, emotion and experience. These include small and large group discussions, role plays, relaxation exercises, visuals of various kinds, art work, drama, games and exercises. These can be used to identify issues, to handle conflict, to encourage participation, to increase group identification and cohesion, and to promote decision-making, planning and action.

While not all of these facilitation skills are available or are used in women's groups, the values and goals outlined by Prendiville (1995) are explicitly aspired to in many women's groups. This was evident in Mulvey's research on 132 funded locally based women's groups in Ireland in 1991, at a time when women's groups had become well established in Ireland. Mulvey writes that groups most often consisted of between 10 and 20 women and were open and fluid in membership. The groups 'usually adopt informal, non-hierarchical and participatory forms of organisation. The tasks involved in organising the activities of the group are shared out amongst all group members. In the process relationships are built, information and knowledge are passed on, new abilities are acquired' (Mulvey, 1994, p. 14).

Groups were funded for a variety of activities designed to promote self-confidence and develop support and educational services for women which would improve the quality of their lives and help to tackle social disadvantage. Most of the groups were aware of the limitations of their work, which arose both because of shortages of resources and because they were relatively new groups. However, they regarded support and development/education as first steps in the process of social change.

This is illustrated in the group discussions and individual interviews undertaken by Mulvey where it is clear that many women gained both self-confidence and skills. Other outcomes identified by Mulvey include social contact, support, self-awareness and self-confidence, family/community benefits, learning opportunities, increased community participation, changed circumstances and conditions, and combating poverty as benefits gained by many of the groups. The following quotes from groups illustrate these benefits:

> The group made you think about yourself and what you became when you got married and had children. It helps you think about yourself again, discover there are things you can do.... your whole sense of self is built up (p. 54).

> Such courses help combat feelings of isolation and powerlessness (p. 55).

> All of the women who had been isolated at home have gained confidence in themselves and a greater awareness of the part they play in the community. Some women have gained confidence to re-enter the work force. It has given women a taste of what they can gain and also a desire to take part in other future courses (p. 57).

> It brought us together. We've all become good friends. The confidentiality of the group has allowed us to open our hearts and reach out to others in need. This has had a remarkable knock-on effect. It has broadened our awareness in so many areas through our many and varied activities. The effects have been positive and even life changing (p. 64).

This research highlights the benefits to women of participation in the groups which she evaluated, emphasizing in particular the development of self-confidence and the breaking of isolation. Many of the respondents moved on to further education and training which enhanced their employment prospects. However, Mulvey notes that only 13 per cent of the groups explicitly named the development of political analysis or consciousness as one of their aims, and both Mulvey and some of the groups themselves were aware of the limited impact they had on the concrete conditions of poverty or on the structural factors associated with women's oppression. Mulvey links these limitations to economic dependency and lack of resources, to the loose and open structure of the groups which inhibits the development of unity and political strength, and to the lack of trained resource people.

Mulvey's research concentrated on women's groups which were for the most part newly formed or had received funding for personal development and educational purposes. As women's groups grew and changed over the years, many of them became more focused on attaining clearer political outcomes at least for their own group, and often for the larger community in which they were embedded (Doyle and Owens, 2003). This shift reflected improvements in resources for women's groups, and also growing critical consciousness among women's groups. This critical consciousness was associated particularly with involvement in education, especially feminist education, which became a key focus for many community-based women's groups (Parsons, O'Connor and Conlon, 2003; Ryan, 2004). Critical education in turn often created more interest in community development, illustrating a process view of political activism. Glanville's (2008) research on community groups who mobilized for political action, which will be discussed more fully in Chapter 7, highlights the continuing relevance of women's groups for developing self-confidence, increasing awareness, obtaining support and encouragement and making connections with others.

Creating community

Community was identified in Chapter 4 as a vital force in sustaining oppressed groups and in providing models for emancipatory activities, particularly in the writings of those who were from marginalized or disadvantaged groups, namely hooks (1993), Pharr (1988), O'Neill (1992) and Maracle (1996). Community was seen as a source of identity and pride, as a vehicle in the provision of support and the forging of solidarity, as an outlet for creative and cultural activity, and as both the context and the focus for political activism. Community traditions could be sources for the development of new practices which challenge dominant traditions – hooks, for example, writes of reclaiming black traditions of community in the effort to develop a life-affirming and empowering spirituality (hooks, 1993).

The communities which are described by these writers may be physically located in a given geographical space, as in the case of the deprived community described by O'Neill (1992). They may be based on a racial/ ethnic grouping as in the case of black women or Native women (hooks, 1993; Maracle, 1996). They may be based on a shared cultural or sexual identity, as in the case of lesbian community (Pharr, 1988). Other bases for community may be involvement in recovery or spiritual development (Kasl, 1997). Perhaps the broadest concept is the generalized concept of 'women's community', used without reference to specific physical, ethnic or other differences. What is clear is that the concept of community is itself a very broad one with many different meanings. Writing in the Irish context Cullen (1994, p. 26) writes that 'the conceptual difficulties of using the term "community" derive from such everyday usage and from its lack of distinct shape or form thus raising questions as to whether it constitutes anything more than myth or ideology'. Yet clearly 'community' has meaning and existence in the writings and experience of very diverse groups and individuals.

What is of interest here are structures and experiences which support the psychological processes of overcoming isolation, developing a sense of solidarity, and becoming part of community. Before proceeding with this discussion, the material aspects of community must first be acknowledged. This is apparent from Cullen's (1994) discussion of community development programmes in the Irish context. Over a period of decades, economic decline, with implications for employment, education, resources and migration had been disruptive of traditional communities, increasing the fragmentation associated with oppression. New suburban communities established without community infrastructures such as shops, recreational facilities, transport, educational, health and other services obviously pose severe difficulties in the creation of community. As economic development was associated with increasing suburban sprawl and the involvement of women in the labour force, the time and resources for involvement in community became increasingly limited, and this was evident both in studies of urban communities and in experiences of women's groups. However, even with these developments there continued to be a strong sense of being part of a local area and of belonging and participation in local community (Murray and Rogers, 2009; Share, Tovey and Corcoran, 2007). Communities continued to differ very widely in resources, with many communities experiencing deprivation and unemployment even during economic growth. The focus in this discussion is on efforts to form women's communities of interest located within a specific context, in order to highlight the processes involved in forming and sustaining communities. As will become clear, community building involves processes that include the interpersonal processes described above, such as providing resources and support to participants, but also involve fundraising and advocacy, thus highlighting community groups as bridges between the personal and the political.

A first example involves the development of a community of interest, namely the Parents Alone Resource Centre (PARC), established in the working-class area of Coolock in Dublin in 1986, changing its name to Doras Buí in 2005. In the first study of PARC, Kelleher (1989) describes some of the features which facilitated PARC's success in establishing itself as a sustainable community of interest, attracting considerable membership and resources. PARC firstly defined itself very clearly as a lone-parent organization, which, while embedded in and sharing interests with the broader community, had its own particular focus and priority. It established clear boundaries between itself and other local organizations. Additionally, it set the clear goal of having autonomous relations with voluntary and statutory organizations. Thus a clear focus, self-definition, and emphasis on autonomy were identified as contributing to its success.

Another feature of PARC which Kelleher (1989) notes is that it defines its interests both in personal terms and in political terms. On a personal level, PARC identifies common interests to include social and economic hardship and the difficulties of being the sole adult in childrearing, but also dependency, loneliness and fear. Thus it clearly acknowledges some of the psychological needs of its target group. At a political level, PARC relates these personal issues to society more generally, including the fact that society gives women total responsibility for childrearing, the difficulties women experience with the intolerant and often controlling reactions of men in their lives when they try to change, women's exclusion from decision-making, and women's economic dependency either on men or on the state.

PARC consciously developed its literature, recruitment strategies, physical environment and activity programmes with the aim of establishing a sense of identification between a woman coming to the centre and the group itself. One way of doing this was to clearly identify itself as consisting of lone parents who themselves understood the experience of lone parenting, and also of making a clear distinction between the membership of PARC and the social workers and other professionals with whom lone parents interact. Another way was actively to encourage the participation of new members in the management and decision-making of PARC. Programmes included personal development, drama and health, which had a clear personal appeal. Family outings were regularly organized to increase group cohesion, solidarity and friendship. Thus PARC's political programme – of fundraising and lobbying – was accompanied by a variety of activities oriented towards increasing and maintaining participation (Kelleher, 1989).

As PARC developed resources and membership, it expanded its programme not just to facilitate greater participation but also to improve the opportunities for making changes in members' lives. In particular, it sought funding from the New Opportunities for Women (NOW) programme to undertake training and employment initiatives which included literacy training, skills acquisition, and enterprise development. This programme included personal development modules on the basis of the explicit recognition of women's psychological needs in a process of capacity-building. Outcomes of PARC's programme included gaining confidence and self-esteem, making connections, and acquiring the necessary skills to make changes, at least in personal lives. The following quotes from Healy (1995) illustrate this last outcome:

> Being on the N.O.W. has made me feel that I can change something out there – if my idea works, I can say 'I did that' – something worthwhile (p. 4).

> I have a basic knowledge of how to go about setting up a business, something I was completely ignorant about before I started the training (p. 9).

> I learned how to at last get my idea going and I realised that it really was a workable idea – it has opened up so many doors to me that it almost takes my breath away (p. 10).

As a result of this programme PARC built up a greater number of members because of the profile that the programme gave it in the community, established links with other community groups, and got more involved in national and international networking. It increased its own skill and resource base as an organization, including developing a pool of skilled women who had gone through its training programme. It facilitated further planning for the development of the organization. PARC continued to develop over the following decade, extending the range of services and activities, networking with other local and national community groups. PARC, or Doras Buí as it is now called, continues to receive funding for its community development programme. This necessitated an expansion of its organizational framework, but also facilitated an increase in services for lone parents and for children and teens and the development of research and policy (Doras Buí, 2007).

A second example from the Irish context is a group formed to support the lesbian community in Dublin, namely Lesbians Organising
Together (LOT). LOT was formed in 1991 with the aim of providing
co-ordination, support and resources for lesbians in Dublin, operating until the late 1990s. Groups and activities associated with LOT
included: Dublin Lesbian Lines and coming-out discussion groups;
campaigns for legislative protection for lesbians and gay men; the
education of the public through outreach, publishing and media
work; the provision of resources and social spaces for lesbians; support
for lesbian mothers and young lesbians. LOT also ran a Community
Enterprise (CE) scheme with an office and a drop-in centre (Moane,
1997b).

LOT began with the priority of providing essential 'frontline' services, namely a telephone line and a discussion group for coming-out
lesbians. The telephone number was listed widely, and occasional public relations (PR) campaigns aimed at a broader audience were undertaken when funding permitted. The next priority was to organize social
events for lesbians, and over the years LOT organized discos, pub quiz-
zes, an annual dinner, and a variety of one-off events which served the
double purpose of creating social opportunities and fund-raising. This
was followed by obtaining premises and starting a community employment scheme, which aided in building up resources and providing
employment for lesbians. The resource centre supported the activities
described above, and also produced a newsletter. LOT estimated that in
a five-year period over 5,000 lesbians made use of LOT services, primarily through social events, use of meeting rooms and telephone services,
and participation in support groups (LOT, 1996).

LOT achieved its goals of providing support and social events for
lesbians, and it contributed to the formation of a lesbian community
through provision of resources, social events, education and written
material. However, like many other community groups, LOT also experienced tension and conflict which had their sources in both external
and internal factors. These tensions obviously arose in part from the
difficulties of organizing in an oppressive political context, and also
from the interpersonal patterns discussed in Chapter 3. Another factor
which created conflict arose from the demands of fund-raising, and
in particular the bureaucratic demands which included the necessity
of setting up a Limited Company, writing annual reports, and so on.
Additionally, the responsibilities and structural demands of running
a community employment scheme created conflict, partly because it
inevitably introduced hierarchical organization. Tensions also arose

internally from personal and political disagreements about the nature and aims of the organization resulting in LOT disbanding.

Another example of lesbian organizing in Ireland is provided by L.inC (Lesbians in Cork), which was established in 1999/2000. L.inC describes itself as

> a network and community resource centre based in Cork city. L.inC as an organisation was set-up in 2000 and it is primarily for women who identify as lesbian or bisexual, including transgender people (or those in transition) who identify as lesbian or bisexual. We welcome the diversity within this space and wish to respect the values, life experiences, and cultural and political views of everyone in L.inC. The current L.inC organisation is the fruit of much labour, and many different women have been part of the process that brought it into being.

This statement highlights the community values espoused by L.inC, which is celebrating its 10th anniversary with a 'photoherstory'. Over the years L.inC has undertaken a variety of activities, most importantly, perhaps, continuing to staff and resource a community centre which provides support for much lesbian, bisexual and transgendered activity in Cork. L.inC's activities have involved both social and support services such as wrtiting groups, education groups, health supports, visiting speakers. It is also involved in political networking and activism, reflecting a balance of activities that aim to contribute towards community building while also facilitating and/or organizing advocacy and mobilization (L.inC, 2003; 2009).

Lesbian organizations, and other community groups, obviously are placed in a wider context of community and society generally. Lesbian community is a local, national and international phenomenon, encompassing a host of individuals and groups across different regions with enormous diversity of values and motives. It consists of physical spaces, social events, social networking, a variety of groups involved in health, education, sports, lobbying, and other activities, romantic fiction, music and music festivals, art, poetry, literature, celebration, and woman-centred spirituality. In Ireland, annual events such as the Irish (formerly Galway) Women's Camp, the Cork Fun Weekend, the Dublin Lesbian Arts Festival (ALAF), Outitude in Sligo and Outburst Arts Festival in Belfast explicitly aim to create community, organizing a variety of workshops and activities designed to bring LGBTs together in as inclusive and accessible a way as possible (Moane, 1997b; O'Donnell, 2008).

The experiences of community discussed in this chapter highlight practical issues which either facilitate or inhibit a sense of identity with or belonging to a community. Practical issues include resources and support, visibility and accessibility. Autonomy and tolerance of diversity and difference are central. Organizational structures which facilitate empowerment may work in small focused groups, while larger groups may require more complex structures, creating a tension between ideals and practice. At a broader level groups such as lone parents or lesbians consist of disparate individuals, some of whom feel part of community and participate or contribute in an individualized way, others of whom see themselves as committed and active in building community in a variety of ways, and others of whom reject community and wish to stand apart. At this level, the role of social and cultural events in creating a sense of connection or community is vital.

Interpersonal processes and liberation

The theory and research discussed in this chapter clearly indicate that women gain a number of benefits from participation in groups and community organizations. These benefits include self-confidence, overcoming isolation and powerlessness, experiencing strong bonds with other women, developing the capacities to enter the labour force or start an enterprise, making connections between their personal experience and social conditions, making changes in their personal lives, dealing more effectively with bureaucracies and other agencies, and feeling part of and contributing to community. Community groups with empowering organizational structures obviously play a vital role in overcoming some of the difficulties created by oppression and in contributing to the psychological processes involved in liberation. Difficulties continue to arise from interpersonal conflict which have their origins not only in personal patterns but also in the differences and diversity which arise in group and community development. Groups and communities are embedded in systems of domination, however well they succeed in establishing structures and processes which aim to counteract this. Groups and communities may emphasize provision of services and supports, which is essential for the process of making connections. Groups and communities can also link individuals and groups into involvement in community and systemic change and are thus an important route to the political level of change.

7
The Political Level: Taking Action

One of the aims of a liberation psychology is to identify processes and practices which will facilitate taking action to bring about change. It appears from the discussion so far that personal, interpersonal and political change are interconnected with each other, but that change at the first two levels can, but does not necessarily, instigate efforts to bring about change in social conditions. The discussion in this chapter will aim to identify further some of the factors which inhibit taking action to bring about social and political change; it will also develop insights into what is involved in taking such action. It will draw primarily on group discussions and interviews with women in the Irish context, and will be further illustrated with examples from the Irish and international women's movement.

The word 'political' is one which has been the subject of enormous debate in many different arenas. Traditional concepts of 'political' tend to define it as being concerned with government or the state, and hence to confine 'political action' to activities that directly engage with government or the state via political parties, lobby groups, and so on (Martín-Baró, 1994). Broader discussions may define 'political' as engaged with structures or institutions of power, again requiring that political action engage with institutions or structures. These concepts of political have received considerable criticism not only at a theoretical level by feminists and others who have undertaken a fundamental reappraisal of power and politics, but also at the practical level by those who consider their work to be political, but find that it is not defined as such by traditional definitions (McAllister, 1988; 1991; Naples and Desai, 2002). These include a variety of individuals active outside the structures and institutions of the state, either in activist campaigns, education or community development. Traditional definitions of 'political' are still dominant, as the following discussion will indicate, and these definitions are part of the mechanism of exclusion from power. Challenging traditional definitions of what is 'political' is therefore one of the processes involved in liberation.

Taking action to bring about change is obviously of vital importance in the liberation process, from a political perspective, but it is also essential from a psychological perspective. The importance of being an agent in the process of change in order to transform the psychological damage associated with oppression was acknowledged by most of the writers reviewed in Chapters 3 and 4. Fanon (1967b), for example, placed being an agent – rather than a passive participant – as a necessary component of the decolonization process. Taking action disrupts the cycle of oppression both by changing the social conditions of oppression and by counterbalancing damaging psychological patterns such as helplessness, alienation and isolation. It is a vital element in the cycle of liberation, because, although it is obviously possible to change only at the personal and interpersonal levels, such change will be limited if social conditions do not change. It feeds the cycle of liberation through personal strengths, such as courage and confidence, which are gained by taking action, and through the interpersonal connections which are made in the course of taking action.

Women's views of political action

Focus group discussions with four groups of women in education and community development contexts focused on the links between the personal and the political, and, in particular, on women's perceptions of their own capacities to take action to bring about change. In all of these groups, women were considerably developed in their awareness and analysis of the social origins of women's oppression, and had also gained personal strengths through their involvement in groups and personal development courses. They were clear that women lacked political power and experienced economic discrimination. They were aware that women's concerns were not a priority on the political agenda. They were frustrated and resentful that their work in the home, as mothers and carers, and as contributors to society, were undervalued and ignored. What emerged quite clearly was that although they had the analysis and the motivation, they felt at a loss when it came to taking action. This was expressed succinctly in the conclusion of one discussion, when all agreed that the fundamental question was 'Where do we go from here?'

Their sense of bafflement about where to go next arose from a number of sources. Firstly, there was a sense of alienation and lack of knowledge about traditional politics. Local authorities and political parties were seen as spheres of activity which were harsh, alienating, competitive and antithetical to the skills and values that they had as women. Their perception of politicians and of political life was that it was corrupt and fraught with conflict. They felt that they would be unwelcome in that arena and that they would be undermined. Furthermore, they felt that they knew very little about how actually to go about getting involved in that arena, or what kinds of activities they would be doing. Unlike the family, the community or the educational system, where they had a sense of a role and a familiarity with how things worked, the world of politics was uncharted territory.

A second theme which emerged as a barrier to political activism was the sense that political and social change was difficult and complex. Change happened slowly and for a variety of reasons: there were many forces at work, there were vested interests in maintaining the status quo, men were generally not willing to change things, and women were often seen to be following their own interests and colluding with the system. There was a sense that they would be overwhelmed by the enormity of it, and that their efforts would be futile. It was clear that the word 'political' evoked a sense of a complex and abstract system which was disconnected from everyday life.

A third theme which emerged was the sense of being immersed in family roles, and of lacking the freedom and resources to engage outside of the family. The responsibilities of childcare in particular were enormously time-consuming. The responsibilities of housekeeping and providing meals for partners and family members were continuously demanding. There was a feeling that their personal needs were always being set aside, and that they were constantly responding to others. At a practical level, the lack of childcare and financial resources meant that they did not have the time or money to get involved in activism. At a more psychological level, the roles of wife and mother became all-consuming, so that women increasingly defined themselves as a wife or mother and lost a sense of being a person outside of those roles.

When the discussion moved to what actions could be taken, it became clear that women did feel that they could play a role in certain ways. The theme that personal change would ultimately lead to political change recurred – 'If we all changed our behaviour we'd get political change.' The kinds of personal change that women thought could have an impact were firstly speaking out, asserting themselves and making demands in their interpersonal relationships. This would have an impact by changing those with whom they had personal relationships, whether it be a husband/partner, family relation, friend or neighbour. A strong theme that emerged was the possibility for change through having an impact on their children, especially girls, by inculcating particular values in their children, teaching their children to be independent, and encouraging them to have high expectations about their lives and about their role in the world. Here there was a feeling of contributing to social change by having an impact on the next generation – 'one generation paves the way for the next'. In moving beyond the personal, there was a feeling that there was a need to move 'beyond the family', and also to acknowledge that women did play active roles in spheres beyond the family. The most frequently mentioned area here was that of education, where women felt that they could and did play a role as parents on committees and boards related to supporting their children's schools and that they had some say in the running of the school. Church involvement was a second area, where it was felt that despite the conservatism of the Catholic Church, the opportunities afforded by the Church allowed women to move beyond the family and have a sense of participation at community level. Women's groups were a third area, and here women again saw women's groups as offering the opportunity for involvement, for the development of personal skills, and also for making connections with other women.

A number of benefits from participation in spheres outside the family were identified which echo many of the themes discussed in the previous two chapters. Firstly there was the opportunity to break the isolation and immersion in the family, and get a sense of themselves as a more rounded person. There was the obtaining of support both at the emotional level, in terms of esteem and liking, and also at the intellectual level, in terms of support for ideas. The opportunity for communication, both in terms of developing communication but also for its enjoyment, was appreciated. Most of all, it was felt that such involvement gave a sense of 'knowing what was going on' and 'seeing how things got done' which helped to counter the feelings of helplessness and lack of knowledge about the world outside the family.

Even at the level of getting involved in education, community groups or the Church, there was a clearly felt need for support in engaging in these activities. In particular, women felt that if they received opposition from family members, children or partner, that this undermined their motivation and made it very difficult to sustain involvement in a particular area. Positive encouragement from families and friends played an important role in enabling them to move beyond the family.

A final theme that emerged in terms of bringing about change was the understanding that women could play a role at the community level in supporting those women who were active in the more traditional public or political sphere. Women who were willing and able to take on public roles were seen as having particular characteristics such as assertiveness and articulacy which enabled them to take on these roles, but they were also seen as depending on the support of the communities from which they came or whom they represented. The women in the discussion groups felt that while they themselves could not get involved at that level, they could support public figures both personally, by encouraging them and expressing support for their views, and more generally by being involved in communities that supported them.

These discussions clearly identified some of the obstacles that women experienced, obstacles which arose particularly from the nature of the political system, and from their roles in the family. However, it also indicated the ways in which women see themselves as agents of change, particularly in the family and the community, and indirectly at the public political level. Thus a model of political change emerged which reflected the three levels of the personal, the interpersonal and the political.

An opportunity to develop further understanding of women's views of political action and political change arose through courses delivered as part of a Certificate in Women's Studies offered through partnership between the Women's Studies programme in University College Dublin and several community based women's groups (see Chapter 8 for further details). The courses involved several group discussions about activism and change, which along with evaluations and essays for the courses, indicated the need for a more women centred view of change.

A first theme in discussions and essays was the need to challenge narrow definitions of 'political' as involving the apparatus of the state, which, as noted above, was alienating and disempowering for women. Such a definition implies that the only way that change can come about is through involvement in the political system. Once the focus shifted to women's involvement in change, a whole new vista of possibilities for action arose. Taking action to bring about change could involve acts as diverse as refusing to cook, changing childrearing practices, speaking out, boycotting, street protests as well as lobbying and voting:

> You never know the impact of anything you do, it could be big or it could be small. Look at <name>…she did one thing and look what

happened. You might not even know that what you did made a difference.

The phrase 'small acts' was used by participants to capture the idea that all people are part of the system and are involved in change, and that even small things such as speaking out can be part of what brings about change:

> If even a few people over there did the same thing it could all add up, it could be like the butterfly, you know, setting something off that got bigger and bigger.

This 'system view' of change, of activism, and of the role of the individual was immensely empowering for women who were used to thinking of themselves as irrelevant and as being unable to have an influence – the very attitudes of alienation and disempowerment which are part of what maintains oppression. Classes and workshops also revealed that almost everyone could identify some area of their lives where they went against the system – by refusing to conform, by supporting other activists, by speaking out – and where they could see themselves as agents of change.

This view of the individual as an active agent taking actions in various contexts that accumulate to create currents of change in an oppressive system linked to the concept of 'niches of resistance'. This concept allowed participants to acknowledge that whereas women and other groups may be oppressed and dominated in a system of oppression, it is also the case that oppressed groups create their own contexts in which they resist oppression and create opportunities for pride, self-expression, solidarity and connection with others. Women felt that friendship and social groups where there was a consciousness about women's oppression and also a sense of strength in being a woman could be seen as niches of resistance:

> I don't care what anyone says, when women get together we can forget about men … I just feel so good, proud of women and what we can do.

The view that all individuals are part of the system and are therefore involved in change, however small, also allowed course participants to recognize that groups and individuals have already developed capacities for action out of their experiences of oppression and out of their resistance to oppression. These strengths that develop under oppression include courage, generosity, perseverance and sense of humour:

> The way women look after each other, we'd share anything even when we have nothing, we've always done that.

> Even at the worst of times we'd always manage to have a good laugh.

Exploring these strengths was empowering because it was a challenge to the view that oppressed people experience only suffering. Along with the concept of niches of resistance it created a view for women that although they experienced oppression they had a history of resistance that provided them with strengths for further action and resistance.

A final element of the courses that is relevant here concerns the development of support and solidarity in relation to other women who have been oppressed, and indeed across the different areas of oppression. Once the concept of a system of oppression was understood, it became clear that such a concept could be applied to different groups in many contexts. For example most of the courses involved white women in poverty or living in deprived communities, but they could identify commonalities with women of colour or with men from oppressed groups. This facilitated a sense of solidarity, compassion and understanding for those who experience oppression:

> I suppose I shouldn't say this but it does help to know that there are people all over the world...the system works against everyone but loads of people work against the system as well.

Exploring change from a bottom-up woman-centred perspective created a different understanding and set of concepts and questions from those generated by more traditional approaches to political change. Themes that emerge include: challenging narrow views of 'political'; developing a system view which allows for many acts, both large and small, to be part of change; acknowledging niches of resistance and strengths from resistance; cultivating solidarity with and support for those who are oppressed.

Political structures and political action

The more complex understanding of the political which emerged from these group discussions is also one which has been articulated by the former Irish President, Mary Robinson, on the basis of her experience as a president who devoted enormous time and energy to supporting

grassroots, local and community-based organizations, that is, organizations which were outside the realm of the political as usually defined. Robinson's presidency coincided with the period when women's community activism achieved significant mobilization. Over the course of her presidency, (1990–97), in which by the nature of the office she was excluded from being involved in or commenting directly on public political affairs, she frequently articulated the nature and the value of the type of politics which she witnessed at the community level. These observations can provide insights into the kinds of political structures which are empowering rather than alienating.

Indicating the diversity of activities and energies at the community level, Robinson writes:

> I could make a composite for you of the hundreds of welcomes I have received, the striking excellence of the committees of management, the co-operatives, the facilitators and support groups which I have been privileged to observe. I have seen these energies in community and information centres, counselling, educational and care groups, creative workshops and artists' collectives (Robinson, 1992, p. 6).

The work of community groups has already been discussed in the previous chapter in terms of their role in the empowerment of women by virtue of their provision of personal development, and through the structures and activities they have evolved to build community. The activities of community groups outlined in the previous chapter were mainly personal development and education. However, in the Irish context community groups more generally, including women's groups, have undertaken an enormous range of activities (Corcoran and Devlin, 2007). Activities range from a focus on housing and accommodation, at the practical level of maintenance and refurbishment, or disposal of sewage, to the provision of training and services. The emphasis of services includes information on health and social welfare, legal services and counselling services. Employment initiatives include the development of training courses, enterprise development, obtaining of funding and partnerships, and job creation. Other activities include tourism and heritage activities, social services to the elderly, supports and services for special interest groups such as lone parents, the unemployed, or battered women. Increasingly, community groups have been involved in networking with each other, and in partnerships with government and business. Much of the activity at community level is funded by a variety of funding agencies, and therefore a considerable amount of energy is given to the bureaucratic demands imposed by this.

In acknowledging the value and contribution of community groups, Robinson suggests that the realm of the political has been fundamentally imbalanced not only in its failure to accord legislative justice and economic equality, but also in its values and priorities. She argues that the liberal agenda, with its emphasis on legislative reforms, or increasing the numbers of women in the labour force or in public life, while important, remains flawed. She writes that 'We must fundamentally reappraise our view of who and what is valuable in our society. We must look with fresh and unprejudiced eyes at the work of women, the views of women, their way of organising and their interpretation of social priorities' (1992, p. 2), suggesting that the real task is to 'accommodate new energies and real creative forces which still remain outside the power structures of the established order' (1992, p. 2).

Robinson contrasts her experiences in law and in the party political system, with its priorities and ways of organizing which are so 'respectful of tradition and governed by precedent' (p. 4) with what she witnessed in community women's groups, finding not only a difference but also a vibrancy and originality which she believes can make an important contribution to the structures already in place. Speaking of the women she has met, she writes: 'Their ability to devise structures, to order priorities, to assemble an agenda and construe a commitment is not only eloquent. To me it often looks distinctive and creative and therefore a style of problem-solving which is different from the ones we are used to in the public and visible power centres of our society' (1992, p. 4).

In articulating the contribution that community politics can make, Robinson notes firstly the vision and vibrancy already referred to. Secondly, she notes the high value given to tolerance, to respect for individuality, to distinctiveness, diversity and even to divergence of opinion, which she argues is a badly needed resource in contemporary politics. Finally she writes that the community is the carrier of imagination and of culture, and that this is something which is vital to the public domain.

Robinson's point that the traditional political establishment excludes or constrains women and the values and priorities of women articulates with a discussion of the political system by Martín-Baró (1994) which can help to illuminate women's sense of alienation from the political system. Martín-Baró writes that for people to become politically active they must see that their needs and interests are connected in some way with those of the political system. Yet the political system is structured to reflect the needs of the ruling class. The question that arises then is how it is that 'social interests are translated into patterns of knowing and valuing; into principles, values and attitudes; into specific ways of speaking and deciding; into specific behaviours in which they are embedded' (p. 56). For him, this is an outcome of political socialization. In Martín-Baró's view one of the functions of political socialization is the social shaping of human needs' (p. 72). This occurs firstly through the shaping of basic biological needs so that they are experienced as specific and contextual: for example, the need for food or sleep is socialized as a need for particular kinds of food or sleep under particular kinds of circumstances. Needs are more easily understood if they are recognized by the political establishment, or if they correspond to the needs of the establishment, and it is easier to articulate clear political objectives in relation to needs which are recognized by the political establishment. If needs fall outside the bounds of the ruling-class interest, then it is harder to be conscious of how one's needs relate to the political system.

This highlights the difficulties for marginalized groups of making connections between their personal needs and the political system. It is particularly relevant to women because of the way in which an area of fundamental relevance to women, namely childcare, caring, and the fostering of growth and development has been marginalized by the political system. As Robinson (1992) points out, women's needs, women's visions and women's ways of organizing have not been accommodated within the political system. The political system has not just controlled political and material resources, its fundamental values and ways of organizing are antithetical to those operating at the community level.

Martín-Baró (1994) also provides a discussion of political activism which can facilitate a broader understanding of the term. In attempting to develop a psychology of politics, which he defines as 'the analysis and psychological understanding of political behaviours and processes' (p. 47), he begins by addressing the question of what constitutes a political act. He dismisses the definition of political as 'to do with the functioning of the state and its various branches' (p. 53) as too narrow. On the other hand, he regards the definition of political as 'actions in which some power is exercised' (p. 53) as too broad, because almost all human behaviour requires the exercise of power in some way. He concludes that 'A behaviour is political when it plays a role in the social confrontation of class and group interests' (p. 55). These interests involve class interests, but also the interests 'of sectors, associations, or groups and even families and persons' (p. 55). This then leads to an analysis of the social interests in a given situation or which are served by particular behaviours. Martín-Baró then concludes that an act may be considered political if 'the actors are embodiments of social interest' (p. 64). Thus an act may be considered political if it is performed on behalf of some group or interest, and if it engages with particular social interests.

A point which Martín-Baró emphasizes is that it is impossible to be completely objective in the definition of political behaviour because meaning inevitably plays a role in political behaviour. He argues that even the act of casting a vote can only be considered political if the actor has some consciousness of political intention. For example, someone who casts a vote simply by marking candidates in alphabetical order without any reference to the consequences may not be considered to be behaving politically. Furthermore, the meaning of a given political action will vary – he points out that to cast a vote under conditions where an election is judged to be fixed is hardly comparable with the casting of a vote in what are seen to be fair and open elections.

What this discussion suggests firstly is that an action can be considered political if it is broadly engaged with social interests. It secondly suggests that an actor must be acting on behalf of an interest group if an act is to be judged political. It thirdly suggests that the intentions of the actors must play a role in what is judged to be a political action. This discussion can help to clarify what is political because it firstly encompasses most actions traditionally considered political, such as voting, lobbying, and so on, yet it also places a boundary on individual acts performed purely out of self-interest. It implies, for example, that the act of 'speaking out' or 'standing up for yourself' can be considered political if the actor sees herself or himself as acting on behalf of a social interest (for example, 'women'), intends this as a political act, and if it confronts the social interests of a particular group (for example, 'men'). These criteria attribute considerable importance to individual consciousness, but they also specify the need to establish that there is a confrontation with particular social interests.

Women's experiences of political activism

The broader view of political activism gained through considering women's understanding of and involvement in political change can be developed through considering research undertaken by Glanville (2008) on women's community activism. Glanville (2008) undertook research on women's activism in Clondalkin, a large urban area in the south west of Dublin with considerable deprivation which has undergone one of the fastest growths in population since 1996. In her research, Glanville aimed to document the development of women's political activism in Clondalkin. Additionally, Glanville aimed to provide an analysis of the match between the approach to oppression and liberation presented in this book, and the experience of women's activism in Clondalkin.

By 2006 Clondalkin had a population of over 43,000, spread over several different areas. Women's groups began in Clondalkin in the early 1980s, and have grown to include 20 women's groups and the Clondalkin Women's Network (CWN), which was established in 2001. The activities of groups include conducting a needs analysis, developing second and third level community-based education, a domestic violence service, a health forum, an annual celebration of International Women's Day and an election campaign (Glanville, 2008). Glanville writes, 'Over the years, the Network has evolved and developed, with its members, to be a strong voice for women's groups' (p. 50). The involvement of women in a partnership with the Women's Studies programme at University College Dublin (UCD) resulted in several cohorts of women participating in an accredited Certificate in Women's Studies that made a significant contribution to consciousness-raising in the community.

In 2007 the Clondalkin Women's Community Education Forum engaged in an extensive consultative process with women's groups in Clondalkin with the aim of involving women in political activism during the forthcoming election campaign. Glanville provides an account of this process based on her own experience and on documentary analysis involving extensive community group and policy documents. A letter setting out the aim of developing a Manifesto that would reflect the needs of the area was circulated along with several policy documents developed by local and national agencies. Following this workshops were held in which agreement was reached on eight key demands which were organized into the Clondalkin Women's Manifesto. This was circulated throughout the Clondalkin areas and used during the forthcoming election campaign. The eight demands are quoted from the Manifesto as follows: Value Care Work; Respect Diverse Clondalkin; Education; Clear Law and Consistent Justice; Responsive Local Government; Women in Power; Social Welfare System; De-Licence Violence against Women; Health. The Manifesto was produced in a colourful one-page document and disseminated widely to women's groups and local groups. It was also distributed door to door, at local shops, the local shopping centre and through local networks. In addition, Clondalkin Women's Network organized two workshops that involved local women's groups meeting candidates going for election in 2007 (Glanville, 2008). The Manifesto thus provided a 'strong collective voice' (quoted in Glanville, 2008, p. 57), and a vehicle for women to inform politicians of their concerns.

In considering the activism of the women's groups with the Manifesto, Glanville first notes that the issues raised during the consultative process and in the Manifesto linked with five of the six modes of control outlined in Chapter 2, namely violence, political exclusion, economic exploitation, cultural control, and control of sexuality. Glanville notes that respect for diversity arose as an important theme that did not readily fit with the six modes, noting also that the area of fragmentation did not arise. The main theme in acknowledging diversity was a recognition that diverse groups had different needs. As Glanville notes: 'Clondalkin women want "equality within equality" – one size does not fit all' (p. 63). The other area that was strongly emphasized in the consultative process is that of education. Glanville concludes this part of her study by describing the development of political activism through the cycle of liberation: 'The stages of the process of the manifesto reverberate with Moane's model. The groups raised awareness of the issues affecting women nationally and locally, developing a feminist consciousness of women's position in society through facilitated sessions on the reading material. The workshops then led women to name and identify issues that were affecting them personally. The community groups connected together to work on a common goal. They made connections with each other through shared consciousness which then forged solidarity. This the led to the collective group of women taking collective political action' (p. 64).

Further to her interest in the ways in which women in Clondalkin came together to identify issues of concern to them, Glanville interviewed six women who were representatives of six women's groups who participated in the consultative process organized to develop the Manifesto. Glanville selected the women with diversity in mind, with variations in age, ethnicity, family status, and forms of activism. All six worked directly with community groups on such issues as domestic violence, education and ethnic minority women. Glanville used a semi-structured interview format based on her experience of political activism and structured around the three areas identified in the cycle of liberation (Moane, 1999; 2009). The interview asked about women's personal history of community activism, and explored the impact of community activism and education at the personal level. At the interpersonal level there were questions about making connections and involvement in community, and at the political level questions about involvement in activism through the development of the Manifesto, and about support for involvement in activism.

Glanville's interviews highlighted steps that women considered to be crucial in becoming more involved: 'activism developed through new awareness, critical education, role models, solidarity and the expansion of connections' (p. 67). Several reasons were given for getting involved in the community. Combating isolation, especially the isolation of being full-time in the home, personal experiences of injustice and lack of resources in the community were important reasons given. Involvement in women's studies provided a critical consciousness about the link between personal experiences and insights into oppression. Several women were inspired by women they knew, including those involved in community activism: 'Women explain the integrity and courage they saw in a local accessible role model and her capacity to encourage them to be involved in community initiatives' (p. 78). Glanville points out locally specific themes, including awareness of local issues, and notes that concern for the community was a key factor in getting involved, along with a sense of giving something back to the community and the motivation and energy gained from involvement in the community.

Glanville's interviews illustrated several ways in which involvement in communities contributed to making connections and developing solidarity. Many of her interviewees were aware of community groups as a route to empowerment, as offering a space in which women could find their voices, express their concerns and act in solidarity to make changes. They spoke of a ripple effect whereby their families, and particularly their children, benefited from their own increasing awareness and political interest: 'A source of inspiration arose from women's knowledge that through their involvement in the community they were having a positive impact on their family' (p. 93). Particular challenges to participation were posed by the need to engage in paid employment, by materialism, by the 'feminist label', unsupportive family members, and government bureaucracy. Glanville notes that many of the women were aware that getting involved went against the grain of individualism and consumerism, highlighting again that women's own awareness influenced their involvement. Themes that emerged strongly in interviews which Glanville argues needs more analysis, were the importance of diversity in community involvement and of experiences in handling conflict.

In exploring women's activism in developing the Manifesto and lobbying public representatives, Glanville's interviews highlight the awareness among the interviewees that an election offered the opportunity to put women's issues on the agenda and pressure politicians to pay attention to these issues. Through organizing collectively they gained a sense that 'a chorus of women's voices were demanding the same thing' (p. 113), and as they used the Manifesto they gained a sense of the power of collective action. They felt empowered to speak and to lobby themselves about the Manifesto, which provided them with a document that reflected the diverse voices in their community: 'The women had a professional document to present to the politicians, eloquence in conversing with them and anticipation of action from them' (p. 117). They also spent many hours explaining the Manifesto to women in the community, observing the changes in women as they found a way to speak out and become involved in activism. The experience with the Manifesto strongly increased their motivation to continue working with the Manifesto to pressurize local and national government, and they also identified new strategies including working with the National Collective of Women's Community-Based Networks and the National Women's Council of Ireland. Overall, the interviews highlighted the sense of passion, of a shared bond with other women, a valuing of the unpaid labour of political activism, and of pride in collective action. In concluding, Glanville presents a definition of women's community activism: 'Women's activism is a method of critical reflection and inquiry and action – always ongoing, discovering things, exposing things to open them up and taking action on them to bring about change' (p. 139).

The development of the women's movement

The broader understanding of political activism developed here means that there are a greater number of options for women to become involved in political activism. Indeed it reinforces the point made by Lerner (1993), Naples and Desai (2002) and others: namely, that women have always been politically involved, either in resisting oppression or in shaping society to their own ends. It means that a variety of acts can be considered political. Some of these acts, particularly those undertaken within the family, have not been considered by some to be political. Yet it may be worthwhile to acknowledge more fully, indeed to claim, actions within this sphere as political, thereby increasing women's sense of political agency and of making a contribution to social change. The variety of political actions in which women have engaged has been documented in the many accounts of women's movement activities in countries all over the world (Basu, 1995; Connolly and O'Toole, 2005; Morgan, 1984; Naples and Desai, 2002).

Historical and contemporary analyses of women's activism high-light the organic nature of women's activism, often, as illustrated above, grounded in specific community concerns, and also involving the establishment of particular political structures such as national representative bodies and non-governmental organizations (NGOs) to advance women's concerns. Connolly (1996; 2002) and Connolly and O'Toole (2005) provide a detailed description and analysis of the women's movement in Ireland. Connolly (1996) notes, like Coulter (1993) and others (Tweedy, 1992) that the women's movement has been active since the mid 1800s as a social movement apart from or overlapping with involvement by women in other political and social activism. Connolly (1996) characterizes 1922 to 1969 as a period of abeyance: 'Abeyance is essentially a holding pattern of a group which continues to mount some challenge even in a non-receptive environment' (p. 49). The activities that continued during this period provided a vital link with the earlier 'first-wave' movement of the late nineteenth century, and also created the necessary networks and strategies which could be drawn upon when the movement became vitalized. An example of this is the Irish Housewife's Association, which, although it pursued a relatively conservative agenda, preserved structures and networks which became resources for the emerging women's movement (Tweedy, 1992).

The 1960s and 1970s saw the emergence of a grassroots women's movement in several areas and also mobilization through trade unions and national organizations. The setting up of the government's First Commission on the Status of Women in 1970 was an outcome of an alliance between a dozen or more organizations which were women only or in which women were active. Following this a variety of groups, ranging from direct activist to established women's groups, proliferated, and women set up sub-groups in trade unions and other organizations. Many different styles of ideology, strategy and organization emerged, and an enormous range of issues were tackled. For example the radical feminist group Irish Women United concentrated on direct action, while others focused on setting up support and advocacy groups, including the Dublin Rape Crisis Centre (McKay, 2005) and Women's Aid (O'Connor and Wilson, 2001).

In the following period Connolly identifies three factors which influenced changes in the women's movement. One was the emergence of a counter-right movement, which confronted the women's movement head-on with a variety of tactics. These included party political and legislative tactics which required resources and expertise to counter. At the same time, some of the early activists withdrew from the movement, and, as the movement grew and became more diffuse, radic-alism became less focused. At the same time, there was a big increase in 'mainstreaming, professionalisation and institutionalisation' of sectors of the movement. During this period the movement had an enormous impact on social change, but also suffered a number of setbacks, includ-ing two defeats in constitutional referenda on abortion and divorce (Mahon, 1995). The outcome of these developments was a feeling of demoralization and lack of coherence in some, and at the same time increased participation of women from many different backgrounds in a variety of different kinds of groups and settings, with many different goals and strategies. By the end of the 1980s Connolly notes a revival of the movement, which received considerable impetus by the election as President of Mary Robinson in 1990. Trends which Connolly identifies are the increasing numbers of community-based women's groups, the development of Women's Studies in Irish universities and adult edu-cation, and the growth in women's publishing. Connolly concludes that the women's movement has moved from being characterized by 'common themes, concepts and goals' to consisting of 'a plurality of feminisms' (p. 71).

Economic and cultural changes since the 1990s have both broadened the scope of women's activism to include, for example, immigrant and refugee issues, and drawn women away from community activism into paid employment. Neo-liberalism has meant on the one hand a degree of greater economic independence for some women, and the establish-ment of equality legislation and other frameworks for the advance-ment of women's rights. However, it has also undermined political commitment, including funding, for local, community and national women's groups which is further threatened by economic recession. Nevertheless, the diversity and resilience of the women's movement is illustrated in Reilly's (2008) review of approaches to women's human rights in Ireland. Reilly details numerous cases of organizations which have adopted a human rights framework in areas as diverse as violence against women, traveller's rights, immigrant rights and reproductive rights.

The National Women's Council of Ireland provides an example of a national organization which aims to provide a structure through which community-based women's groups and NGOs can link into the tradi-tional political system (Reilly, 2008). The NWCI is the national repre-sentative body for women and for women's groups. It was originally set up to be an organization which could present the views of women at government level by acting as representative for the many individual community and national organizations which are affiliated to it. It currently has 165 women's groups, networks, NGOs, trade union and service agencies affiliated, representing over 300,000 women. It has a representative structure which involves a central executive elected by representatives from each of its constituent organizations, and a limited number of committees formed by the executive. Broad policy decisions are made at annual general meetings where motions are proposed and voted upon. The NWCI thus aims to bridge the gap between community groups and government. It should be noted here of course that many of its constituent organizations themselves make direct representations to government organizations autonomously from the NWCI. The NWCI has initiated and continues to develop policies in a variety of areas, including childcare, economic equality, reproductive rights and violence against women. Reilly (2008) notes that increasingly the NWCI has incorporated an approach based on equality and human rights for women as well as approaches influenced by national policy.

Examples of the continuing mobilization of women all over the world are provided by Naples (1998) and by Naples and Desai (2002), who note the enormous variety of contexts and activities of women. Contexts range through local specific action groups, regional associations, transnational NGOs, and numerous local, national and transnational networks. Naples (1998) notes that community is often the primary focus of women's activism, yet often community activism is not recognized as political. Women's specific concerns around motherhood, childcare, health and education are often the focus of activity, yet again may not be recognized as such. Areas of activism include economic issues such as adequate wages, funding and resources for local communities, and people-centred economic development. There are numerous responses to violence against women that include offering shelter and support, lobbying for legislative changes and undertaking public awareness about the forms of violence against women. Diversity forms an important focus for organizing, including immigrant rights, racism and homophobia. Sustainable economics, reproductive rights, education are other examples of areas of activism. A common theme is the need for women's issues and concerns to be placed on the political agenda in recognition that these issues are vital for the development of society and the viability of the planet.

Obviously these actions cover an enormous range, from electoral politics to separatist peace camps. The diversity of activities is described particularly by McAllister (1988; 1991), who provides a historical overview of nonviolent political tactics, arguing not only that these are more desirable in principle, but that commitment to nonviolence leads to more innovative and ultimately more effective political action. The activities she describes are taken from all over the world, and include 'strikes, physical obstruction, sanctuary, hunger strikes, petitions, protest demonstration, tax resistance, boycotts, and civil disobedience' (p. 7).

Many of the actions described by McAllister are familiar forms of political action such as marches and demonstrations, protests to parliaments and other legislative bodies, petitions, sit-ins and occupations. She also provides examples of what she labels '[t]he strike of a sex' (p. 53), actions which are based on women's roles. These include sex strikes by Nicaraguan women in 1530, by Iroquois women around 1600, by Russian women in the early 1920s, by Chinese women in the 1940s, and by French, Italian, Sicilian, Indian and Finnish women in the 1970s and 1980s. Women's domestic work as well as their role in the economy was highlighted by a 'Day off for Women' in Iceland in 1985 which was organized to protest women's economic inequality. McAllister (1991) provides many examples of boycotts and other actions that take advantage of women's power as consumers. In one such example, women in Burkina Faso in West Africa organized a 'Market day for men' in which they insisted that men do the daily task of going to the market. McAllister (1991) notes that women's bodies have often been a 'battleground for social change' (p. ix), especially in the areas of reproductive rights. She cites many examples of women using their body and clothing as a form of protest, citing refusal to shave body hair or wear the veil as examples of resistance. McAllister suggests that each action plays a role in the process of change, writing that 'the continuity of women's courage has forged its own path like water that wears away the rock' (1991, p. 8).

The variety of actions outlined so far are increasingly being enhanced as the women's movement grows and diversifies worldwide. Post-modern, global and third-wave feminist writings and activism have opened up further possibilities for agency and action that include deconstructing popular culture, networks that link the local and the global and strategic consumerism (Naples and Bojar, 2002; Valenti, 2007). In the Irish context for example, new activist groups in such areas as reproductive rights (choiceireland.org) and LGBT rights (lgbtnoise.ie) use social networking sites, mobile phones and other internet technologies to enhance more traditional political methods. Globally, the work of Mary Robinson continues to engage with local and global issues through her New York based but also web active organization Realizing Rights, the Ethical Global Initiative (realizingrights.

org). This advocates actions that include supporting Fairtrade, recycling, writing or emailing newspapers and politicians, and supporting migrant rights.

Taking action to bring about change

The discussion in this chapter explored factors which both act as barriers to taking action and which facilitate taking action. Political action to bring about change was characterized in a broad sense as involving actions which are undertaken on behalf of a particular social group with the intention of confronting the social interests of another social group. A variety of actions undertaken by women conform to this understanding of political action, and range from speaking out to engaging in political lobbying. A developmental model of political action suggested that while actions at the personal level are relatively accessible to women, greater difficulties arise when it comes to joining a women's group or seeking out education with a political content, and even greater difficulties arise in taking actions which involve engaging with structures of power or participating in organized political campaigns or movements. These difficulties can be related to both macro or structural factors and psychological factors.

Structural factors can obviously include the six modes of control and other patterns outlined in Chapter 2. More specifically, structural factors include firstly the nature of traditional political institutions, whose structures, values, priorities and ways of working are not compatible with the structures and ways of working which have evolved in community and group settings, and which have been identified as empowering or as facilitating high levels of participation by women and other groups. Structural factors also include the lack of education and resources for groups which are operating outside the mainstream political structures. In the case of women, structural factors also include the failure to provide childcare and indeed other forms of institutional care; this places the responsibility for providing care in women's hands. Gender operates through male domination of political and other structures, but is also embodied in the actions of individual men, especially family members, who create barriers to women's political participation through lack of support, violence, and other controlling behaviours. Class, ethnicity and other dimensions of oppression also operate through the control of political and other institutions, and also through marginalization and lack of economic resources, which itself is a barrier to political activism.

At the psychological level, the many forms of psychological damage associated with oppression obviously act as barriers to action. These have been explored in Chapter 3, and include lack of self-confidence and self-worth. However, it is also clear that those who are marginalized or oppressed have considerable resources and motivation for involvement in political action, as discussed in Chapter 4.

Women's role in the home can be seen as a factor which involves the structural and the psychological. It is obviously structural in so far as it is an outcome of the political and other patterns which structure women's roles in particular ways. The isolation that it creates is a barrier to taking action, but where opportunities are created through the formation of women's groups, isolation can act as a motivation for women to join such groups. The submersion in the role of wife and mother which women experience creates considerable psychological barriers to getting involved and taking action, but can also act as a motivation to look for opportunities outside the sphere of the family.

Taking action obviously requires awareness, and personal capacities and strengths such as confidence and courage. It requires interpersonal contexts such as groups and communities which provide support and solidarity. The analysis in this chapter suggests that at the immediate level taking action requires firstly appropriate structures which can provide a context for taking action. Analysis which makes clear links between the personal and the political is a second element in taking action, while a third element is the provision of support both in terms of material resources and in terms of encouragement from family and others. Finally, as the historical analysis shows, the social climate plays an important role.

8
Liberation Psychologies in Action: Local and Global Examples

So far this book has presented an approach to liberation psychology with three components: an analysis of society as a whole; an exploration of psychological patterns associated with oppression; and a model for change that links the personal and the political. Society was characterized as a hierarchical system of domination with six modes of control – violence, political exclusion, economic exploitation, cultural control, control of sexuality and fragmentation (divide and conquer) – and other dynamics, which served to maintain power differences. An exploration of the link between systems of domination and psychological patterns – the cycle of oppression – was provided through a review of selected writings on feminism, colonialism and oppression-liberation. These writings also provided insights into processes of liberation, which were elaborated on the basis of writing and experiences in women's liberation movements, especially the Irish women's liberation movement. A cycle of liberation was posited involving three levels of change: the personal, the interpersonal and the political. Processes and practices were identified at each level which could facilitate transforming or counterbalancing the psychological damage associated with the cycle of oppression and facilitate taking action to bring about change. Key processes identified were developing awareness, building strengths, making connections and taking action.

This chapter will firstly describe the application of this model in courses and workshops on liberation psychology that have been delivered in the Irish context over the years since the first edition of this book was published. It will then provide an overview of recent developments in liberation approaches in psychology. These developments have occurred around the world and include Latin American liberation psychologies, feminist liberation psychologies, approaches in community and critical psychologies, and developments in psychotherapy and counselling with a social justice orientation.

Courses and workshops in liberation psychology in Ireland

Previous chapters have described the emergence of women's groups in Ireland and their involvement in community-based support, resources and activism from the 1970s on. Many of these groups were aware of the importance of education, and of the barriers for women in accessing education, especially third level education. They had worked with national policy agencies to obtain recognition and resources for this area and by the 1990s the need for further education was recognized at a national policy level, partly linked to labour market needs (Parsons, O'Connor and Conlon, 2003). Several community women's groups accessed funding and approached the women's studies programme at University College Dublin (UCD), which ran a Women's Education Research and Resource Centre (WERRC). WERRC also sought and received funding to further develop and deliver the outreach education programme that would provide a Certificate in Women's Studies.

One of the aims of the group involved in establishing the women's studies programme in UCD in 1990 had been to provide outreach education to women in communities and develop access routes through third and fourth (postgraduate) level education. The women's studies programme in UCD was already connected to what was then called adult education, which was well developed through a longstanding commitment of UCD to exra-mural courses and part-time degree programmes. An extra-mural course, Women and Society, had been started in the early 1980s, and was followed by a course on Women and Psychology. These courses were offered in UCD; it was clear that further development and outreach would be needed to meet the interest of community-based women's groups.

The Certificate was based on a feminist ethos of participatory teaching and learning strategies and was developed in partnership with community-based women's groups (Parsons, O'Connor and Conlon, 2003). It consisted of four modules, with Liberation Psychology for Women as one of the optional modules. WERRC received funding from several national agencies which enabled it to employ a fulltime coordinator who developed the programme through consultation with community groups, coordinated tutors and also employed a learning skills tutor who provided mentoring and support in terms of reading, writing and research skills. Local and community women's groups who obtained funding, again from several sources, formed a partnership with WERRC, providing a community resource centre where the courses could be delivered, and where there was an employed resource person who provided practical support, organized study groups and other inputs and coordinated the community groups who were taking the Certificate. An attraction of the Certificate (and the Diploma which was developed later) was that it was fully accredited by UCD and by the National University of Ireland, thus providing a progression route through third level education. Over the last decade, the Certificate in Women's Studies has been delivered to women's groups in around a dozen areas in Dublin, which had experienced poverty and deprivation, and in over a dozen urban and rural centres outside Dublin.

Courses in liberation psychology

The Certificate in Women's Studies thus provided a feminist and community context for the development of a course in psychology for women that would reflect feminist and liberation psychology principles. Prior to the development of the Certificate I had had several opportunities to present the approach described in this book to students in the Women and Psychology course taught in UCD. From that experience it was clear that a systematic analysis of society was of great benefit even to students in psychology courses. It provided a context in which psychological theory and research could be more fully understood. Many of the women who took this course had a strong interest in social justice, and found the social analysis helpful in developing their political analysis. The use of colonialism as a model for understanding oppression was particularly useful, as it drew on the Irish experience of colonization and provided a framework in which the complexities of oppression could be explored. This experience also highlighted the value of participatory approaches to lifelong learning, and the need for groupwork skills to facilitate participation.

For the Certificate I designed a course outline centred around the three components developed in this book, namely: a social analysis (Ch. 2), a cycle of oppression that focused on areas of psychological functioning that included self-worth and body image, anger, sexuality and spirituality (Chs 3, 5); an analysis of change (cycle of liberation) that focused on community (Ch. 6) and social change (Ch. 7). Unlike many psychology courses, this course thus started with a social analysis; this provided a framework for the psychological aspects of the course.

Specific and accessible readings from diverse authors were offered for each topic, including extracts from the first edition of this book and chapters, articles and extracts from feminist writers, writers on colonialism and Irish writers. There was considerable interest in a psychology course that was clearly critical of traditional psychology; that was oriented towards oppression and liberation, and that aimed to link the personal and the political. Course sizes varied from 9 to 20.

In the five community settings where the course was delivered, the initial session of the course focused on groupwork issues regarding the group contract, expectations for the course, modifying the course outline to suit the specific interests of the course participants, and negotiating the assessment for the course. In all cases students chose to write essays reflecting on a specific personal experience (preferably but not necessarily their own) and linking this experience to the social analysis of oppression and liberation. Only the analysis part of the essay was assessed. Topics chosen for the essay often reflected the course content. For example, many participants wrote of body image, linking to the social analysis of advertising and media images. Others wrote of experiences of sexual assault and violence, of humiliations experienced from welfare officers and other agencies, of work experiences that linked to economic exploitation. Topics that linked to liberation included speaking out or self-assertion, and experiences in community groups or NGOs.

Methods used on the courses included a short (10–15 minutes) structured input or mini-lecture on the topic; this involves setting out key ideas for consideration by participants. Open discussion involves the entire group, with participants expressing their views on a topic, which are recorded on a flipchart. In a group brainstorm, participants are asked to provide short responses (word or phrase) to a topic in a short period (5–15 minutes), also recorded on a flipchart. The entire group can also break into small groups (3–5) and discuss a topic. The themes of their discussion may be fed back to the larger group through a verbal report or through recording the small group discussion which is then shared with the larger group. Pair discussions (or buzzes) can also provide an opportunity for participants to share their reactions to a topic. Other experiential methods such as role plays and image theatre were also used. A form completed at the end of the course provided feedback about the course and included open-ended questions about the course. Flipcharts, essays, discussions, informal feedback and the responses to the open-ended questions in the feedback form all provide sources for the following description of course content, process and outcomes.

As noted above, each of the courses started with a course outline that was developed further with course participants into a 10-week programmed, with three hours per week. After this first week, the course focused on the social analysis, aiming to provide a clear analysis of oppression and domination. The concept of society as a pyramid was first presented for consideration, facilitating a discussion of hierarchy and power dynamics. Colonialism provided a particular example of a system of domination, which was familiar to participants partly due to the Irish experience of colonization. It allowed participants to identify social patterns associated with oppression, and also to explore the more complex dynamics of oppression. This was followed by one or two structured sessions in which students broke into small groups to exemplify the modes of control that were presented to them. Each small group focused on one mode and identified specific examples of how it operated in terms of social structures and everyday life and then gave feedback to the class, thus creating an overall picture of a system of domination with specific examples. Given the experiences and social conditions of the students, this was a task that was readily completed, with most small groups having no difficulty recognizing the modes of control and their manifestation. Figure 1 lists the six modes identified in Chapter 2 with examples from class discussions.

Violence, rape, sexual assault and domestic violence were readily identified, and the role of police, the legal system, public attitudes and resources for women who had been victimized were noted. In the

Mode	Colonialism	Patriarchy
Violence	Military and police violence	Rape, assault, battery
Political exclusion	No voting rights, restrictions on assembly	Access to voting, selection of candidates, attitudes
Economic exploitation	Seizure of land, low/unpaid labour, charges/taxes	Ownership of wealth, low/unpaid labour
Cultural control	Control of education, stereotypes	Erasure from history, media images
Control of sexuality	Control of marriage, enforced motherhood	Marriage laws, birth control
Fragmentation	Enforced migration	Tokenism, competition

Figure 1 Examples of six modes of control found in colonialism and patriarchy

case of economic exploitation, the direct experience of students with employment and poverty provided ready examples and was linked to an understanding of class issues, ownership of resources, workers rights, discrimination, unemployment and women's roles in the family and in the work place. Political exclusion was again readily understood, given women's experience of both local and national politics, and their awareness of the ways in which the political system often excludes women and fails to respond to their concerns. Limited access, exclusion and invisibility in relation to education provided a concrete example of cultural control, with links also made to history, literature and mass media. The control of sexuality, particularly of reproductive rights, by church and state in the Irish context was obvious, along with marriage and gender roles within and outside marriage. Experiences of fragmentation linked to housing, employment or unemployment and under-resourced communities were also apparent.

In the two to four weeks following the social analysis, the course focused on the psychological analysis, where psychological areas were nominated or chosen from a list for more detailed consideration, each in a single class session. Topics included sexual assault and violence (SAV), self-worth, body image, anger, sexuality, motherhood, spirituality/religion, physical and mental health. In most cases the session began with an input and open discussion of the social structures and discourses associated with the area, thus illustrating the ways in which the area was socially shaped or constructed. This was followed by a consideration of less restricted or new possibilities for experiences or expressions in this area. Experiential methodologies were often used for this part of the session, often linked to short readings that were supplied in advance. The case of anger illustrates this approach: Miller's (1981) chapter on 'the construction of anger in women and men' provided a basis for discussion and understanding of how women's anger is shaped. Personal experiences and observations about anger in men and in women provided examples of social shaping of anger. Role plays and image theatre provided opportunities to explore alternative expressions of anger. This often involved identifying the reasons for anger, viewing anger as a positive force for change, and, importantly for women, where possible directing anger outward rather than inward. This section of the course thus provided a psychological analysis of oppression and also explored possibilities for new approaches in each area. Negative psychological patterns or vulnerabilities were linked to systems level, and psychological strengths were also identified. Figure 2 provides examples of vulnerabilities and strengths that were identified across courses and workshops.

Vulnerabilities	Strengths
Lack of self-worth	Pride
Alienation	Agency
Hopelessness	Hope
Anger	Camaraderie
Fear	Solidarity
Conflict, confusion	Sense of history
Isolation	Tolerance
Distrust	Courage
Tension	Humour
Health problems	Perseverance
Dependency	Generosity
Depression	
Addiction	

Figure 2   Psychological vulnerabilities and strengths: The cycle of oppression

This part of the course opened up the possibility of making changes at the personal or individual level. The course then moved on in the remaining weeks to considering women's involvements in groups and communities and the nature of change through the cycle of liberation. This began by exploring possibilities for change in terms of the three levels of the personal, the interpersonal and the political. The length of time and the methods used to explore this area varied depending on the interests and experiences of participants. It could be done through a brainstorming exercise focused on change at each level, or through small groups discussions with each small group taking one level, and then feeding back to the larger group. In some cases, the main focus was on the personal level where students could see possibilities for change that would benefit them and that they could implement. There was recognition of the overall principle that there is a need for change at all three levels, and that there were interconnections between the three levels whereby change at one level could filter through to change at other levels. The experience of the class itself provided one example of the benefit of making connections at the interpersonal level; improvements in community resources was another example of change at this level. However, while change at the personal and interpersonal levels were readily accessible, there was a general view, as discussed in Chapter 7, that women could have little impact on state-related politics, leading to an exploration of other options for action. In some cases, particularly in a Diploma group who had already completed the Certificate, there was a big interest in understanding and being involved in change, and this part of the course focused particularly on exploring the nature of change, of women's roles in change and of the variety of possible actions as discussed in Chapter 7. Figure 3 provides a summary of options for changes considered over all courses and workshops.

At the end of the course, participants completed an evaluation and feedback form, some of which was designed and used by WERRC and the community group and some of which I designed to assess the topics, methodologies and outcomes of the courses. Students often gave structured inputs high rankings while also expressing enthusiasm about participatory methods, highlighting the value of receiving relevant theory and research as well as developing their own understandings. In terms of course content, students frequently ranked the social analysis as

Political	Taking action	Vision
		Lobbying, voting, advocacy
		Social movements, NGOs
		Consumer-based actions
		Education and awareness
		Variety of actions
		Systems view of change
		Social analysis
Interpersonal	Making connections	Niches of resistance
		Groups and communities
		Diversity
		Solidarity
		Support
		Sharing experiences
		Breaking isolation
Personal	Building strengths	Speaking out
		Sense of history
		Spirituality
		Sexuality
		Positive role models
		Agency
		Pride
		Courage
		Hope
		Self-confidence and self-worth
		Release self-blame

Figure 3   Changes in the personal, interpersonal and political spheres: The cycle of liberation

most helpful followed by varied rankings for the different psychological topics. In the beginning, the analysis of change was not as well developed and did not receive high rankings. It became a particular interest in some of the later courses, becoming a primary focus for one course that was delivered at Diploma level. Four additional open-ended questions in the evaluation form asked participants about the social analysis, the connections between the personal and the political, and their involvement in change. A number of evaluations of the Certificate programme were also carried out by various agencies. All of these sources indicated that the course was highly popular, had a very high participation and completion rate, and was considered very relevant and helpful to participants (Parsons, O'Connor and Conlon, 2003).

It was clear from class participation, feedback and from essays that participants found the overall framework and approach accessible and helpful. It drew on their knowledge and experience of oppression, of psychological patterns, and of support and solidarity, and provided a framework for critical analysis and development of insight and understanding. The social analysis provided a clear understanding of society as a system of domination and made explicit what participants already knew. Feedback indicated that participants found this helpful rather than overwhelming, with participants using phrases in written feedback such as: 'found it helpful', 'very clear', 'gave a language to analyze oppression', 'put things in perspective', 'helped to make connections with other groups', 'helped me understand personal experiences'.

Participants also indicated that the course made connections between the personal and the political and that this: 'helped me to understand the past', 'I could see what some conflicts were about', 'see what was causing anxiety', 'saw how society impacted', 'stopped self blame', 'increased confidence'. Participants saw possibility for making changes at the personal level: 'increase confidence', 'hope for a better future', 'enriching', 'able to make changes', 'not accepting the norm', 'see others in different ways', 'sense of possibility'. Participants also expressed more interest in groups and communities: 'helped to reconnect', 'saw the value of a group', 'can be part of change', 'look for and give more support', 'play a more active role'. While there was a clear sense of valuing community groups and resources, there were often reservations about getting involved in more politically oriented groups: 'might at some point', 'will think about it', 'if I had more time, yes'.

The delivery of these courses was a learning experience for all involved, providing increasing insights into the nature of oppression, its impact on our lives and the ways in which we could be involved in transformation.

The structural analysis combined with a systems perspective offered a framework in which the broader social system could be recognized, and also linked the modes of control to personal experiences at the micro level, allowing a more context specific understanding to emerge. The psychological analysis was more general in the courses, but allowed links to personal patterns, and developed possibilities for choices at the personal level. The broader understanding of change that evolved over the courses opened up many possibilities for involvement in change, creating a greater sense of agency.

An opportunity to deliver a liberation psychology course also arose through a Certificate in Lesbian Studies and Queer Culture, which was launched by WERRC in 2000. The first Certificate was delivered in UCD and later delivered in community resource centres. The Certificate was informed by a feminist ethos of inclusion, safety and participation. It consisted of four modules, some of which were delivered as courses over 10 weeks and others as intensive weekend modules, with modules taken by participants at their own pace. Participants identified as lesbian, gay, bisexual or transgendered (LGBT), and had varying involvements with the LGBT community, ranging from attending social events to involvement in community and political organizations. As a member of and activist in the LGBT community I was particularly interested in this opportunity, and offered a course entitled Liberation Psychology: Lesbian and Queer Perspectives which was delivered in UCD over a 10 week period to 10 participants who identified as lesbian or bisexual.

In this case the course content was modified for LGBT participants while retaining the basic structure of a social analysis, a psychological analysis and a cycle of liberation. The social analysis first of all focused on society as a hierarchy drawing on colonialism as a model with parallels to heterosexism and homophobia. A more detailed exploration of religion, education, medicine and mass media as particular sources of oppression for LGBTs followed. The psychological analysis included some of the areas described above, and also offered a session specifically on shame as a particular element in homophobia. This session focused on the social origins of shame, experiences of shame, and methods for transforming shame. In the LGBT context, pride has evolved as a central concept in LGBT activism. In this course it could be seen as an antidote to shame, as well as a strategy for social transformation. This analysis thus highlighted the possibilities for personal changes as well as the importance of community for cultivating and expressing pride. The exploration of sexuality focused particularly on sexuality as fluid, multidimensional and changing over time as an alternative to the fixed view of sexual orientation (and gender) as binary opposites. In exploring the cycle of liberation, the LGBT community and political activism provided many examples of change at the interpersonal and political levels, which will be discussed more fully below.

Although formal evaluations were not obtained for this course, informal and written feedback indicated that the course had been of value for several participants. It had increased their understanding and awareness of the impact of heterosexism and homophobia and increased their motivation to take counteractive steps both in their personal life and through involvement in groups and communities. In an evaluation of the Certificate as a whole by an external evaluator participants specifically indicated that the course had been of personal and practical use. Overall, those who took Certificate courses were much more likely to have increased their involvement in LGBT groups and organizations (Sheehan, 2003). This course thus provides an example of how the three component model can be adapted for use in different contexts.

Workshops on liberation psychology

Between 2002 and 2007 several opportunities arose to offer workshops varying in size from 12 to 22 participants in liberation psychology, some for the Certificate in Lesbian Studies and Queer Culture and others to community groups. A course was firstly offered in a weekend (non-residential) workshop format as part of the Certificate. Working with Joni Crone, a lesbian activist, community worker and psychodrama therapist (Crone, 2004), we adapted the model for a workshop using a variety of participatory and experiential methodologies, including role play and image theatre. I also delivered several other workshops on a day-long basis again following the format of the social analysis, the psychological analysis and the cycle of liberation. The workshops were mostly supported by or located in community centres as a resource for the LGBT community and involved lesbian and in some instances bisexual and transgendered persons who identified as lesbian. In partnership with resource centres, the aim was to provide education and awareness and to foster insight, self-worth, agency and greater involvement in LGBT communities.

The workshop provides a very different context for applying liberation psychology. Whether over a day or a weekend, workshops provide a more intense and focused experience in which there is more sharing of personal experiences, values and perspectives, and also greater opportunities for spontaneity, fun, support and solidarity. The workshops involved groupwork methods that foster inclusion and equality of participation. There was an emphasis on safety, on confidentiality and on creating a supportive environment. There was an expectation that the workshop would be an enjoyable as well as useful experience. As with other courses and workshops, discussions were recorded on flipcharts, and I also distributed questionnaires to participants that included questions about the social analysis, the connections between the personal and the political, and their involvement in change.

The approach to the three components had to be adapted for a workshop format, as, unlike a course, which is dispersed over 10 or 12 weeks, all three components are condensed into one or two days, or even into one or two hours. In a short (2–3 hour) workshop the three components are addressed through open questions in a brainstorm format. First, questions in relation to homophobia (the social analysis) include: what is it, where does it come from, what are the sources or origins of homophobia? Secondly, questions regarding the impact (cycle of oppression) include: what is the impact of homophobia on us, how does it make us feel, what are the reactions to homophobia? Thirdly, the analysis of change (cycle of liberation) can include questions such as: what needs to change, how can things change, how can we be involved in change? Longer workshops obviously allow more detailed analysis using a variety of methodologies to allow more process and participation.

In most workshops, following introductions and group agreements, the workshops began with open discussion of society as a pyramid and the implications in terms of domination and modes of control. This served as a background to a more focused identification of the specific structures and institutions associated with homophobia and heterosexism. These could be readily identified as participants were generally very aware of the role of religion, health and medicine (including psychiatry and psychology), mass media and education in producing homophobia. Anti-gay statements by the Vatican or right-wing Christians were named, along with medical and psychological views. Stereotypes in mass media, exclusion from education, general prejudice and occasional assaults had all been experienced by participants, sometimes involving families and communities of origin. This session stirred up several emotions, of which anger and outrage were the most obvious, with sadness also evident. A clear sense of a shared oppression and of having the opportunity to explicitly name something that was part of being lesbian was often evident in these sessions, and later stated in feedback questionnaires.

The psychological analysis focused on these and other reactions to homophobia. It began by asking for examples of negative psychological reactions to these social patterns based on personal experience or on general reactions. The first part of this session therefore maintained a focus on oppression, allowing participants to name and sometimes vent a range of reactions that included anger, shame, sadness, conflict about being out, isolation and lack of support. Hearing these reactions created a sense both of differences and diversities in experiences of and reactions to homophobia, and also of the commonalities. This contributed to greater understanding of difference and diversity and also of shared experiences, solidarity and support. Identification of negative patterns or vulnerabilities was immediately followed by a session on strengths associated with being lesbian, usually resulting in a list of strengths that included hope, pride, courage, sense of being outside the box, sense of belonging to a community, and pride in the history of LGBT activism. The naming of strengths most often shifted the workshop from a negative to a positive focus. In several workshops, strengths were seen as antidotes to negative patterns, providing a motive to further develop strengths. The discussion of strengths provided an important counterbalance to the negative patterns and reconnected participants with their pride in being lesbian and with many positive experiences of love, sexuality, friendship, solidarity and sense of belonging.

The analysis of change varied depending on the context. In some daylong or short workshops the focus was specifically on exploring sexuality. Here the session considered sexuality in terms of how it was constructed, and then explored an alternative holistic approach that provided a positive view of sexuality, explored complexity and fluidity and used an energy exercise to create a positive group experience. In longer workshops the three levels of change were explored. At the personal level a clear strategy was to value personal strengths, which included hope, pride and courage. Taking steps to increase self-worth and reduce self-blame linked to developing pride. The development of pride at a personal level was linked to being proactive about including positive images and positive culture (books, DVDs, art) in daily life, or valuing LGBT culture and history. Challenging fixed views of gender and of sexuality and speaking out and expressing views were also examples of changes that particpants identified on a personal level. Coming out in daily life was an important theme, linking into specific fears about coming out as well as understanding the personal, social and political value of coming out. Both coming out and pride also involved the interpersonal level, breaking isolation and making connections with others. Coming out also highlighted the need for and value of support in taking this step. The group itself also provided an experience and increased appreciation of group support that in turn increased a sense of solidarity with others and appreciation of diversity. The importance of connecting with the LGBT community in some way became apparent, if only to break isolation but more positively to develop a sense of belonging. At the political level a range of possibilities for action were identified. In some cases participants had a clear interest in joining groups or being involved in activism in some way. Others did not see direct action as a possibility, but saw that they could play a role by supporting political action, while some did not have an interest in engaging at this level.

Responses to feedback questionnaires for several workshops indicated several benefits were gained. Participants indicated that they found the social analysis very clear and helpful, writing that it was: 'a very clear analysis', 'an eye-opener', 'strengthened my understanding of oppression', 'was a very powerful way to show things', 'equipped me to see our society more clearly', 'it was great to see the bigger picture'. The course also enabled the participants to see the connection between their own personal patterns and the social pattern discussed in the social analysis: 'I learnt about myself and about domination', 'more aware of how I can be determined by society', 'how my surroundings affect me'. Several wrote of being relieved of self-blame: 'I feel a lot of relief that there is nothing wrong with me', 'I stopped beating myself over the head, blaming myself', 'I wasn't so hard on myself'. Finally, a sense of solidarity with others was expressed 'a sense that we all run up against the same hurdles', 'helped me to understand the connections, how we react the same'.

The majority of participants indicated that they could see changes that they could make in their lives at a personal level, and that this provided them with hope and inspiration: 'it lifted my heart and gave me hope for a better future', 'I found it inspiring', 'it gives me a sense of possibility', 'aware that I'm in a position to change things', 'I can see small changes and big changes'. They felt increased confidence and strength: 'I feel stronger and better equipped', 'I feel able to start to make changes'. Some participants wrote of a sense of understanding and connecting better with others: 'yes we all count', 'see myself and others in a different way', 'it will make me more supportive'. There was an awareness that being visible and speaking out were important areas of change: 'I want to reveal myself in a more open way', 'I want to speak out and be more forthright, challenge people'.

At the political level, those participants who were already involved in groups, organizations and communities oriented towards social change felt re-energized by the course/workshop experience: 'It renews my commitment to community involvement', 'the course validated my work in the community, I feel re-energized', 'I can see myself in further community roles'. Others expressed a strong interest in or saw the value of involvement in change: 'it has reinforced my commitment and belief in activism', 'I can see the value of working with like-minded people', 'I would like to be more involved in the community'. However, some were more ambivalent about more involvement: 'I'm coming to terms with the idea that I can be part of change', 'would look at it in the future'.

Further insights into the experience of the workshops is provided in an evaluatation by an MA student who participated in a daylong workshop and who later wrote a thesis (Keane, 2006). This evaluation involved in-depth interviews with 7 of the 13 participants, and thus provides a richer understanding of the processes and outcomes involved. Keane placed the workshops in the context of psychological writings on the benefits of groups, as well as in the framework of liberation psychology.

Interviews firstly highlighted the benefits of the greater awareness of oppression gained from the workshop. Participants felt that they could understand the systemic nature of oppression and had a better analysis that they could apply not only to homophobia but also to other areas of their lives. They felt that the opportunity to focus on oppression was beneficial. Rather than increasing the negative impact of oppression, such awareness helped to remove self-blame, and broaden a sense of understanding and solidarity. Their understanding of oppression gave them more choices and enabled them to be clearer about their lives.

Participants also benefited from seeing the connection between the personal and political, both in the sense of their identity and emotions being shaped by oppression, and in the sense that the personal level of change is linked to the political. Interviews again revealed a common theme here of relief that 'it's not all my fault' gained by realizing that some of their emotional experiences were related to external sources of oppression rather than some intrinsic weakness. They were also able to observe the reactions of others in the group, which validated their own experience. Observing the varied reactions and experiences in the group was also associated with appreciation of diversity. Sharing of experiences thus led to greater understanding, tolerance and solidarity.

Finally participants also expressed a strong wish for more involvement in change. They saw that they could shift the dynamic of oppression in their own lives through a variety of actions. These could involve taking steps to develop a broader and more positive view of lesbian existence through cultural activities such as reading, education and video, being out and speaking up more as a lesbian, wanting to be more involved and supportive of lesbian and gay community, and looking for opportunities to get involved in political activism. However, rather than pressure to 'take on the world' they felt more focused in where they could take action.

Informal feedback as well as the in-depth interviews indicated that the group context was itself a source of support and solidarity for participants and increased their appreciation of the value and importance of support and solidarity. Participants made connections through forming friendships and contacts in the community, and some later did indeed participate more in community events and in activism. These workshops thus facilitated movement through the cycle of liberation from awareness to taking action.

Overall the workshops involved a more context specific application of the three component model, with all elements adapted for each group. For example specific sources of homophobia in society were identified, as were several vulnerabilities and strengths associated with homophobia. Additionally, the cycle of liberation focused specifically on areas of change linked to being lesbian, creating a somewhat different profile to that identified in the courses described above.

Another application of the model will further illustrate its adaptation for specific contexts, namely workshops on pornography. Here the social analysis examined pornography as an industry, explored economic, political and cultural aspects of pornography, and focused on the content of pornography. The psychological analysis explored women's reactions to pornography. The cycle of liberation identified options for action specifically in relation to pornography at the personal, interpersonal and political levels. Workshops were delivered on several occasions over a 5-year period to groups of between 8 and 20 women.

Evaluations firstly indicated that participants benefited from the opportunity to examine pornography and explore their own reactions and values. Many of the participants felt silenced and unable to express their concerns, and did not have a clear analysis. The social analysis provided research and knowledge that raised their awareness and enhanced their ability to voice their concerns. The main reactions that were articulated in the cycle of oppression focused on the degradation and humiliation that was present in pornography and which many women experienced when they encountered pornography in public places or through the internet. Other reactions included negative impacts on body image and sexuality, anger and sadness particularly regarding the impact of pornography on young people. Participants expressed considerable relief at the opportunity to explore and express these reactions and from hearing the reactions of other women. This could reinforce their own responses or highlight individual differences. As in other workshops, hearing the differing reactions thus increased a sense of solidarity and also an appreciation of difference and diversity.

The cycle of liberation starts with change at the personal level, and here women felt empowered to voice their objections and take action to exclude pornography from their personal lives. They could also see the value of speaking out and voicing concerns more generally, and exercising their power as consumers. Options for action also included lobbying, campaigning and providing education and awareness. The workshop as a whole could thus facilitate awareness and analysis, increased participants strength and confidence in relation to this area, and increased their sense of solidarity and agency.

Taken as a whole these examples illustrate the application of liberation psychology in several community contexts using the three component model as a framework. They demonstrate the possibility of co-creating analyses of oppression and liberation that facilitates the processes of developing awareness, building strengths, making connections and taking action. Between them they contributed to the development of a fuller understanding of the three elements. In most cases the social analysis (Figure 1) was adapted in several ways by participants and illustrated with specific experiences. Several vulnerabilities associated with oppression were identified, but participants were also very aware of psychological strengths (Figure 2) and this provided an important balance to the emphasis on negative patterns found in many approaches to oppression. As the understanding of change was developed over many courses and workshops, a bottom up view of change emerged along with many examples of activism in different spheres (Figure 3). The implications for understanding oppression and liberation based on these experiences and on further theory and research will be considered in Chapter 9.

The development of liberation approaches in psychology globally

In this section I will focus more specifically on the field of psychology itself, and on developments that share an explicit analysis of oppression and of resistance to oppression, and an emphasis on transformation, activism and interventions that have explicitly aimed to engage with oppression and marginalization. Many of these approaches have been influenced by the authors reviewed in Chapters 3 and 4. Thus approaches to the psychology of colonization, and in particular Fanon (1967) and Memmi (1968) who wrote of the impact of colonization on both colonized and colonizers, were influential. Post-colonial contexts include Ireland (Moane, 1994; 1999; Ruth, 1988) and South Africa (Biko, 1986; Nicholas and Cooper, 1990), where writers attempted to understand the impact of oppression at individual and societal levels with a view to transforming oppression. Feminist critiques of psychology led to the development of feminist psychology (Wilkinson, 1986), including feminist psychotherapy (Miller, 1986), feminist community psychology (Mulvey, 1988) and lesbian and gay psychology (Brown, 1992). A psychology of liberation was also developed in African-American (Bulhan, 1985; Jones, 1991) and Native-American contexts (Duran and Duran, 1995).

The most sustained development of liberation approaches has been in South and Central America, where the phrase 'liberation psychology' was used by Martín-Baró (1994). This context was characterized by totalitarian military regimes and large-scale poverty where Freire (1970), Martín-Baró (1994) and others were developing radical approaches to education as well as examining the role of psychology both as an instrument of oppression (where, e.g., psychologists are involved in torture and psychiatric abuse) and as an aid in liberation (where, e.g., psychologists were involved in empowering local communities).

In the last ten years a substantial body of theoretical and applied work has been published reflecting developments and applications of liberation approaches all over the globe. Feminist approaches have responded to critiques of white and ethnocentric bias (Bhavnani and Phoenix, 1994) and have expanded into an enormous variety of feminist approaches to and in psychology, to allow for complex transnational and local multicultural and multi-ethnic perspectives, reflecting changes in the women's movement itself. Several recently published edited collections provide examples of such feminist praxis that aims to be inclusive and transformative (Hesse-Biber, 2007; Landrine and Russo, 2009; Lykes and Moane, 2009). Liberation psychologies have also expanded to combine perspectives from around the globe as well as developing locally specific practices that engage with difference and diversity. Examples of such work include a recently published collection edited by Montero and Sonn (2009), as well as several monographs (Rosado, 2007; Ruth, 2006; Watkins and Shulman, 2008). Many areas of psychology, notably community, political and peace psychology, as well as counselling psychology, have drawn on feminist and liberation psychologies to develop further understandings of social justice, wellness and emancipatory theory and practice (Deutsch, 2006; Goodman et al., 2004; Nelson and Prilleltensky, 2004; Reich et al., 2007). Critical psychologies have also focused explicitly on social justice and transformation (Fox, Prilleltensky and Austin, 2009).

Many of these approaches draw on a variety of psychological models as well writers outlined in Chapters 3 and 4 of this book, and have developed further understandings through working with groups and communities in contexts of marginalization, including poverty, homelessness, migration and armed conflict. They are of course highly critical of the traditional field of psychology, agreeing with the critiques put forward by Bulhan (1985) and others outlined in Chapter 1. Psychological approaches that are individualistic and acontextual are seen as exclusionary and as reproducing inequalities associated with oppressive social conditions. A psychology that works for and with people involves participation. Such a psychology often aims to be bottom up, with psychologists and researchers engaging in the co-creation of knowledge, strategies and interventions with participants in specific contexts.

Forms of research, particularly feminist and participatory action research, have developed that enable participants to record and share experiences, provide witness and testimony, accompany and support each other, develop skills and implement strategies for transformation. Participatory action research in particular, involves, as Lykes, Coquillon and Rabenstein (2009, pp. 62) note, firstly a 'recognition of and collaboration with communities' local or indigenous resources' and secondly 'emphasis on bringing forward the voice of participants in both the research endeavours and in broader struggles for social change'. Collaboration, participation, diversity of methods and a focus on change are thus key elements of feminist and liberation psychology approaches. Working with individuals and groups in marginalized and oppressed contexts also highlights the power and privilege that many psychologists have access to, requiring critical self-reflection (Fine 2006).

Emancipatory approaches also make links to structural inequalities, recognizing that individual and group contexts are embedded in the larger macro system, which in turn manifests in the specific situation through the particular intersections of class, gender, ethnicity and other dimensions of inequality. The development of critical consciousness, that is, the awareness of the links between individual and group experiences and social patterns of oppression, is itself seen as central to liberation. Critical consciousness develops through dialogue, in group and community contexts, and has transformative action as its goal.

Emancipatory approaches, as Montero (2007) notes, are relational, and therefore ethical. These themes will be evident in the following examples of liberation psychologies in action.

Psychologies of liberation

The recent collection of essays edited by Montero and Sonn (2009) contains 16 chapters documenting developments in psychologies of liberation in Latin American countries (Colombia, Mexico, Panama, Peru, Venezuela), South Africa, Australia, the Philipines, Malaysia, Ireland, England and Spain. While such a diverse collection obviously draws on many different sources, almost all of them are have been influenced by the work of Freire, Martín Baró and related developments in Latin America. The work of Martín Baró, who wrote explicitly of liberation psychology, has been particularly influential, partly because he provided a critique of psychology but also wrote of the need for a new approach. Drawing on the ideas of Freire and of liberation theology, he set out his ideas in several papers and conference presentations during the 1980s, until he was assassinated in 1989, that had an important influence on psychologists in several Latin American contexts.

Several chapters in this collection provide outlines and summaries both of the ideas of Martín Baró (1994) and of others that developed in Latin American contexts (Montero and Sonn, 2009). Additionally, Montero in particular has published several articles in Spanish and English developing further understandings of liberation psychology (Montero, 1994; 1997; 2007). As noted in Chapter 4, Martín Baró, like others in Latin American countries, was particularly aware of the conditions of warfare, poverty, class domination and totalitarian regimes that created enormously oppressive conditons for the majority of people (the oppressed majority). He drew attention to the individualistic and hierarchical nature of the psychology that had been developed in North America and Europe. Martín Baró challenged the objectivity of psychology and was particularly scathing of its obsession with scientific, or more specifically, positivist and quantitative methods. He sought to 'de-centre psychology's attention from its own scientific status in order to devote itself to the urgent problems of the oppressed majorities in Latin America' (Martín-Baró, 1994, p. 141).

Martín Baró and others aimed instead to produce a psychology for the people, a psychology with social relevance and practical applications that would contribute to liberation. The process of conscientization or developing awareness about the world through dialogue and transformative action is central. De-ideologization, or decoding dominant ideologies and allowing people to realize their own knowedge of their situation is part of this process. Other concepts of Martín Baró that were briefly discussed in Chapter 4 include political socialization, recovery of historical memory, and the virtues of oppressed peoples. Martín Baró thus set the broad outlines of an approach to psychology that inspired further critical developments in Latin American countries. There are limited critiques of Martín Baró's ideas, partly because many of his writings set out broad themes. He did not have an analysis of gender, and he was also criticized for his adherence to empirical methods, traditional scientific tools, in particular survey and other research, rather than to action research (Jiminez-Dominguez, 2009).

Osorio (2009) provides further contextualization of approaches to liberation in Latin America generally, including theory of dependency, liberation theology, philosophy of liberation, Freire's approach to education and other influences. These brought attention to the broader economic and political conditions in Latin American countries and to capitalism as a global system. The concept of praxis as combining theory and reflection in a relational and dialogical manner was developed by Freire and Martín Baró, and also by critical sociologist Fals Borda (1986), who wrote extensively on participatory action research (PAR). Like other approaches to action and participatory research, PAR involves several epistemological assumptions, with the fundamental idea, similar to Martín Baró, that knowledge is produced through dialogical processes involving the people's participation, and with a further aim of feeding this knowledge to intellectuals and other groups with power and resources who could ally with the people to bring about social change.

Montero (2009) places social transformation at the centre of liberation psychology, and argues that conscientization and problematization are vital forces in social transformation. Providing a detailed discussion of the meanings of conscientization, she notes that it involves both emotional and cognitive elements. It involves critical questioning in dialogue, and therefore is intrinsically relational. She writes that 'participation is a basis for liberation' (p. 132), and explores PAR as a particular example of participation. PAR places power within the hands of the groups involved, who are in control of what or how knowledge is created. It works with the resources of the group themselves, drawing on existing relationships, networks and community resources in order 'to transform their living conditons, their immediate environment and the power relations established with other groups or institutions in their society' (Montero, 2009, p. 134). She discusses the practical difficulties of techniques for liberation. Practical methods identified for psychologists by Montero include listening, dialogue that involves humility and respect, critique, and specific concrete situations. The use of problematizing questions that go beyond everyday understandings is discussed in detail as a form of conscientization in group settings.

Several other chapters from Latin American countries provide reviews of theory and also detailed examples of the practices and challenges of applying liberation psychology. Sapene-Chapellín (2009) describes participatory action research with children in Caracas, using games and dramatization in a series of reflection-action-reflections, showing that children make connections from their immediate situation to the socio-political situation. Llorens (2009) describes the difficulties and tensions of participatory research with street children in Caracas, supporting the children in their search for resources while negotiating policies with various agencies. Hernández (2009) sets out the need for a psychology of liberation in Panama that can promote community participation and coexistence in contexts of conflict, suggesting that psychology can at least play a role in the generation of new meanings that disrupt traditional lines of conflict.

The process of accompaniment in the reconstruction of traumatized communities is developed in two chapters, where accompaniment involves psychologists entering the lives of participants, listening to and/or recording their stories, and offering supportive company during contacts, including those involving community services. In Peru Chauca-Sabroso and Fuentes-Polar (2009) describe the collection of testimonies from survivors of war and armed conflict in a process that involved becoming part of the community through providing one-day workshops and emotional and psychosocial accompaniment. They chart a healing process of recovery of historical memory in which testimonies are recorded and returned to participants who are supported to participate in group mobilization. Sacipa-Rodríguez et al. (2009) also develop understandings and practices for accompaniment of women and youth in Bogota, describing 'everyday chats, actively listening, working and teaching' among their activities.

Writing from a European perspective, Burton and Kagan (2009) provide an overview of concepts in liberation psychology, and then consider the implications for what they call Core Capitalist Countries (CCC), a term they use to describe Western Europe, North America, Australia, New Zealand and Japan. Ireland is included as both post-colonial and newly CCC. Aligning liberation psychology concepts with critical community psychologies that have developed internationally, they describe several examples of action-oriented research with marginalized groups.

For example in working with people who have intellectual impairment they examine the ways in which the disabling aspects of social arrangements may be improved. They call for the development of a 'real social psychology' in CCCs that would offer true understandings of the societal and develop interventions for change based on a valuing of 'wellness, equality and empowerment' (p. 66). Other contributions from Europe include my own chapter on the Irish context (Moane, 2009), and a chapter by Luque-Ribelles, García-Ramírez and Portillo (2009) analyzing a university community partnership with women from marginalized neighbourhoods in Seville in Spain. Using PAR methods of group discussion, participant observation and community meetings they facilitated identification of problems and actions to address these problems, and described the development of critical consciousness which enable women to work towards change.

Approaches to a psychology of liberation also have roots in South Africa, as illustrated in the chapter by Duncan and Bowman (2009). Psychology as a field was implicated in apartheid, and at the same time many in the field were opposing apartheid and developing emancipatory approaches. The use of intelligence tests and other psychological research to reinforce racism, the role of psychologists in the psychiatric system and in interrogation and torture are among the oppressive practices documented by Duncan and Bowman. The supposed scientific neutrality of psychology helped to justify and mystify psychology's complicity with apartheid. Critical and dissenting approaches that were in the minority during apartheid began to develop as a stronger presence especially after 1994. Many of these drew on the work of Fanon in particular, and were also inspired by Biko (1986). Duncan and Bowman describe one example of a practice designed to address the under-representation of blacks in publications in psychology, namely the formation of the Psychology Research and Authorship Forum.

Three remaining chapters broaden the discussion to other contexts. Sonn and Lewis (2009) set out to articulate a liberation perspective for working with race and migration issues in Australia, specifically with South Africans in Australia. They draw on critical whiteness studies and critical race theory, focusing on the role of whiteness in privilege and dominance as well as the construction of race and racism in the experience of South African immigrants. Montiel and Rodriguez (2009) use a multi-layered (ecological) model involving micro, meso and macro levels to chart the changing relations at each level between social movements and the state during the transition to democracy in the Philippines. Noor (2009) advocates a critical analysis of the Hijab in a Malaysian context through empowering women to make their own decisions regarding the Hijab, and considering examples from the Muslim world in which women can use the Hijab to their own advantage.

This edited collection thus provides many examples of liberation psychology drawing particularly on Latin American ideas. Several other books have developed a broad perspective and offer a variey of approaches to psychologies of liberation. Although outside the scope of this overview, which focuses on the field of psychology, Mullaly's book on critical social work draws on a range of writers, including many covered in this book. Writing in the Australian context, Mullaly advocates anti-oppressive social work practice at personal, cultural and structural levels, and also attends to dominator patterns (Mullaly, 2002). Two other books of relevance here provide approaches to liberation psychology that draw on integral and depth psychology as well as feminist and Latin American liberation psychologies. Based on his experiences in community mental health and community activism, especially in the Puerto Rican context, Rosado (2007) provides an approach to liberation using Integral Psychology. He provides a structural and systems analysis of 'the cyclone of oppression' (p. 79) and its relation to internalized oppression. He develops a detailed, social identity-based approach to liberation, describing an outward spiral of action and transformation. Watkins and Shulman (2008) bring together a wide range of literature in depth psychology, trauma and participatory practices of liberation psychology. Locating their analysis in the global context of colonial related war, transnational corporations and massive global inequalities, and based on their own interrogation of traditional therapeutic and research paradigms they draw together many different strands that aim to heal the traumas related to colonialism and global domination at individual, group and collective levels.

An approach that also attends to those in positons of dominance is Ruth (2006), who has developed his theory and practice in the Irish context, drawing on co-counselling, colonialism and radical psychologies, including feminism. Ruth works with community groups and NGOs among others, and is particularly focused on the dynamics of leadership in organization and community contexts, and also in relation to social inequalities such as classism, sexism and racism. He has also developed an analysis of the dynamics of oppressor status, with particular attention to middle class and men's experiences, arguing that an awareness of oppressor identities is essential for acting in alliances towards liberation. Ruth develops a model and identifies several strategies for effective leadership in organizations and communities.

There are several emancipatory approaches in psychology in Ireland. Examples that explicitly use liberation psychology include: Carroll's (2010) use of Art to facilitate work on anti-racism with women in communities; Kelleher's (2008) PhotoVoice project that engages LGBT youth in documenting their experiences of stress; Reygan's (2010) interviews with LGBT participants on the meaning of spirituality; the international collaboration of Veale et al. (2008) which involved formerly abducted girl-mother soldiers in Uganda and Sierra Leone in decision-making and managing of resources, thus facilitating their economic and social re-integration. Participatory research aproaches with children are described by Hennessy and Heary (2005), while McCarthy, Quayle and Alwyn (2008) include examples of applications of psychology with a social justice orientation. Approaches in critical health and clinical psychology (Bates et al., 2009; Guilfoyle, 2009; MacLachlan, 2005), feminist psychology (Greene, 2003), social psychology (O'Connell, 2001) and several others reviewed in Madden and Moane (2006) seek to develop understanding and interventions that incorporate the socio-political level.

Feminist liberation psychologies

While feminist psychologies have had emancipatory aims since their emergence in the contexts of women's liberation movements, there have been several developments that specifically integrate the contribution of Latin American liberation psychology, particularly the work of Martín Baró. This includes the work that I have described above, using participatory pedagogy in a community context. The work of Lykes and colleagues in Guatemala provides an early example which combines feminist and liberation psychology approaches using PAR. Following a 36-year period of civil war that included government terror and silencing, attacks on the indigenous Mayan communities and war related sexual assault and violence, Lykes and colleagues were able to forge alliances with indigenous Mayan women over a period of 15 years. As the women themselves engaged in rebuilding their lives, they became interested in documenting the effects of war on their community, and on making their stories of oppression and survival known both inside their own community and also more widely, with the aim of contributing towards healing and the prevention of further violence. Lykes, who was already working and known in the area, was invited to collaborate, and was involved for several years as advisor and advocate (Lykes, 1997). A research team involving Mayan women of Chajul and Lykes evolved a strategy of using photographs and storytelling that enabled them to document and record their experiences. Over many workshops selecting photos and recording stories and accounts, deeper understandings emerged regarding both the traumas experienced by the women (and children) and their political aims. These could be shared with each other and with other communities, and also published to a wider, global community. The PhotoVoice project facilitated personal and collective healing as well as collective action for change. For Lykes, as for others working across boundaries, it presented challenges such as building relationships, self-disclosure, negotiating individual and cultural differences, language and communication issues, collaborative writing, and the impact of the project on gender and other relations in the local community (Women of ADMI and Lykes, 2000; Lykes, Coquillon and Rabenstein, 2009).

The recent Special Issue of *Feminism & Psychology* contains 14 articles providing contributions involving 15 countries, namely the USA, the Netherlands, Portugal, England, Ireland, South Africa, Democratic Repubic of Congo, Uganda, India, Pakistan, Palestine, Guatemala, Colombia, Peru and El Salvador (Lykes and Moane, 2009). Contributions combine a variety of methods and perspectives, including PAR and participatory pedagogy, and also present critical and innovative perspectives on the praxis of feminist liberation psychology. Contributions share a focus on the role that psychology can play in detailing the specificities of social context while acknowledging the impact of structural inequalities, and on understanding and where possible contributing to the exercise of agency.

Crosby's (2009) contribution describes further work with Lykes and colleagues in developing the praxis of accompaniment. Aiming to take the further step of facilitating transformative action with accompaniers, Lykes and colleagues brought together psychologists, lawyers, researchers and activists from Peru, Guatemala and Colombia who were working with and accompanying women survivors of sexual assault. Drawing on participatory action research methods, Crosby describes the challenges of accompanying in a context where rape had been used as a weapon of war and where perpetrators have had impunity. Using creative methodologies that included mask making and theatre, Crosby and colleagues created a dialogical space in which accompaniers could consider their shared experiences of witnessing and testimony, and of their own experiences of threat and assault linked to their participation in bringing experiences of rape and sexual assault into the public domain. A particular feature of this article is its description of the attempts to build solidarity across national boundaries often fraught with historical and contemporary conflict.

Madrigal and Tejeda (2009) describe another strategy to address sexual assault and violence in San Salvador, namely a participatory education and awareness programme for men that examines masculinity itself as a risk factor for perpetrating gender-based violence (GBV). They combine liberation psychology concepts with feminist analyses of gender and of gender-based violence, to create a workshop-based dialogical space where men can work together to prevent GBV. As men share their personal experiences and consider the impact of men's violence on their own lives and communities, they develop awareness of their own capacity for violence and develop strategies for how they can act together to prevent GBV.

In another example of the use of a workshop format using participatory action research, this time in the USA, Billies et al. (2009) describe the formation of the Welfare Warriors' Research Collaborative of low-income lesbian, gay, bisexual, transgendered and gender nonconforming individuals who are involved in a variety of ways with a homeless shelter in New York City. They set out to document experiences of structural and everyday violence linked to poverty, gender and sexual orientation, and also of homeless shelter staff abuse and neglect. Using collaborative methods that include videotaping group discussions, interviews and a survey, the group provided a context for individuals to describe and record their experiences and develop strategies for enabling homeless LGBTs to exercise agency and influence in the homeless shelter through, for example, aiding each other in asserting their rights. In such a space they mobilize the dual consciousness or second sight discussed by DuBois (1963) to create more fluid spaces that challenge the binaries of sexual orientation and gender.

An example of research interviews drawing on ethnography and PAR is offered by Chaudhry and Bertram (2009), who provide a rich and detailed description of the specific contexts and strategies of Mohajir or migrant women in Karachi, Pakistan. Combining themes from transnational feminisms and from liberation psychology Chaudhry and Bertram document the ways in which women exercise agency despite the limits imposed by the intersections or configurations of class, ethnicity and gender. These configurations are linked to structural inequalities that manifest in everyday violence and deprivation. Chaudhry and Bertram describe the strategies that women use to survive assaults on themselves and their family members, provide material resources and support for their family and community.

White and Rostagi (2009) also document the strategies of women who are targets of physical and sexual assault, again at the intersections of class, ethnicity and gender in Banda in India. In this context the breakdown of police, community and family systems of security leaves women exposed to sexual assault and violence, grabbing of land and resources, and demands for sex in return for welfare and other resources. Through interviews and documentary material, White and Rostagi describe a group of women who form a vigilante group in response to this violence, exploring the rationale and activities of the vigilante group in terms of feminist discussion of retributive and restorative justice. White and Rostagi argue that vigilante groups can be a form of agency exercised under constraint, motivated partly by the need for retaliatory actions to prevent violence, but also by values of fairness and justice, contributing to their community through provision of food, jobs, shelter, and other resources.

Two research studies using in-depth interviews aim to record and document experiences of discrimination and oppression. Shalhoub-Kevorkian (2009) reports on focus group discussions with children who have suffered house demolitions in Palestine, giving voice to the pain and confusion of children under conditions of ongoing military assault, and also showing their resilience and hope for the future. Lorasdagi (2009) uses one-to-one interviews to allow Muslim women in Amsterdam to explore and express the meanings associated with wearing a headscarf. Their words convey complex and context specific understandings that both acknowledge the limits of wearing a headscarf and also the emancipatory opportunities that it can offer, especially when framed in relation to their own religious and geographic location.

Working as part of a multinational aid community in the Democratic Republic of Congo and in Uganda, Lindorfer (2009) provides a reflection on trauma work that incorporates the critical insights of liberation psychology. She challenges the individualistic nature of much NGO assistance based on trauma models, and outlines how working with such models pressurizes women to identify as victims, and through focusing on individual women contributes toward breaking up community-based helping networks. She calls on aid and psychosocial trauma workers to challenge both governments and NGOs to critically examine their practices.

DeOliveira and colleagues (deOliveira et al., 2009) document the influence of Latin American liberation ideas on the women's movement in Portugal, providing a historical account of the convergences between feminist and liberation psychology approaches to knowledge production and praxis. Interviews with women reflecting on their involvement in the women's liberation movement in Portugal illustrate the convergences of feminist and liberation psychology approaches in emphasizing a structural analysis that links to personal experiences.

A theme that recurs throughout several of these articles is the need to develop methodologies that can encompass class, ethnicity, privilege and multiple dimensions of difference. Torre and Ayala (2009) explore this in detail drawing on the work of Gloria Anzeldua (1999). Rather than be constrained by binary oppositions, they seek the development of a space in which the binaries of 'we' and 'other' are challenged. This requires spaces and group processes characterized by fluidity in which new understandings can emerge through listening, opening up to uncertainty and engaging with conflict. Several other articles provide reflections on practice in a variety of contexts. Ostrove, Cole and Oliva (2009) explore both challenges and positive experiences of building alliances between deaf and hearing colleagues in the USA. Carolissen and Swartz (2009) provide a critical analysis of community psychology in South Africa. They note that in focusing on the single category of race, community psychology in South Africa has overlooked the marginalization of women They argue that to be emancipatory it is necessary to consider multiple positionings. Writing in a British context, Whelan and Lawthom (2009) integrate feminist pedagogical practices with community psychology to demonstrate the potential of pedagogical practices in the community, especially in contexts of diversity and marginalization.

Several other developments in feminist psychology provide both a critical reflection on psychology as a field and offer emancipatory and participatory approaches that engage with structural dimensions of inequality. Writings in Hesse-Biber (2007) place feminist research in the context of standpoint epistemology, ethnography, grounded theory and poststructural approaches, as well as black, post-colonial and transnational perspectives. Landrine and Russo (2009) provide a comprehensive collection which reviews feminist research and practice across multiple dimensions of gender diversity, including ethnicity, race, sexual orientation, age, health, migration, violence and poverty, concluding with several discussions of policy and advocacy. Critical considerations of power, gender and intersections with political psychology are provided by Unger (2004) and Capdevila and Unger (2006). Burman (2008) and Greene (2003) engage in critical analysis of developmental psychology, aiming to reconceptualize key concepts such as time, age and development and to address multiculturalism and globalization. In a rare combination of personal reflection and theory, Lott and Bullock (2006) consider their own experiences of class and also integrate theory and research on class. MacLeod (2006) integrates critical, post-colonial and feminist perspectives to consider emancipatory practice in South Africa.

A great deal of feminist analysis has been applied in the context of psychotherapy and counselling, with several attempts from the early days of the women's movement to link therapy and counselling with consciousness-raising. Goodman et al. make this connection, defining consciousness-raising as 'helping clients understand the extent to which individual and private problems are rooted in larger historical social and political forces' (Goodman et al., 2004, p. 804). They and others (Sue and Sue, 2007) provide an extended discussion and critique of individualistic approaches to psychological distress. They advocate critical reflection by practitioners of class, ethnicity and gender biases and the development of interventions that facilitate clients in seeing the connections to group, community and structural forces. They also see an emancipatory role for psychotherapists and counsellors through acting as allies and advocates both in their own practice and through their professional organizations. Their proposals thus challenge many of the fundamental assumptions around objectivity, non-judgementalism and professionalism in psychotherapy and counselling.

Other liberation approaches in psychology

The field of community psychology took an early interest in empowerment and social justice (Burton and Kagan, 2005). The field initially emphasized a two-tiered approach that focused on empowerment (often at the individual level) and social support (at the community level). As the limitations of these approaches became apparent, several multi-levelled approaches developed, with increasing recognition of the importance of a socio-political analysis and developing multi-level approaches to understanding and intervention. Watts and Serrano-Garcia's (2003) co-edited special issue of the *American Journal of Community Psychology* provided a diverse collection of approaches to liberation and contributed to the development of the socio-political level of analysis. Prilleltensky in particular develops the concept of 'psychopolitical validity' (Prilleltensky 2003, p. 195) or validity that depends on integrating the psychological and the political. Taking this further, Nelson and Prilleltensky (2004) bring together important concepts and writings for a community psychology that will advance liberation and well-being. They write that: 'Psychopolitical validity, then, derives from the concurrent consideration and interaction of power dynamics in psychological and political domains at various levels of analysis' (p. 122). They develop a clear link between social justice and wellness: 'Wellness is a positive state of affairs brought about by the simultaneous satisfaction of personal, relational and collective needs' (p. 276). Liberation psychology is increasingly recognized in the fields of community psychology in Britain (Burton and Kagan, 2005; Orford, 2008) and internationally (Reich et al., 2007).

The field of critical psychology has also had a longstanding interest in feminist, liberation and emancipatory approaches, as the edited collection of Fox, Prilleltensky and Austin (2009) demonstrates. This collection provides comprehensive critiques of most of the mainstream areas of psychology, with several chapters devoted to 'critical social issues' (p. vi), including race, class, gender, disabilty, trauma, colonialism and mental health. The development of PAR and other critical and action approaches to research is evident in the collection edited by Reason and Bradbury (2008), who, in their introduction also advocate approaches that take account of the personal, interpersonal and political levels. Other areas have also paid increasing attention to oppression and liberation, recognizing the importance of psychological approaches extending their analysis and intervention beyond personal and community levels. These include peace and political psychology (Dawes, 2001; Deutsch, 2006), theory and psychology (Teo, 2005), and lesbian, gay and queer psychologies (Clarke and Peele, 2007). Recent psychological analyses of globalization and climate change have also emerged that explore their psychological impact and the role that psychology can play, again advocating multilevel approaches that engage with the socio-political level (Hermans and DiMaggio, 2007; Stokols et al., 2009).

As noted above, feminist, liberation and multicultural perspectives have been combined in several approaches that aim to move models of clinical practice away from individualistic approaches and acknowledge the structural origins of inequality involved in ethnicity, race, class and other dimensions of inequality and oppression (Aldorondo, 2007; Costigan, 2004; Goodman et al., 2004; McAuliffe et al., 2008; Sue and Sue, 2007). The authors in these collections provide several arguments for the importance of psychologists, counsellors and psychotherapists becoming agents of change at community and socio-political levels through practices ranging from accessible fees and display of relevant literature through developing and advocating evidence-based policies that are linked to social justice. Goodman et al. capture the implications of the link between wellness and social justice, writing, in the context of counselling psychology that 'a commitment to social justice ... means an expansion of our professional activities beyong counseling and psychotherapy to advocacy and intervention at the community and policy levels' (Goodman et al., 2004, p. 821).

Psychology and liberation

The theory, research and practices described in this chapter illustrate the possibilities for the involvement of psychology in transformation using the approaches developed in several different areas of psychology. As liberation psychology is practised in diverse settings, the impact of oppression on daily lives is clear. Structural inequalities, war related violence and sexual assaults, ethnic conflicts, breakdowns in justice and security systems and everyday poverty are found in every part of the world, and also demonstrate massive global inequalities. Histories of resistance, examples of resilience, support and solidarity, strong commitments to communities and actions for transformation are evident. Psychologists can offer many skills and resources that can facilitate making changes in conditions of oppression, can play a role in documenting and inscribing such experiences, and also make links between groups and with structures of inequality. Participatory pedagogy and participatory research methods form cornerstones for approaches in liberation psychology, along with several other themes whch have been explored throughout this book and which will be discussed more fully in Chapter 9.

9
Interconnections between Personal and Political Change: Towards an Egalitarian Society

Gender and colonial relations have been central features of global developments in economics, politics and culture, and have been the focus of an enormous body of writing and research. Both gender and colonialism involve social systems in which power differentials are institutionalized so that some have considerable access to power and resources while others have little access to power and resources. The importance of psychological factors in the maintenance of these differentials, as well of course as material and cultural factors, has been acknowledged by the range of writers, researchers and practitioners discussed in this book. A liberation psychology which aims to facilitate transformative action requires a social analysis that can incorporate macro or global levels as well as micro or local levels. Such a psychology would aim to link psychological patterns to power differentials, and develop practices that are grounded in the social origins of psychological patterns and that are clearly focused on the capacity to take action. This involves practices that interconnect individual, group, community and collective levels and are informed by principles of emancipatory practice that have emerged in the development of liberation psychologies.

Liberation psychology and emancipatory practice

This book adopted an approach to liberation psychology that is grounded in an analysis of social conditions and that emphasizes transformation at the personal, interpersonal and political levels. The importance of structural inequalities, their impact on the immediate social conditions in which people live their lives, the strengths and vulnerabilities associated with these conditions, and the processes and practices involved in making changes were documented throughout the book. Several elements of emancipatory practice were identified based on this approach and illustrated by the many examples of liberation psychology described in Chapter 8.

It is clear that liberation psychologies are firstly *critical* of traditional psychology, developing the critiques outlined in Chapter 1 through the work described in Chapter 8. The assumptions made in psychology about the nature of human beings (ontology), about knowledge production (epistemology) and about methods and practices (methodology) have been critically examined along with specific critiques of the many paradigms that have evolved in psychology. A fundamental feature of such critiques from a liberation psychology perspective is the individualistic nature of much theory and practice in psychology. The person is viewed as an individual unit, possibly in a family and community context, but rarely as embedded in the broader macro systems which have such a profound influence in their lives.

Liberation psychologies are also *participatory*, involving individuals and groups in the production of knowledge and strategies for change. Whether this is in one-to-one, group or community settings, involving education or research, participatory methods emphasize inclusion, giving voice, recording individual perspectives and appreciating diversity. This again is in contrast to established practices in psychology, which view the psychologist as an expert in a position of authority with regard to clients, aiming to use objective scientific techniques for knowledge production. Such participatory practices, especially in a group context, have an element of unpredictability and fluidity; this itself is part of liberation psychology practice. It involves practitioners *interrogating* their own *privilege* and developing their awareness about dominator practices, as well as using privilege to provide resources and to support making links with other groups, undertaking advocacy and inscribing the experiences of those marginalized from dominant discourses.

The importance of the *structural*, socio-political or macro level of society is recognized by liberation psychologies. Several approaches to developing a view of structural inequalities and their impact on local conditions were described. Conversely, liberation psychologies aim to develop interventions which will link to different levels of oppression and liberation, and to contribute to socio-political change as well as to improving immediate social conditions. Liberation psychologies are also specific to particular contexts, social conditions or limit-situations, and it follows that *specificity* is an important principle which is also linked to the participative nature of liberation psychology. Specificity is linked to appreciation of diversity and to the unique perspectives and experiences of different individuals and groups.

A key process in liberation psychology is the development of the *link* between *the personal and the political*. The feminist movement has used the term consciousness-raising to refer to a process whereby women in groups gained an understanding of the common basis of oppression by sharing their experiences and then becoming involved in action. In the Latin American context, the interrelationship between *consciousness and action* became uniquely captured in the phrase conscientization, referring to a cyclical process in which awareness and action feed each other. This process must be grounded in the lived experience of the oppressed, and should arise out of their own experience of reflection and action (praxis). It follows from this that liberation psychology approaches change from the *bottom up*, aiming to empower people to develop agency on their own behalf. This is in contrast to many traditional approaches to political change, which emphasize top down influences on change. Liberation is a necessarily *relational and collective* enterprise that involves relationships, or relatedness. It is through interaction with each other, with discourses and the state that oppression is enacted and liberation is attained. Interpersonal relationships, group and community contexts and acting in solidarity are examples of relational processes involved in liberation that are the opposite of the isolation and fragmentation that accompany oppression. Developing support and solidarity and acting in groups are thus further elements in liberation.

These assumptions have implications for individualistic approaches to psychology and to change. If psyche and society are interlinked, then it follows that the social conditions in which people live their lives have profound implications for psychological functioning. Changes in psychological patterns will therefore require changes in social conditions and vice versa. Breaking out of oppression, whether at the personal level or at the political level, requires changes in both psychological and social patterns. Attempting to break out of internalized oppression by focusing on personal development without attending to the need for change in social conditions will be fraught with difficulty as the social conditions associated with oppression continue to impinge on individuals and shape psychological functioning in oppressive ways. On the other hand, attempts to break out of oppression through political means without reference to the need for psychological change will be undermined by the negative psychological patterns associated with oppression.

A further element in this analysis of personal and political change is the recognition that interpersonal relationships, whether through one-to-one contact, groups or communities, are an important vehicle for psychological change and development. In the cycle of liberation presented in this book the interpersonal level was seen as bridging the personal and the political levels. Change at the personal level is stimulated, encouraged, supported and maintained by interpersonal relationships, while efforts to bring about political change almost always involve working with others in groups, organizations and communities. The vital role of interpersonal relationships highlights further the need for personal change in order to accomplish political change, because, as many of the writers on oppression indicate, a number of difficulties in political organizing are related to the psychological patterns associated with oppression which create problems in relationships and in groups.

A fundamental theme to emerge is *the importance of analysis* in a liberation psychology, because it is through analysis that links are made between personal experiences and features of the social context. The insight that subjective experiences, such as lack of self-worth or frustration and anger have their origins in social conditions both counteracts the focus on the individual which is part of the ideology of psychology and psychotherapism, and opens the way for practices which can transform these patterns. Analysis is itself interactional, because it involves engagement either in one-to-one or group situations, or with culture and discourse. Reflection based on individual experience plays a central role, and therefore analysis must engage with individual experience.

A liberation psychology *acknowledges diversity and complexity* in power differentials, and makes the assumption that status and subjectivity are shaped by multiple factors that include gender, race, class, religion, sexual orientation, disability, age and other dimensions, some of which are advantageous and others of which are disadvantageous. Some individuals are highly favoured and therefore privileged, others are highly disadvantaged, and therefore marginalized and underprivileged, while for others the balance of factors may not be so clearcut. Furthermore, individuals have some degree of choice, however limited, in relation to their status, and can collude with or attempt to change the status quo. Individuals are not seen as passive recipients of oppressive social forces, but as active agents who can negotiate with and mediate these forces, albeit with varying degrees of choice. These observations raise several questions about agency and justice which were alluded to in Chapter 8.

A liberation psychology attends to those in positions of dominance as well as to those who are oppressed. This is in part because individuals who occupy positions of power or who are favoured by power differentials are obviously an important part of the social context and of social change. Writers in liberation psychology highlight the complementary relationship between those who are in dominant positions and those who are oppressed. Change in one group will be limited if it is not matched by change in the other group. Additionally, many of the writers on the psychological aspects of domination emphasize the negative patterns associated with domination, highlighting the benefits to both dominants and subordinates of psychological and social transformation.

Systems of domination, the cycle of oppression and the cycle of liberation

This book began by arguing that since psychological patterns are related to social conditions, it was essential firstly to understand these conditions. It presented a structural and systemic view of society as a system of domination which shaped psychological functioning through its impact on day-to-day life or the micro level. The experience of the courses and workshops and of liberation psychology examples from around the world both reinforced the value of this approach, and also emphasized the importance of specificity and diversity. Individuals and groups exist at the micro level in environments that are constantly changing and within which they are engaged in many different ways that are unique to them. Liberation psychology offers a more fluid and dynamic understanding of the relationship between individuals and the environment, and a more balanced view of individuals as experiencing both vulnerabilities and strengths. Individuals are engaged with modes of control which interact with each other and impact on the micro environment and the psychological functioning of individuals. However, individuals are linked in to kin and friendship networks as well as many kinds of groups and communities which also impact on the micro environment and psychological functioning.

The analysis in this book viewed society as a *system of domination* with six modes of control (Fig. 1, p. 180), namely violence, political exclusion, economic exploitation, cultural control, control of sexuality and fragmentation. It involves a patriarchal system of domination, that is, one which favours men. It can also been seen as a system of race domination (racism and imperialism), and of heterosexual domination (hetero-patriarchy). It was analysed in Chapter 2 as a system of domination which was constantly evolving over time, so that current patterns of domination bear the legacies of historical developments, and are also laying the ground for future patterns.

Further dynamics of systems of domination were also described. In particular, the modes of control were seen as interconnected with each other so that they reinforced each other. For example, violence provides the underpinning for political exclusion and often for economic and sexual exploitation. Fragmentation creates obstacles to political organizing and to cultural expression, and so forth. Systems of domination almost always develop an ideology in which dominants are regarded as superior and subordinates as inferior, and this is usually regarded as natural or biologically based. Another dynamic is that of the interrelationship between those in positions of domination and those in positions of subordination, already referred to above. Resistance and collusion were two other dynamics identified. Some offer resistance to domination in a variety of ways which were explored in the book, while others cooperate with those in positions of domination, sometimes by choice and sometimes through coercion.

Modes of control have an impact in a variety of ways on the micro level in which individuals and groups live their lives. At the psychological level, as the above discussion indicates, individuals are seen as embedded in a system of domination. The mechanisms of control and other patterns which are characteristic of systems of domination manifest themselves at the individual level through their impact on the day-to-day life of the individual: in experiences of threat or of violence and harassment; in opportunities for political participation; in the features of paid and unpaid work or the experience of poverty; in access to contraception or freedom of sexual choice; in exposure to stereotypes or silence and erasure; in isolation and competition. These examples highlight the pervasive nature of oppression. Given the multiple patterns of domination and their interrelationships, it is clear that there are an enormous variety of ways in which oppression impinges on the individual.

As the many writers reviewed in this book indicate, psychological patterns can be linked to oppression to form a *cycle of oppression*, whereby the psychological vulnerabilities associated with oppression undermine capacities for action or involvement in change. The psychological vulnerabilities listed in Figure 2 (p. 182) are illustrative, and can be linked to those identified by writers in Chapter 3. They include lack of self-worth, alienation, hopelessness and confusion, anger and fear. Given the complexities discussed above, it is clear that some or none of these patterns may be manifested, or may be context specific.

However, some of these psychological reactions can create genuine difficulties at the individual level and also pose problems for groups and communities involved in change. This combination of social and psychological pressure can thus create a downward spiral. Figure 2 also provides examples of strengths that are linked to experiences of living with oppression and of resisting oppression, and to engaging with the cycle of liberation. Strengths include courage, perseverance, humour, support and solidarity. Strengths and vulnerabilities can coexist, contradict and interact with each other. They are not necessarily qualities of individuals although they may become so, as some of the research presented in this book illustrates; they can also be seen as qualities that are evoked in different environments over time and place.

Some of the writers reviewed in this book also identified patterns associated with being dominant. These patterns could also be linked to modes of control. For example, dehumanization and brutalization can be associated with violence; omnipotence, sense of importance and arrogance may accompany political power; sense of confidence and economic security may arise from economic wealth; restrictions on sexuality and emotional vulnerability may be linked to sexual exploitation; sense of superiority may develop from stereotypes of superiority; and isolation and personal insecurity may be created by fragmentation. A strong theme in writings on psychological aspects of domination is the isolation and alienation which can arise because of restrictions on emotional awareness and emotional expression.

Figure 3 (p. 183) presents a *cycle of liberation* as involving three levels of the environment. They are the personal level of building strengths, the interpersonal level of making connections, and the political level of taking action. Developing awareness through analysis plays a central role at all three levels. Figure 3 charts a bottom up approach to change or a cyclical approach. It shows the variety of elements involved in bringing about change as they have emerged through the theory and research reviewed in this book, and also through the courses and workshops. Although the levels are presented as if they are separate from each other, the analysis presented in this book, the experience of workshops and courses, and the research and analysis presented in Chapter 8 demonstrate the interconnections and overlaps between the three areas, which from an ecological perspective would be better understood as spheres. There is also a developmental perspective in the analysis, acknowledging that some individuals and groups, for many reasons, may seek to build strength at the personal level before engaging with groups, communities or political organizing. Of course this is not always possible, as the descriptions of the many oppressive contexts described in Chapter 8 indicate – for many, it is a matter of survival to engage with groups and communities. The cycle of liberation encompasses the overlaps between the personal, interpersonal and the political, and thus highlights the interconnections between change at different levels.

At the *personal* level there is obviously an interest in health, and the self, with an emphasis on self-determination, self-worth and self-expression. These areas have obviously been the focus of massive self-help industries involving such well-worn concepts as diet, nutrition, assertiveness training and self-esteem. Yet physical exhaustion, malnutrition, lack of self-worth and difficulties with direct action were repeatedly identified in writings on oppression, and the importance of physical health and feelings of self-worth must be acknowledged. Unlike practices characteristic of the self-help industry, the practices identified in this book were linked to the social origins of these negative patterns. They included questioning social norms and counteracting the negative representations and messages of inferiority characteristic of systems of domination. Developing a sense of history, especially a history of resistance to oppression, identifying positive role models and images, and valuing unpaid or poorly paid labour are examples of practices which originated in acknowledging the social origins of self-worth. Similarly practices in the areas of sexuality and spirituality focused on their role in transforming disconnections and dissociations associated with oppression, in creating connections with others, and in creating culture and community, which are cornerstones of political action.

At the *interpersonal* level, making connections with others is essential for overcoming the individual and cultural isolation which is associated with oppression. Such isolation arises particularly from the social mechanism of fragmentation, as well as from the other mechanisms of control, and it is exacerbated by the negative psychological and interpersonal patterns such as displaced anger. Furthermore, interpersonal relationships play an essential role in psychological and political change. The practices identified are aimed at facilitating supportive and enduring relationships, gaining skills, self-confidence and support in groups, and developing a sense of solidarity with a larger group or community. They derived both from an analysis of the social origins of isolation and other negative interpersonal patterns, and also from experiences of groups and communities involved in liberation described in Chapters 6 and 8. Since groups and communities are interpersonal in their nature, it is here that engagement with diversity and difference occurs.

At the *political* level, taking action is facilitated by developments in the personal and interpersonal areas outlined above, and can involve individual actions such as voting or group and collective actions. The discussion in Chapter 7 emphasized collective action, the accumulation of change over time, and the linking of groups and communities into structures that could advocate and lobby. A broader definition of 'political', and awareness of the varieties of political action, facilitated the development of a sense of agency, which could counteract the feelings of alienation and powerlessness associated with oppression. The importance of having a vision as well as strategies and policies is emphasized in writings reviewed in Chapter 3 and 4, with many writers identifying tendencies to reproduce dominator patterns when positions of power are gained.

The three component framework developed in this book aims to allow for dynamic engagement and fluidity rather than a linear sequence. A cycle of oppression is described in which modes of control undermine psychological functioning, and a cycle of liberation is described which involves change at the three levels of the personal, the interpersonal and the political. Change in these spheres can accumulate to bring changes in the modes of control. The cycle of liberation suggests that engagement with change for liberation in the personal, interpersonal or political spheres can build up psychological strengths. Such a reading emphasizes the value of engaging with groups and communities towards resistance and transformation. In particular, it suggests that actively seeking out environments or niches of resistance can be part of liberation psychology. A niche of resistance refers to a space or context in which individuals and groups can create a safe and supportive space which offers temporary respite from the everyday intrusion of the modes of control. In a niche of resistance, individuals and groups can create their own environment in which listening, respect, tolerance, pride, hope, courage and humour can prosper.

Making links between oppressions

While the analysis presented in this book focused primarily on women's oppression, it may also be applicable in other areas. The book drew on writers on feminism and colonialism from a variety of different backgrounds in terms of gender, race, class, sexual orientation, ethnicity and nationality. These writers identified many common themes in relation to psychological aspects of oppression. Writers as diverse in historical time, race, nationality and experience as Frantz Fanon, a black man who was also a psychiatrist writing in Algeria in the 1950s, and Cathleen O'Neill, a white working-class woman writing in Ireland in the 1990s, identified psychological patterns such as lack of self-worth, anger and vulnerability to addiction, linking these to lack of power, violence and humiliation, and control of culture. While this suggests that different situations of oppression can share some common features, it is also vital to recognize that there are clearly specificities in the experience of oppression and in reactions to them – for example, the white women interviewed by O'Neill (1992) did not experience the racial hatred described by Fanon (1967a).

The recognition of commonality would seem to be vital for solidarity, which plays an important role in the cycle of liberation both for over-coming the sense of isolation associated with oppression and for coop-erating for effective action. Yet an emphasis on commonality can lead to universalizing tendencies which ignore local variations and impose a white Western framework on culturally specific conditions (Lindorfer, 2009; Mohanty, 2003). Indeed it is mostly Western scholars, including those in psychology, women's studies, cultural studies and post-colonial studies, who have been criticized for universalizing. Universalizing, it has been argued, is itself an imperialist pattern, or a pattern of domi-nation, because patterns found in the dominant group are judged to be the norm in comparison with which patterns found in subordinate groups are usually found to be lacking.

The counterpoint to universalizing is specificity, where the uniqueness of each individual and each location or context is acknowledged. Yet while it is essential to acknowledge specificity, this has led some of those interested in difference and diversity to question any possibility for gen-eralization or commonality. This questioning of commonality was first seen as undermining identity, solidarity, and the capacity for political action (Brodribb, 1992). However, the call for specificity when made by feminist writers from southern countries is a challenge to Westerners to recognize what Narayan (1991, p. 10) first called 'the global imbalance of ignorance', that, partly as a result of colonialism, those in formerly colonized countries are more exposed to the culture of formerly coloniz-ing countries than vice versa. There is a general lack of information in European and North American societies about conditions in African, South American and Asian societies, which itself makes overgeneraliza-tion possible. Specificity implies that oppression must be described from the viewpoint of those actually experiencing it, in their own language and from their own frame of reference (Hesse-Biber, 2007).

This recognition of specificity as well as of commonality is a central theme in global and transnational feminist writings, which combine a global perspective with an emphasis on local conditions (Landrine and Russo, 2008). A global perspective recognizes that patriarchy, capitalism, imperialism and other systems of domination are global systems, that is, they are not confined to one country or region of the world, but span different regions in an interconnected way. Regions, countries and localities are part of this global system, and are influenced by it, while at the same time there are obviously enormous local variations because of nationality, ethnicity, religion, economic resources, history and a host of other factors. Furthermore, a particular local area will itself contain considerable diversity in terms of class, race, ethnicity, gender, disability, sexual orientation, religion and so forth.

Making links between oppressions will therefore involve both identifying commonalities and acknowledging specificities across different experiences of oppression. The six modes of control may provide a useful starting point for such an exploration, as long as, of course, it is seen as an open framework which can be adapted. Almost all of the writers reviewed in Chapters 3 and 4 – who, it may be recalled, included Native American, African American, lesbian, working-class, North American, Irish, Martinique, Tunisian, Indian, Brazilian and El Salvadoran writers – made reference to social conditions of oppression which included some or all of the six modes of control. Violence, political exclusion, economic exploitation, cultural control and fragmentation or divisions are referred to in numerous accounts of oppression. The addition of sexual exploitation highlights the specific uses of sexuality in maintaining oppression. Oppressed individuals or groups may further their analysis of their own oppression by documenting the six modes of control as each operates in relation to their situation, and may also develop solidarity with other groups by exploring differences and similarities in the patterns relating to each mechanism.

The example of violence may illustrate these points. Violence has been recognized as a feature of women's oppression in almost every country in the world, and there are movements against violence in many countries, and also international networks aimed at combating violence against women. Davies writes that 'The threat of male violence is a fundamental experience that unites women across barriers of race, culture and class throughout the world' (1994, p. vii). Yet as Davies' own collection of articles illustrates, there are enormous variations in the forms of violence and in the political reactions to violence. Culturally specific forms of violence include, for example, war-related rape in Bosnia, genital mutilation in some

Central African countries and serial killing in the USA. Vulnerability to violence is influenced by factors such as armed conflict, foreign status and development issues. Responses to violence vary from theatre and popular education in Jamaica to women's police stations in Brazil.

Violence and trauma have been documented and experienced across other dimensions of oppression – class, race, nationality, ethnicity, sexual orientation, disability, religion. Again, different groups obviously experience violence differently – gay men and lesbians, for example, differ from men and women with disability in a variety of ways, even in terms of their experience of a specific form of violence such as assault. They differ in their vulnerability to violence, the grounds for violence, the specifics of their violations, their reactions to violence, the reactions of those around them, and the role and response of state agencies. Yet writings on the psychological aspects of violence share a number of common themes.

Just as links can be made through the social conditions of oppression, so can links be made through the processes and practices of liberation. Many groups, for example, have developed a sense of solidarity with each other through common histories of resistance, in particular, resistance to colonization. Jayawardena's (1986) exploration of the impact of colonialism on the women's movements in formerly colonized countries of Asia and Africa is an example of making links through historical analysis. Jayawardena's analysis firstly highlighted commonalities in the nationalist movements in these countries of the late nineteenth and early twentieth century. The movements had in common that they were male dominated and primarily led by the emerging bourgeoisie, but in each country women from all classes were involved in street demonstrations and other forms of political protest. Specificity was also highlighted in Jayawardena's analysis, which showed that women's participation varied systematically depending on, for example, the status of women in each society in pre-colonial times. The analysis highlighted women's ongoing involvement in resistance to colonialism in many different countries, and encouraged a search for that involvement in countries which were not included in the analysis. Another common theme uncovered by Jayawardena was that women were actively excluded from participation in the newly emerging bourgeois administrations in many of these countries, a finding which placed the origins of this exclusion in the newly emerging post-colonial male-dominated administrations rather than in the women's lack of participation or organization. Finally, in many of these countries, and also in Ireland, women's involvement in resistance to colonialism laid the basis for women's organizing in the post-colonial state.

Similarly, the many examples of liberation psychology presented in Chapter 8 highlight commonalities across many different countries with enormous variations in history, economic status, the nature of violence and political regimes and the degrees of isolation and trauma associated with specific local conditions. Each example discussed in Chapter 8 was unique in several respects, and described specific applications of liberation psychology. Yet common themes included the importance of opportunities for people to come together in a safe environment where they could give voice and listen to each other. They also highlighted the enormous variety of political activities that ranged from documenting their experiences and sharing this with other groups, contributing through art and drama and developing platforms, manifestos and strategies for action (Lykes and Moane, 2009; Montero and Sonn, 2009).

Making such links can facilitate the key processes of liberation, namely developing awareness, building strengths, making connections, and taking action. While these processes may be recognized as common processes in the cycle of liberation, the particular practices which facilitate these processes will obviously vary from one situation and from one group to the next. Indeed, not only the recognition of specificity, but also the principle that each individual or group should be agents in their own process of change indicate that liberation involves each individual or group evolving their own practices of liberation. Since culture and community play such a vital role in liberation, and since each group has their own unique and dynamic forms of culture, these practices are likely to be culturally specific, although they may also be inspirational in other contexts.

Recognition of commonalities between oppressions has obviously resulted in many fruitful as well as conflicted coalitions between different groups, as well as giving rise to an enormous number of transnational and global networks. There is obviously a danger of replicating sexism, racism and imperialism as the patterns of domination and subordination identified and described in this book are enacted in these arenas. Personal and interpersonal transformations are therefore necessary for effective action in these spheres, just as they are for more localized contexts.

Visions for liberation

The importance of vision was a central theme in the writings on oppression and liberation reviewed in this book, not only because vision offers goals and hopes for the future, but because it provides a counterbalance to the tendency to adopt dominator patterns when a degree of liberation (or decolonization) has been obtained. This is particularly discussed by Fanon, who identified a Manichean mentality in which the world was seen in oppositional binaries that included the binary of being 'on top' or 'on the bottom'. Fanon warned against the tendency of oppressed groups to adopt dominator or oppressor patterns once they have gained some level of power and/or independence. The emphasis on fluidity and on challenging binaries are examples of efforts to move beyond binaries and to create new consciousness that can in turn create new social forms (Anzeldua, 1999).

Feminist visions for liberation have spanned the personal, the interpersonal and the political, as the writings reviewed in this book have illustrated. These and many other feminist writers have attempted to expand visions of human potential, set out ideals for interpersonal relationships, and develop new models for political organization based on the principles of equality. Among the fundamental principles of equality are that every individual should be valued equally, and be afforded equality of opportunity. Equality is thus antithetical to domination–subordination, as the analysis in Chapter 2 indicated. Domination–subordination is almost inevitably associated with dynamics of superiority–inferiority, as well, of course, as with violence, control and the other patterns discussed in Chapter 2. Elimination or minimalization of domination–subordination is not just a political goal which is linked to justice and equality, it is also essential for the full development of human potential. Domination–subordination, as the analysis of Chapter 3 indicates, is associated with damaging psychological patterns in both those in subordinate positions and those in dominant positions. It fosters qualities such as aggression, fear and competition, and acts as a block to personal and spiritual development, as fear is antithetical to joy and ecstasy. Many feminist visions connect the personal and the political, emphasizing the need for change in the personal as well as the political sphere.

The authors reviewed in Chapters 3 and 4 placed a high value on relational as opposed to individualist aspects of psychological functioning (hooks, 1993; Maracle, 1996; Miller, 1986). Miller and Stiver (1986) in particular argue that there is a need to place a much higher value on the capacities involved in fostering growth and development, which include empathy and nurturance. Maracle (1996) and hooks (1993) placed a high value on personal qualities such as love and compassion. hooks (2002a) writes of the need to recognize and cherish personal qualities which are associated with living under conditions of oppression and working for social change, such as courage, perseverance, tolerance and cooperation. At a more idealistic level, Daly calls for a new way of being which involves connection with nature and development of psychic capacities. She captures this vision in the title of her book *Pure Lust* (Daly, 1984, p. 3):

> Pure Lust names the high humour, hope, and cosmic accord/ harmony of those women who choose to escape, to follow our hearts deepest desire and bound out of the State of Bondage, Wanderlusting and Wonderlusting with the elements, connecting with the auras of animals and plants, moving in planetary communion with the farthest stars. This Lust is in its essence astral. It is pure Passion: unadulterated absolute, simple sheer striving for abundance of being. It is unlimited, unlimiting desire/fire.

Daly (1984; 2005), Starhawk (1979; 2005) and others see connection with nature as essential in such a new consciousness, in contrast to the disconnection or estrangement which is characteristic of patriarchy. Starhawk (2005) argues that if we wish to create new forms of social organization and new relations with nature and the planet, we must also create a new consciousness, which she argues must then be put into action to bring about social change.

At the political level, much feminist writing envisions a society free of violence and exploitation, with freedom of choice in sexuality and culture, and empowering political structures. A framework which offers a way of integrating the personal and political, the local and global, is that of human rights. The human rights framework is one which has gained widespread recognition in groups as diverse as the Hawaiian sovereignty movement and lesbians and gay men although it has been subject to a great deal of criticism, particularly for its reliance on state intervention and on a particular Western and individualistic view of rights. The aim of this discussion is not to advocate the human rights model as a political method, but to present the concept of human rights, as developed by feminists, as a model which can inform political activism. As Reilly (1997, p. 4) writes: 'The idea of universal human rights evokes a vision of justice that has global resonance.'

Feminist approaches to human rights challenge the narrow focus of traditional human rights frameworks for their emphasis on civil and political rights, their concepts of state responsibility, and their reliance on mechanisms of law and government. Their initial aim of broadening the concept of human rights to deal with violence against women expanded into the aim of developing a comprehensive set of rights, which would encompass civil and political rights but also include bodily, cultural and economic rights; they also aimed to extend the application of these rights to all areas of life, including the family and the workplace.

Reilly and others (Reilly, 2007; 2008) have developed a categorization of human rights which articulates with the six modes of control described in Chapter 2. The first category is rights related to 'Bodily integrity and security of person'. These rights include the right to freedom from violence and assault, freedom of movement, and the right to live in safety, and these rights are obviously violated by violence and by the fear and restrictions that accompany violence against women. The right to bodily integrity has also been interpreted by feminists to mean control over reproductive and sexual functioning. Sexual exploitation is therefore also a violation of these rights. The second category involves rights related to 'Democracy, citizenship and participation', which includes not just civil liberties and the right to vote, but also the right to political structures which are empowering. Political exclusion obviously violates these rights. Rights related to 'Economic discrimination and exploitation' (the third category) refer to the right of access to fairly paid work, to education and training, to involvement in decision-making, and also to childcare, and to acknowledgement of the economic value of unpaid work. These rights are obviously violated by the forms of economic exploitation described in Chapter 2. The fourth category of rights is 'Cultural rights, human expression and social exclusion', which are violated by control of culture and by fragmentation. This includes rights involving freedom of expression, access to education and culture, and also education about difference and diversity.

Thus the value of this framework for the present discussion lies in its elucidation of a conceptual model to guide political action which articulates with the analysis of oppression presented in this book. The framework can be adapted for specific concerns and/or by particular groups. Reilly (2008) describes six approaches to human rights that have been used in Irish (and transnational) contexts since the early 1990s. She argues that the human rights framework fosters 'awareness of the need to take account of the global framework in developing analyses and strategies on local–global issues' (p. 227).

Obviously the use of feminist human rights to inform political vision does not necessitate engagement with the formal mechanisms associated with human rights. It has provided a model which has found support among feminists across the globe, facilitating international networking and local activism. It offers a positive framework for political activism, as Butega notes: 'The fundamental difference with working within a human rights framework is the fact that you are starting from a position of entitlement – that you are not begging or calling on someone's benevolence, that you are demanding something that you are entitled to by virtue of being a human being' (1997, p. 14).

Concepts of human rights also integrate the personal and the political, since much of the discourse on human rights justifies them with reference either to concepts of justice or to human potential. For example the UN Universal Declaration of Human Rights (United Nations, 1948) makes frequent reference to 'the inherent dignity of the human person' and 'free development of personality'. Liberation psychology offers the possibility of expanding this concept of the person through its elaboration of the strengths that people demonstrate under conditions of oppression, which have been discussed in detail throughout this book. Such strengths include courage, hope, generosity and pride, along with capacities for support and solidarity. These qualities highlight the positive potential in humans, in contrast to biologically based narratives of 'human nature' which emhasize competition and aggression. The qualities identified in liberation psychology also articulate with emerging research in psychology on flourishing and other strengths, which, despite the individualistic and positivist nature of the analysis, can offer further elaboration of human potential.

Colonialism and changes in Irish society

During the 1990s Ireland was still emerging from a prolonged recession in which unemployment reached a high of 18 per cent, with mass emigration that has been a feature of Irish history for centuries. Debates about colonialism were highly contentious, partly reflecting the continuing conflict on the island regarding the status of Northern Ireland, but also reflecting an ongoing reappraisal of Ireland's colonial history. The social transformations that occurred from the mid 1990s seem to have cleared the way for a more open approach both to our colonial history and to its impact on Irish society today. At the same time global and economic developments, particularly the Bush era in the USA and the global economic downturn, have exposed a world order that is clearly linked to colonialism, continuing global patterns of military domination, economic exploitation and cultural imperialism. The global majority is faced with the possibility of increasing poverty and planetary breakdown even as the wealthy elite regroup and seem intent on business as usual. In this world order, where multinational corporations have enormous influence, it would seem that consumer power, where it exists, can be an important, if not vital, instrument for exercising political power, and can take its place along with the variety of political actions discussed in this book.

As historical studies show, Ireland has always been embedded in global historical developments, and today finds itself faced with its own version of the economic downturn that is occurring globally. The boom of the mid 1990s to 2008, referred to as the Celtic Tiger, was part of the process of globalization that happened worldwide, and seemed to create unprecedented wealth in Ireland, supposedly placing it among the top wealthy countries globally. By the early twenty-first century it was possible to see the impact of neo-liberal economics and the emphasis on economic growth. On the one hand there was very low unemployment, a construction boom and the development of consumer culture and individualism in a way that had not been seen on a large-scale in Ireland. On other other hand there was increasing inequality between rich and poor with many areas of deprivation. Exclusive focus on economic growth was associated with predictable social problems of alienation, fragmentation, high levels of drug and alcohol use and increasing levels of violence, although the a sense of belonging to a community and of community values persisted.

There has been an enormous development of scholarship and research on Irish society over this time period; here I will reference several monographs or collections that make explicit links to colonialism, oppression, liberation and social justice. These include: economic and social critiques of the Celtic Tiger (Allen, 2007; Kirby, Gibbons and Cronin, 2002); studies of racism, immigration and multiculturalism (Fanning, 2009; Lentin and McVeigh, 2002; McVeigh and Rolston, 2009; Zappone, 2003); discussions of modernity and globalization (O'Connell, 2001; Inglis, 2008; Keohane and Kuhling, 2004; Share, Tovey and Corcoran, 2007); analysis of post-colonial patterns in Irish society (Carroll and King, 2003), studies in feminism and gender (Barry, 2008; Gray, 2004; Hayes and Pelan, 2005; MacCurtain, 2008; O'Connor, 2002); and explorations of equality and social justice (Baker et al., 2009; Lynch, Baker and Lyons, 2009).

The global economic downturn of the last two years has obviously had an impact in Ireland, with familiar patterns of a credit crunch related to banking difficulties, collapse of the construction industry, and increasingly widespread unemployment which has already reached over 12 per cent. The downturn in Ireland has exposed an elite of bankers, developers and the political class that created a property bubble and inflationary policies in excess of many comparable countries, leading to the prospect of more than a decade of severe economic recession. This alliance between politics and finance (referred to colloquially as crony capitalism) has been strengthened by a feature of our post-colonial history, namely that the same political party has been in power for over 60 of the 88 years since the Republic of Ireland gained political independence. This is an example of an argument I have made elsewhere, namely that Ireland's post-colonial status may exacerbate some of the more oppressive aspects of globalization, while at the same time the long history of resistance and countercultural activities provides a rich resource for action and transformation (Moane 2002). Here I would like to consider several other features of Irish society that have been shaped by colonial history, in terms of the changes they have undergone and the possibilities they create for a more open and egalitarian society.

Historical developments, namely the 150th anniversary of the famine of 1845–49 (see Chapter 2), prompted a public reappraisal of Ireland's history of colonization both in Ireland and among the Irish diaspora internationally. The famine had not been previously a focus for commemoration, a pattern that itself can be linked to post-colonial patterns in Irish society. At the 150th anniversary there was a strong public commitment to commemoration, with funds available to local, national and international groups and communities. This generated considerable public discussion in Ireland and among the Irish diaspora regarding such issues as the responsibility for the tragedy, the nature and role of forgiveness, the role of commemoration and the processes involved in healing from historical trauma. It seemed that Ireland's long history of mass emigration, which had endured since the famine through the 1980s, looked as if it might end, with the possibility that Ireland might not only welcome but seek immigration into the country.

By the 1990s there had been continuing conflict about partition on the island since 1921, when partition was established in a political agreement with Britain. This was immediately followed by a civil war in the Republic of Ireland which has only been publicly discussed in the last decade. Northern Ireland was established as a separate territory in a union with Britain, and has a been a site of conflict since, culminating in over 30 years of armed conflict. Intensive efforts (the Peace Process) resulted in the negotiation of a new agreement that reshaped political and constitutional relations between the Republic of Ireland, Northern

Ireland and Britain. The agreement also created all-island economic, political and cultural institutions. These, along with existing all island organizations as well as longstanding cultural and political links, have the potential to create new relations on the island.

The 1990s also saw the beginning of the economic boom which, despite its artificial nature, created a decade or more of economic development in many sectors. Growth in sectors such as information technology and the pharmaceutical industry were dominated by multinational corporations, while retail and other areas became consolidated in large conglomerates. The growth of urban areas has resulted in just over a majority of people living in urban areas, with farming and other rural communities now under threat. At the same time, there were considerable increases in funding for community development and education which facilitated the mobilization of communities and movements for social justice, resulting in, for example, the establishment of an Equality Authority and comprehensive equality legislation. The voluntary, community and NGO sector in Ireland, which has longstanding roots in resistance, has thus benefited from over a decade of experience and resourcing which could provide further impetus for progressive change.

An impact of these development was a large increase in immigration, initially linked to greater economic development. Ireland's history of emigration and limited immigration had left a largely white population in place, with a minority ethnic group of Travellers who, by the 1990s, had experienced decades of marginalization and discrimination. Increasing immigration through the 1990s and the expansion of the European Union in 2002 has resulted in a large number of new communities from all over the world, particularly from Eastern Europe but also from Asia, Africa and South America. This development has also exposed levels of racism in Irish society. Attitudes and behaviours have reflected, in part, the experience of Irish people over generations who themselves were a target of racism in the countries to which they emigrated and who in turn became racist themselves. There have also, of course, been many efforts to support and welcome immigrants, particularly linked to the strength of community-based activism in Ireland.

The Catholic Church has held a strong place in Irish society, its dominance linked to the role that religion played in colonization. In the decades following independence the Catholic Church consolidated its power in Irish society, establishing control of health, education and social services, and exercising enormous influence on social policy, particularly related to sexuality and reproductive rights. Its power began

to decline in the 1990s with increasing reports of sexual abuse of children by priests, and also of cover-ups by the Church. In the late 1990s a series of revelations led to a detailed investigation of abuse in industrial schools and other institutions run by Catholic religious congregations involving hundreds of thousands of children. Survivors of abuse in these institutions still await legal, education and health resources, and have endured a decade of efforts to silence them. Following an exhaustive investigation (see p. 31), the Ryan Report (Ryan, 2009) details a regime of abuse that has resulted in ongoing reappraisal of Catholicism, of the alliance of Church and state, and of the capacities of Irish society for collusion and denial, and of spirituality itself which is also creating an openness to new forms of spirituality.

The role of women (see Chapter 2) has also been shaped by colonial patterns that deprived women of independence and led to large numbers of women migrating from rural areas. Post-colonial farming and land patterns (along with the Catholic Church) placed an emphasis on control of women and of women's sexuality and reproductive capacities, a pattern which has continued throughout the twentieth century. One impact of economic development has been the growth of the sex industry and the commodification of sex, with continuing double standards regarding women. Another post-colonial pattern has been the exclusion of women from public life, despite their involvement in struggles for independence, which has been broken somewhat by the election of two women presidents in the Republic of Ireland. A major impact of economic growth has been greater involvement of women in paid employment, albeit much of it part-time, with greater access to economic resources. Along with paid employment has come greater involvement in education, health, community development, art and culture, with ongoing challenging of traditional gender roles. Women have become increasingly involved in community and political activism in many spheres from the local to national and international, and have greater capacity than ever to be agents of social change.

In examining these changes from the perspective of colonialism and liberation psychology, it is also possible to identify psychosocial patterns, that is, patterns which bridge the psychological and the social. Elsewhere I have presented evidence that there are psychosocial vulnerabilities and strengths in Irish society, which have also been identified by many writers, that I have linked to colonialism (Moane, 2002). Psychosocial vulnerabilities include very high alcohol consumption, patterns of denial and doublethink, and ambivalence about law, authority and the environment. Psychosocial strengths include creativity, imagination, solidarity and support. These patterns coexist and can reinforce or undermine each other. Along with other forces, they can contribute to the tendency in Irish society to re-enact dominator patterns of control and exploitation, or they can open up possibilities for new and creative forms of social organization that can move towards a society based on values of equality, vision and social justice. Such a society is surely possible for a very small relatively wealthy country, a society where basic needs are met, where there is equality of opportunity, where diversity and creativity are encouraged, a society which encourages our potential for compassion, cooperation, generosity, support and solidarity.

Conclusion

This book began with the aim of exploring the insight that 'the personal is political', demonstrating both how the political shapes the personal and also how the personal can shape the political. Oppression was analysed by placing individuals and groups in the context of a system of domination that is both unjust and unsustainable; this system has local and global manifestations that impact on day-to-day lives and in many cases create severe psychological suffering. Domination is a key feature of oppression, operating to creative massive local and global inequalities in living conditions and contributing to increasingly pressing global climate and resource problems. This system has reached a crisis point, as indicated by ongoing economic, social and environmental instability. Liberation was conceptualized as building on strengths gained through histories and experiences of resistance and developing transformative actions and visions that would aim to create sustainable egalitarian social organization.

The attainment of egalitarian social organization requires not just the elimination of inequality in social conditions, but also a rejection of patterns of domination and the development of new modes at the personal, interpersonal and political levels. Moving towards an egalitarian society involves the development and implementation of visions, policies and practices at each of these levels. In this book numerous examples of practices based on participative and egalitarian principles were described. A liberation psychology aims to facilitate transformation through participatory practices, rather than through individual and private personal development. It advocates a bottom up view of knowledge and of change. It regards action and engagement as keys to personal and social wellbeing. It takes the view that individual wellbeing is interconnected with collective wellbeing, and aims to facilitate transformation through the exercise of agency at multiple levels of the environment from the personal to the global. An enormous variety of different possibilities for taking action to bring about change were outlined at the individual, group, community and political levels, offering many possibilities for all of us to shape a better future.

References

Agarwal, B. 1988. *Structures of Patriarchy*. New Delhi: Kali for Women.

Aldarondo, E. (ed.), 2007. *Advancing Social Justice in Clinical Practice*. New Jersey: Lawrence Erlbaum Associates.

Allen, J. (ed.), 1990. *Lesbian Philosophies and Cultures*. New York: State University of New York Press.

Allen, K. 2007. *The Corporate Takeover of Ireland*. Dublin: Irish Academic Press.

Allen, P.G. 1986. *The Sacred Hoop: Recovering the Feminine in American Indian Traditions*. Boston, MA: Beacon Press.

Alston, P. and Robinson, M. 2005. *Human Rights and Development: Towards Mutual Reinforcement*. Oxford: Oxford University Press.

Ang-Lygate, M., Corrin, C. and Henry, M. (eds), 1996. *Desperately Seeking Sisterhood: Still Challenging and Building*. London: Taylor & Francis.

Ani, M. 1994. *Yurugu: An African-Centered Critique of European Cultural Thought and Behaviour*. Trenton, NJ: Africa World Press.

Anzeldua, G. 1999. *Borderlands/La Frontera*. San Francisco, CA: Aunt Lute Publishers. First published 1987.

Apfelbaum, E. 1979. 'Relations of Domination and Movements for Liberation: An Analysis of Power between Groups'. In W.G. Austin and S. Worchel (eds), *The Social Psychology of Intergroup Relations*. Belmont: Brooks Cole.

Apfelbaum, E. 1999. 'Twenty Years Later'. *Feminism and Psychology*, 9, 267–72.

Ashcroft, B., Griffiths, G. and Tiffin, H. 1989. *The Empire Writes Back: Theory and Practice in Post-Colonial Literatures*. London: Routledge.

Ashcroft, B., Griffith, G. and Tiffin, H. (eds). 2006. *The Post-Colonial Studies Reader*. Second Edition. London: Routledge.

Baker, J. 1987. *Arguing for Equality*. London: Verso.

Baker, J., Lynch K., Cantillon S. and Walsh J. 2009. Second Edition. *Equality: From Theory to Action*. Basingstoke: Palgrave Macmillan.

Barry, K. 1979. *Female Sexual Slavery*. New York: New York University Press.

Barry, K. 1995. *The Prostitution of Sexuality*. New York: New York University Press.

Barry, U. 1992. 'Movement, Change and Reaction: The Struggle over Reproductive Rights in Ireland'. In A. Smyth (ed.), *The Abortion Papers*: Ireland. Dublin: Attic Press.

Barry, U. 1996. Trends and Prospects for Women's Employment in Ireland in the 1990's. UMIST Working Papers, University of Manchester.

Barry, U. (ed.), 2008. *Where are We Now?: New Feminist Perspectives on Women in Contemporary Ireland*. Dublin: New Island.

Bartky, S.L. 1990. *Femininity and Domination: Studies in the Phenomenology of Oppression*. London: Routledge.

Bass, E. and Davis, L. 2008. *The Courage to Heal*. New York: Harper & Row.

Basu, A. (ed.), 1995. *The Challenge of Local Feminisms: Women's Movements in Global Perspective*. Boulder, CO: Westview Press.

Bates, T., Illback, R. J., Scanlan, F. and Carroll, L. 2009. *Somewhere To Turn To, Someone To Talk To.* Headstrong – The National Centre for Youth Mental Health. Dublin: Headstrong.

Beale, J. 1986. *Women in Ireland: Voices of Change.* London: Macmillan.

Bean, K. 2007. *Post-Backlash Feminism: Women and the Media since Reagan–Bush.* North Carolina: McFarland & Company, Inc.

Beasley, M. 1994. 'Maltreatment of Maids in Kuwait'. In M. Davies (ed.), *Women and Violence: Issues and Responses Worldwide.* London: Zed Books.

Belenkey, M.F., Clinchy, B.M., Goldberger, N.R. and Tarule, J. 1986. *Women's Ways of Knowing: The Development of Self, Voice, and Mind.* New York: Basic Books.

Bell, D. and Klein, R. (eds), 1996. *Radically Speaking: Feminism Reclaimed.* London: Zed Books.

Bem, S. 1993. *The Lenses of Gender: Transforming the Debate on Sexual Inequality.* New Haven, CT: Yale University Press.

Beneria, L. 2003. *Gender, Development, and Globalization: Economics as if all People Mattered.* New York; London: Routledge.

Benjamin, J. 1988. *The Bonds of Love: Psychoanalysis, Feminism, and the Problem of Domination.* New York: Pantheon.

Benson, C. 1994. 'A Psychological Perspective on Art and Irish National Identity'. *Irish Journal of Psychology,* 15(2,3), 316–30.

Bergalli, R. and Sumner, C. (eds), 1997. *Social Control and Political Order: European Perspectives at the End of the Century.* London: Sage.

Bernard, J. 1981. *The Female World.* New York: Free Press.

Beteille, A. 1983. *The Idea of Natural Inequality and Other Essays.* Oxford: Oxford University Press.

Bhavnani, K.K. (2007). 'Interconnections and Configurations, Towards a Feminist Ethnography'. In S. Hesse-Biber (ed.), *Handbook of Feminist Research: Theory and Praxis.* Thousand Oaks, CA: Sage Publications.

Bhavnani, K. and Phoenix, A. 1994. 'Shifting Identities Shifting Racisms: An Introduction'. *Feminism and Psychology* 4(1), 5–18.

Biko, S. 1986. *I Write what I Like.* San Francisco: Harper & Row.

Billies, M., Johnson, J., Murungi, K. and Pugh, R. 2009. 'Naming Our Reality: Low Income LGBT People Documenting Violence, Discrimination and Assertions of Justice'. *Feminism and Psychology,* 19(3), 375–80.

Black, D. (ed.), 1984. 'Social Control as a Dependent Variable'. In D. Black (ed.), *Toward a General Theory of Social Control.* Vol. 1. London: Academic Press.

Blackwell, J., O'Shea, E., Moane, G. and Murray, P. 1992. *Care Provision and Cost Measurement: Dependent Elderly People at Home and in Geriatric Hospitals.* Dublin: Economic and Social Research Institute.

Blickle, P. 1997. *Resistance, Representation and Community.* Oxford: Clarendon Press.

Boahen, A.A. 1987. *African Perspectives on Colonialism.* London: Johns Hopkins University Press.

Boal, A. 1993. *Theatre of the Oppressed.* London: Pluto Press.

Bohan, J.S. (ed.), 1992. *Seldom Seen, Rarely Heard: Women's Place in Psychology.* Boulder, CO: Westview Press.

Boland, E. 1989. *A Kind of Scar: The Woman Poet in a National Tradition.* Dublin: Attic Press.

Boland, E. 1995. *Object Lessons: The Life of the Woman Poet in our Time*. Manchester: Carcanet.

Boland, E. 2007. *Irish Writers on Writing*. Texas: Trinity University Press.

Boston Women's Health Collective. 2005. *The New 'Our Bodies Our Selves'*. New York: Simon & Schuster. (First Published 1969.)

Bourke, A. 1995. 'Reading a Woman's Death: Colonial Text and Oral Tradition in Nineteenth-Century Ireland'. *Feminist Studies*, 21(3), 553–86.

Brabeck, K. 2003. 'Testimonio: A Strategy for Collective Resistance, Cultural Survival and Building Solidarity'. *Feminism and Psychology*, 13(2), 252–8.

Brabeck, M.M. 2000. *Practicing Feminist Ethics in Psychology*. Washington, D.C.: American Psychological Society.

Bradley, C. 1994. 'Why Male Violence against Women is a Development Issue: Reflections from Papua New Guinea'. In M. Davies (ed.), *Women and Violence, Issues and Responses Worldwide*. London: Zed Books.

Brannen, J. and Wilson, G. (eds), 1987. *Give and Take in Families: Studies in Resource Allocation*. London: Allen & Unwin.

Brodribb, S. 1992. *Nothing Mat(t)ers: A Feminist Critique of Post-Modernism*. New York: New York University Press.

Bronfenbrenner, U. 1979. *The Ecology of Human Development*. Cambridge, MA: Harvard University Press.

Bronfenbrenner, U. (ed.), 2004. *Making Human Beings Human: Bioecological Perspectives on Human Development*. California: Sage Publications.

Brown, L. 1992. 'While Waiting for the Revolution: The Case for a Lesbian Feminist Psychotherapy'. *Feminism and Psychology*, 2(2), 239–53.

Brown, L. and Burman, E. 1997. Editors' introduction: 'The Delayed Memory Debate: Why Feminist Voices Matter'. Special Issue, 'Feminist Responses to the "False Memory" Debate'. *Feminism and Psychology*, 7, 7–17.

Brown, L.M. and Gilligan, C. 1992. *Meeting at the Crossroads: Women's Psychology and Girls' Development*. Cambridge, MA: Harvard University Press.

Brownmiller, S. 1975. *Against our Will*. New York: Simon & Schuster.

Buikema, R. and Smelik, A. (eds), 1995. *Women's Studies and Culture: A Feminist Introduction*. London: Zed Books.

Bulhan, H.A. 1985. *Frantz Fanon and the Psychology of Oppression*. New York: Plenum Press.

Bunch, C. 1990. 'Women's Rights as Human Rights: Towards a Re-vision of Human Rights'. *Human Rights Quarterly*, 12, 486–98.

Bunch, C. and Reilly, N. 1994. *Demanding Accountability: The Global Campaign and Vienna Tribunal for Women's Human Rights*. New York: UNIFEM.

Burman, E. (ed.), 1990. *Feminists and Psychological Practice*. London: Sage.

Burman, E. 2008. *Deconstructing Developmental Psychology*. Second Edition. East Sussex: Routledge.

Burman, E., Alldred, P., Bewley, C., Goldberg, B., Heenan, C., Marks, D., Marshall, J., Taylor, K., Ullah, R. and Warner, S. 1996. *Challenging Women: Psychology's Exclusion, Feminist Possibilities*. Buckingham: Open University Press.

Burstow, B. 1992. *Radical Feminist Therapy: Working in the Context of Violence*. Newbury, CA: Sage.

Burton, M. and Kagan, C. 2005. 'Liberation Social Psychology: Learning from Latin America'. *Journal of Community and Applied Social Psychology*, 15, 63–78.

Burton, M. and Kagan, C. 2009. 'Towards a Really Social Psychology: The Legacy of Racism and the Pursuit of Representative Knowledge Production'. In M. Montero and C.C. Sonn (eds), *Psychology of Liberation: Theory and Applications*. New York: Springer.

Butega, F. 1997. 'Women Taking Action to Advance their Human Rights: The Case of Africa'. In N. Reilly (ed.), *Women's Rights as Human Rights: Local and Global Perspectives*. Dublin: Irish Council for Civil Liberties.

Butler, S. and Wintram, C. 1991. *Feminist Groupwork*. London: Sage.

Buzawa, E.S. and Buzawa, C.G. 1996. *Domestic Violence: The Criminal Justice Response*. London: Sage.

Byrne, N. 1996. 'The Uneasy Relationship Between Feminism and Community'. In A. Smyth (ed.), *Feminism, Politics, Community*. University College Dublin: Women's Education Research and Resource Centre.

Byrne, N. and McCarthy, I.C. 1995. 'Abuse, Risk and Protection: A Fifth Province Approach to an Adolescent Sexual Offence'. In C. Buck and B. Speed (eds), *Gender, Power and Relationships*. London: Routledge.

Bystsydziensky, J. (ed.), 1992. *Women Transforming Politics: Worldwide Strategies for Empowerment*. Bloomington: Indiana University Press.

Caherty, T., Storey, A., Gavin, M., Molloy, M. and Ruane, C. (eds), 1992. *Is Ireland a Third World Country?* Belfast: Beyond the Pale Publications.

Cairns, E., Hewstone, M., Niens, U. and Tam, T. 2005. 'Intergroup Forgiveness and Intergroup Conflict: Northern Ireland, A Case Study'. In E.L. Worthington (ed.), *Handbook of Forgiveness*. New York: Brunner-Routledge, pp. 461–76.

Cairns, D. and Richards, S. 1988. *Writing Ireland: Colonialism, Nationalism, and Culture*. Manchester: Manchester University Press.

Cameron, J. 1995. *The Artist's Way: A Course in Discovering and Recovering your Creative Self*. London: Pan Books.

Cantillon, S., Corrigan, C., Kirby, P. and O'Flynn, J. 2001. *Rich and Poor: Perspectives on Tackling Inequality in Ireland*. Dublin: Oak Tree Press in association with Combat Poverty Agency.

Cantillon, S., Gannon, B. and Nolan, B. (eds), 2004. *Sharing Household Resources: Learning from Non-monetary Indicators*. Dublin: Institute of Public Administration/ Combat Poverty Agency.

Cantillon, S. 2005. 'Equality in Economic and other Dimensions'. In J.O. Hagan and C. Newman (eds), *Economy of Ireland*, Ninth Edition. Gill and Macmillan.

Capdevila, R. and Unger, R. 2006. 'Editors' Introduction: Feminism without Borders: Exploring the Relationships between Feminist and Political Psychology'. *Feminism and Psychology*, 16(1), 5–12.

Carolissen, R. and Swartz, L. 2009. 'Removing the Splinters from our own Eyes: A Commentary on Identities and Power in South African Community Psychology'. *Feminism and Psychology*, 19(3), 407–13.

Carroll, T. (2010). *A Model for using Arts in Community Development Based on Liberation Psychology and IPA: The Example of Anti-racism*. University College Dublin: PhD Thesis.

Carroll, C. and King, P. (eds), 2003. *Ireland and Post-Colonial Theory*. Cork: Cork University Press.

Casey, M. 2007. On Bloods: Of Womb and Tomb, Blood Mysteries and Blood Sacrifice. Conference Paper, Centre for Gender and Women Studies and Institute of Feminism and Religion, Trinity College Dublin.

Chauca-Sabroso, R.L. and Fuentas-Polar, S. 2009. 'Development of Historical Memory as a Psychosocial Recovery Process'. In M. Montero, and C.C. Sonn, (eds), *Psychology of Liberation: Theory and Applications*. New York: Springer.

Chaudry, L. and Bertram, C. 2009. 'Narrating Trauma and Reconstruction in Post-Conflict Karachi: Feminist Liberation Psychology and the Contours of Agency in the Margins'. *Feminism and Psychology*, 19(3), 298–312.

Chesler, P. 1972. *Women and Madness*. New York: Doubleday.

Chesler, P. 1986. *Mothers on Trial*. Seattle, WA: Seal Press.

Chesler, P. 2006. *Women and Madness*. Revised updated edition. London: Palgrave Macmillan.

Chinweizu, A. 1987. *Decolonizing the African Mind*. Lagos, Nigeria: SUNDOOR.

Chodorow, N. 1978. *The Reproduction of Mothering*. Berkeley: University of California Press.

Chodorow, N. 1994. *Femininities, Masculinities, Sexualities: Freud and Beyond*. Lexington, KY: University Press of Kentucky.

Christie, D.J., Wagner, R.V. and Winter, D.D. (eds), 2001. *Peace, Conflict and Violence, Peace Psychololgy for the 21st Century*. New Jersey: Prentice Hall.

Claffey, U. 1993. *The Women Who Won*. Dublin: Attic Press.

Clarke, V. and Peel. E. 2007. *Out in Psychology: Lesbian, Gay, Bisexual, Trans and Queer Perspectives*. Oxford: John Wiley and Sons.

Cleary, J. and Connolly, C. (eds), 2005. *The Cambridge Companion to Modern Irish Culture*. Cambridge: Cambridge University Press.

Clough, P.T. 1994. *Feminist Thought: Desire, Power and Academic Discourse*. Oxford: Blackwell.

Cockburn, C. and Mulholland, M. 2000. 'Analytical Action, Committed Research: What Does a Feminist Action Research Partnership Mean in Practice?' In A. Byrne and R. Lentin (eds), *Researching Women: Feminist Research Methodologies in the Social Sciences in Ireland*. Dublin: Institute for Public Administration.

Cole, E. and Henderson Daniel, J. (eds), 2005. *Featuring Females: Feminist Analyses of Media*. Washington, DC: American Psychological Association.

Collins, L.H., Dunlap, M.R. and Chrisler, J.C. (eds), 2002. *Charting a New Course for Feminist Psychology*. Westport, CT: Greenwood Publishing Group, Inc.

Collins, P. 1990. *Black Feminist Thought*. London: Unwin Hyman.

Comas-Díaz, L., Lykes, M.B. and Alarcon, R.D. 1998. 'Ethnic Conflict and the Psychology of Liberation in Guatemala, Peru, and Puerto Rico'. *American Psychologist*, 53(7), 778–91.

Condren, M. 1989. *The Serpent and the Goddess: Women and the Church in Celtic Ireland*. San Francisco: Harper SanFrancisco.

Condren, M. 2002. *The Serpent and the Goddess: Women, Religion, and Power in Celtic Ireland*. Dublin: New Island.

Connolly, B. 1997. 'Women in Community Education and Development– Liberation or Domestication?' In A. Byrne and M. Leonard (eds), *Women and Irish Society: A Sociological Reader*. Belfast: Beyond the Pale Publications.

Connolly, L. 1996. 'The Women's Movement in Ireland 1970–1995: A Social Movement's Analysis'. *Irish Journal of Feminist Studies*, 1(1), 43–77.

Connolly, L. 2002. *The Irish Women's Movement: From Revolution to Devolution*. Dublin: The Lilliput Press.

Connolly, L. and O'Toole, T. 2005. *Documenting Irish Feminisms: The Second Wave*. Dublin: The Woodfield Press.

Cook, R.J. 1995. 'International Human Rights and Women's Reproductive Health'. In J. Peters and A. Wolper (eds), *Women's Rights, Human Rights*. London: Routledge.

Corcoran, M. and Devlin, M. (eds.) (2007). 'Special Issue: Communities'. *Irish Journal of Sociology*, 16(2).

Costigan, L. 2004. Social Awareness in Counselling: A Critique of Mainstream Counselling from a Feminist Counselling, Cross-cultural Counselling, and Liberation Psychology Perspective. United States: Iuniverse.com.

Coulter, C. 1993. *The Hidden Tradition: Feminism, Women, and Nationalism*. Cork: Cork University Press.

Crawford, M. and Unger, R. 2004. *Women and Gender: A Feminist Perspective*. Fourth Edition. New York: McGraw Hill.

Crawley, M. 1996. 'The Reality of Women's Studies in Community-Based Education'. In A. Smyth (ed.), *Feminism, Politics, Community*. University College Dublin: Women's Education Research and Resource Centre.

Crone, J. 1988. 'A History of Lesbian Feminism in Ireland'. *Women's Studies International Forum*, 11, 112–19.

Crone, J. 2004. *Drama, Action, Politics: Dramatic Action Methods for Social Change in the Work of Boal ad Moreno*. Unpublished Masters Thesis. Equality Studies Centre, University College Dublin.

Crosby, A. 2009. 'Anatomy of a Workshop: Women's Struggles for Transformative Participation in Latin America'. *Feminism and Psychology*, 19(3), 343–53.

Cullen, B. 1994. *A Programme in the Making: A Review of the Community Development Programme*. Dublin: Combat Poverty Agency.

Cullen, M. and Luddy, M. 1995. *Women, Power and Consciousness in 19th Century Ireland*. Dublin: Attic Press.

Curtin, C. and Varley, T. 1995. 'Community Action and the State'. In P. Clancy, S. Drudy, K. Lynch and L. O'Dowd (eds), *Irish Society: Sociological Perspectives*. Dublin: Institute of Public Administration.

Curtis, L. 1994. *The Cause of Ireland: From the United Irishmen to Partition*. Belfast: Beyond the Pale Publications.

Curtis, L. 1996. *Nothing but the Same Old Story: Studies in Anti-Irish Racism*. Belfast: Sasta.

Cutts, M. 1996. *The Plain English Guide*. Oxford: Oxford University Press.

Daly, M. 1968. *The Church and the Second Sex*. New York: Harper & Row.

Daly, M. 1973. *Beyond God the Father: Towards a Philosophy of Women's Liberation*. Boston, MA: Beacon Press.

Daly, M. 1978. *Gyn/Ecology: The Metaethics of Radical Feminism*. Boston, MA: Beacon Press.

Daly, M. 1984. *Pure Lust: Elemental Feminist Philosophy*. Boston, MA: Beacon Press.

Daly, M. 1985. 'Original Reintroduction'. In *Beyond God the Father: Toward a Philosophy of Women's Liberation*. With an Original Reintroduction by the Author. Boston, MA: Beacon Press.

Daly, M. 1993. *Outercourse: The Be-Dazzling Voyage*. San Francisco: Harper San Francisco.

Daly, M. 2005. *Amazon Grace: Re-Calling the Courage to Sin Big*. New York: Palgrave Macmillan.

D'Augelli, A.R. 2003. 'Coming Out in Community Psychology: Personal Narrative and Disciplinary Change'. *American Journal of Community Psychology*, 31(3/4), 343–54.

D'Augelli, A.R. and Patterson, C.J. (eds), 1995. *Lesbian, Gay, and Bisexual Identities over the Lifespan*. New York: Oxford University Press.

Davies, M. (ed.), 1983. *Third World, Second Sex*. London: Zed Books.

Davies, M. (ed.), 1994. *Women and Violence*. London: Zed Books.

Dawes, A. 2001. 'Psychololgy for Liberation: Views from Elsewhere'. In K.J. Christsie, R.V. Wagner and D.D. Winter (eds), *Peace, Conflict and Violence, Peace Psychology for the 21st Century*. NJ: Prentice Hall, pp. 295–306.

de Beauvoir, S. 1961. *The Second Sex*. New York: Bantam. (Original French edition, 1949.)

Delphy, C. and Leonard, D. 1992. *Familiar Exploitation*. London: Polity Press.

Denmark, F. and Paludi, M. (eds) 2007. *Psychology of Women: A Handbook of Issues and Theories*. New York: Praeger.

deOliveira, J.M., Neves, S., Nogueira, C. and De Koning, M. 2009. 'Present but Un-Named: Feminist Liberation Psychology in Portugal'. *Feminism and Psychology*, 19(3), 394–406.

Deutsch, M. 2006. 'A Framework for Thinking about Oppression and its Change'. *Social Justice Research*, 19(1), 7–41.

Diamond, L.M. 2008. *Sexual Fluidity, Understanding Women's Love and Desire*. Harvard: Harvard University Press.

Dillon, B. and Collins, E. 2004. *Mental Health: Lesbians and Gay Men; Developing Strategies to Counter the Impact of Social Exclusion and Stigmatization*. Dublin: GLEN.

Dimsdale, J.E. (ed.), 1980. *Survivors, Victims and Perpetrators: Essays on the Nazi Holocaust*. New York: Hemisphere.

Dirks, N.B. (ed.), 1992. *Colonialism and Culture*. Anne Arbor: University of Michigan Press.

Dobash, R.E. and Dobash, R.P. 1992. *Women, Violence and Social Change*. London: Routledge.

Dominelli, L. 1991. *Women Across Continents: Feminist Comparative Social Policy*. London: Harvester Wheatsheaf.

Donaldson, L.E. 1992. *Decolonizing Feminisms: Race, Gender and Empire Building*. London: Routledge.

Doras Buí. 2007. *Annual Report*. Coolock, Dublin.

Dorf, J. and Perez, G.C. 1995. 'Discrimination and the Tolerance of Difference: International Lesbian Human Rights'. In J. Peters and A. Wolper (eds), *Women's Rights, Human Rights*. London: Routledge.

Dorkenoo, E. and Elworthy, S. 1994. 'Female Genital Mutilation'. In M. Davies (ed.), *Women and Violence*. London: Zed Books.

Douglas, C.A. 1990. *Love and Politics: Radical Feminist and Lesbian Theories*. San Francisco: Ism Press.

Doyle, R. and Owens, M. 2003. *Organising for Change: A Handbook for Women Participating in Local, Social Partnership*. Galway Community Worker's Cooperative.

Drakulic, S. 1994. 'The Rape of Women in Bosnia'. In M. Davies (ed.), *Women and Violence*. London: Zed Books.

Du Bois, W.E.B. 1963. *An ABC of Color: Selections from Over a Half Century of the Writings of W. E. B. Du Bois*. New York: Penguin.

Duncan, N. and Bowman, B. 2009. 'Liberating South African Psychology: The Legacy of Racism and the Pursuit of Representative Knowledge Production'. In M. Montero and C.C. Sonn (eds), *Psychology of Liberation: Theory and Applications*. New York: Springer.

Dunne, E. 2006. *The Views of Adult Users of the Public Sector Mental Health Services: Report of a Survey for the Mental Health Commission*. Dublin: Mental Health Commission.

Duran, E. and Duran, B. 1995. *Native American Postcolonial Psychology*. New York: State University Press.

Dworkin, A. 1981. *Pornography: Men Possessing Women*. London: Women's Press.

Ehrenberg, M.R. 1989. *Women in Prehistory*. London: British Museum Publications.

Eisenstein, Z. (ed.), 1979. *Capitalist Patriarchy*. New York: Monthly Review Press.

Eisler, R. 1987. *The Chalice and the Blade: Our History, Our Future*. San Francisco: Harper & Row.

Eisler, R. 1995. *Sacred Pleasure: Sex, Myth and the Politics of the Body*. San Francisco: Harper SanFrancisco.

Emberley. J.V. 1993. *Thresholds of Difference*. Toronto: University of Toronto Press.

Enloe, C. 1989. *Bananas, Beaches and Bases: Making Feminist Sense of International Politics*. Berkeley: University of California Press.

Enloe, C. 2004. *The Curious Feminist: Searching for Women in a New Age of Empire*. London: University of California Press.

Enloe, C. 2007. *Globalization and Militarism: Feminists Make the Link*. Plymouth: Rowman & Littlefield.

Ernst, S. and Goodison, L. 1981. *In our Own Hands: A Book of Self-Help Therapy*. London: Women's Press.

Faderman, L. 1981. *Surpassing the Love of Men: Romantic Friendship between Women from the Renaissance to the Present*. London: Junction Books.

Fadiman, J. and Frager, R. 2005. *Personality and Personal Growth*. NY: Harper & Collins.

Fagan, B. M. 1995. *People of the Earth: An Introduction to World Prehistory*. New York: Harper Collins.

Fahey, T., Russell, H. and Whelan, C.T. (eds), 2007. *Best of Times? The Social Impact of the Celtic Tiger*. Dublin: Institute of Public Administration.

Fahy, B. 1999. *Freedom of Angels – Surviving Goldenbridge*. Dublin: O'Brien Press.

Fals Borda, O. (ed.) 1986. *The Challenge of Social Change*. London: Sage Publications.

Faludi, S. 1992. *Backlash: The Undeclared War against Women*. London: Chatto & Windus.

Fanning, B. 2002. *Racism and Social Change in the Republic of Ireland*. Manchester: Manchester University Press.

Fanning, B. 2009. *New Guests of the Irish Nation*. Dublin: Irish Academic Press.

Fanon, F. 1967a. *Black Skin, White Masks*. New York: Grove Press. (Original French edition, 1952.)

Fanon, F. 1967b. *The Wretched of the Earth*. London: Penguin. (Original French edition, 1961.)

Ferree, M.M. and Hess, B.B. 1985. *Controversy and Coalition: The New Feminist Movement*. Boston, MA: Twayne Publishers.

Ferriter, D. 2005. *The Transformation of Ireland 1900–2000*. London: Profile Books.

Ferro, M. 1997. *Colonization: A Global History*. London: Routledge.

Fetherston, B. and Kelly, R. 2007. 'Conflict Resolution and Transformative Pedagogy: A Grounded Theory Research Project on Learning in Higher Education'. *Journal of Transformative Education*, 5, 262–85.

Fine, M. 1992. *Disruptive Voices: The Possibilities of Feminist Research*. Anne Arbor, MI: The University of Michigan Press.

Fine, M. 2006. 'Bearing Witness: Methods for Researching Oppression and Resistance–A Textbook for Critical Research'. *Social Justice Research*, 19(1), 83–108.

Fine, M. and Burns, A. 2003. 'Class Notes: Toward a Critical Psychology of Class and Schooling'. *Journal of Social Issues*, 59(4), 841–60.

Fine, M., Weis, L., Powell Pruitt, L. and Burns, A. (eds), 2004. *Off White: Readings on Race, Privilege and Resistance*. NY: Routledge.

Finkel, N.J. and Moghaddam, F.M. (eds), 2005. *The Psychology of Rights and Duties: Empirical Contributions and Normative Commentaries*. Washington, DC: American Psychological Association.

Fonow, M. and Cook, J. 1991. *Beyond Methodology*. Bloomington, IN: University of Indiana Press.

Ford-Smith, H. 1994. 'No! to Sexual Violence in Jamaica'. In M. Davies (ed.), *Women and Violence*. London: Zed Books.

Fox, D.R. and Prilleltensky, I. (eds), 1997. *Critical Psychology, an Introduction*. London, Sage.

Fox, D., Prilleltensky, I. and Austin, S. (eds), 2009. *Critical Psychology: An Introduction*. Second Edition. London: Sage.

Fox-Genovese, E. 1994. 'Difference, Diversity and Divisions in an Agenda for the Women's Movement'. In G. Young and B. Dickerson (eds), *Color, Class and Country*. London: Zed Books.

Frankenberg, R. 1993. *White Women, Race Matters: The Social Construction of Whiteness*. London: Routledge.

Freeman, J. 1975. *The Politics of Women's Liberation*. New York: David McKaly and Company.

Freeman, M.A. 1995. 'The Human Rights of Women in the Family: Issues and Recommendations for Implementation of the Women's Convention'. In J. Peters and A. Wolper (eds), *Women's Rights, Human Rights*. London: Routledge.

Freire, P. 1970. *Pedagogy of the Oppressed*. London: Penguin Books.

Freire, P. 1993. *Pedagogy of the Oppressed*. Second Edition. New York: Continuum. (Original Spanish edition, 1970.)

French, M. 1985. *Beyond Power: On Women, Men, and Morals*. New York: Ballantine Books.

Frye, M. 1983. *The Politics of Reality*. New York: Crossing Press.

Gadon, E.W. 1989. *The Once and Future Goddess*. San Francisco, CA: Harper SanFrancisco.

Gardiner, F. 1993. 'Political Interest and Participation of Irish Women 1922–1992: The Unfinished Revolution'. In A. Smyth (ed.), *Irish Women's Studies Reader*. Dublin: Attic Press.

Garner, S. 2004. *Racism in the Irish Experience*. London: Pluto Press.

Gergen, M.M. 2001. *Feminist Reconstructions in Psychology: Narrative, Gender, and Performance*. California: Sage Publications.

Giddens, A. 2006. *Sociology*. Fifth Edition. Oxford: Polity Press.

Gilbert, S. and Gubar, S. 1979. *The Madwoman in the Attic: The Woman Writer and the Nineteenth Century Imagination*. New Haven, CT: Yale University Press.

Gilligan, A.L. and Zappone, K. 2008. *Our Lives Out Loud: In Pursuit of Justice and Equality*. Dublin: O'Brien Press.

Gilligan, C. 1982. *In a Different Voice*. Cambridge, MA: Harvard University Press.

Gilligan, C. 1994. 'Afterword: the Power to Name'. *Feminism and Psychology*, 4(3), 420–5.

Gimbutas, M. 1989. *The Language of the Goddess*. London: Thames and Hudson.

Gimbutas, M. 1991. *The Civilization of the Goddess: The World of Old Europe*. San Francisco, CA: Harper SanFrancisco.

Gimbutas, M. 1999. *The Living Goddesses*. Edited and supplemented by M.R. Dexter. Los Angeles: University California Press.

Giroux, H.A. (ed.), 1989. *Critical Pedagogy, The State and Cultural Struggle*. Albany: State University of New York Press.

Glanville, G. 2008. 'Clondalkin Women's Manifesto: A Study of Women's Community Activism'. M.A. Thesis. Masters in Women's Studies, University College Dublin.

Goodchilds, J. (ed.), 1991. *Psychological Perspectives on Human Diversity in America: Master Lectures*. Washington, DC: American Psychological Society.

Goodman, L.A., Liang, B., Helms, J., Latta, R., Sparks, E. and Weintraub, S. 2004. 'Training Counseling Psychologists as Social Justice Agents: Feminist and Multicultural Principles in Action'. *The Counseling Psychologist*, 32, 793–837.

Goonatilake, S. 1982. *Crippled Minds: An Exploration into Colonial Cultures*. New Delhi: Vikas Publishing House.

Gordon, M. and Riger, C. 1989. *The Female Fear*. Urbana: University of Illinois Press.

Gray, B. 2004. *Women and the Irish Diaspora*. London: Routledge.

Greene, B. and Herek, G.M. (eds), 1994. *Lesbian and Gay Psychology, Theory, Research and Clinical Applications*. London: Sage.

Greene, B. and Croom, G.L. (eds), 2000. *Education, Research and Practice in Lesbian, Gay, Bisexual and Transgendered Psychology: A Resource Manual*. Thousand Oaks, CA: Sage.

Greene, S. 2003. *The Psychological Development of Girls and Women: Rethinking Change in Time*. London, New York, Routledge.

Greenspan, M. 1983. *A New Approach to Women and Therapy*. New York: McGraw-Hill.

Guilfoyle, M. 2009. 'Therapeutic Discourse and Eating Disorders in the Context of Power. In H. Malson and M. Burns (eds), *Critical Feminist Approaches to Eating Disorders: An International Reader*. London: Psychology Press, pp. 196–206.

Haaken, J. and Reavey, P. (eds), 2009. *Memory Matters: Contexts for Understanding Sexual Abuse Recollections*. London: Routledge.

Hamilton, S., Whitehouse, R.D. and Wright, K.I. (eds), 2006. *Archaeology and Women: Ancient and Modern Issues*. London: Left Coat Press.

Hanisch, C. 1971. 'The Personal is Political'. In J. Aget (ed.), *The Radical Therapist*. New York: Ballantine.

Harding, S. 1986. *The Science Question in Feminism*. Ithaca, NY: Cornell University Press.

Harlow, B. 1987. *Resistance Literature*. London: Methuen.

Harper, G.W. and Schneider, M. 2003. 'Oppression and Discrimination among Lesbian, Gay, Bisexual, and Transgendered People and Communities: A Challenge for Community Psychology'. *American Journal of Community Psychology*, 31(1/2), 243–52.

Hart, M. 1990. 'Liberation through Consciousness-Raising'. In J. Mezirow (ed.), *Fostering Critical Reflection in Adulthood*. Oxford: Jossey Bass.

Hasford, W.S. and Kozol, W. (eds), 2005. *Just Advocacy? Women's Human Rights, Transnational Feminisms, and the Politics of Representation*. New Brunswick, NJ: Rutgers University Press.

Hayes, A. and Pelan, R. (eds), 2005. *Women Emerging: A Decade of Irish Feminist Scholarship*. Galway: Women's Studies Centre.

Haynes, A., Devereux, E. and Breen, M. 2006. 'Fear, Framing and Foreigners'. *International Journal of Critical Psychology*, Spring, Special Edition on 'White Fear'.

Healy, G. 1995. *Women and Enterprise Network: An Evaluation Report*. Dublin: Parents Alone Resource Centre in co-operation with the Northside Partnership.

Hennessy, E. and Heary, C. 2005. 'Exploring Children's Views through Focus Groups'. In S. Greene and D. Hogan (eds), *Researching Children's Experience*. London: Sage.

Henwood, K., Griffin, C. and Phoenix, A. (eds), 1998. *Standpoints and Differences: Essays in the Practice of Feminist Psychology*. London: Sage.

Herman, J.L. 1981. *Father–Daughter Incest*. Cambridge, MA: Harvard University Press.

Herman, J.L. 1997. *Trauma and Recovery*. New York: Basic Books.

Hermans, H.J. and Dimaggio, G. 2007. Self, Identity, and Globalization in Times of Uncertainty: A Dialogical Analysis'. *Review of General Psychology*, 11, 31–61.

Hernández, E. 2009. 'New Challenges for the Psychology of Liberation: Building Frameworks for Social Coexistence'. In M. Montero, and C.C. Sonn (eds), *Psychology of Liberation: Theory and Applications*. New York: Springer.

Hesse-Biber, S. (ed.), 2007. *Handbook of Feminist Research: Theory and Praxis*. Thousand Oaks, CA: Sage, pp. 297–326.

Hoagland, S. 1988. *Lesbian Ethics*. Palo Alto, CA: Institute of Lesbian Studies.

Hochschild, A.R. 1983. *The Managed Heart: The Commercialization of Human Feelings*. Berkeley: University of California Press.

Hodgkenson, H.L. 1990. *The Demographics of American Indians: One Percent of the People; Fifty Percent of the Diversity*. Washington, DC: Institute for Educational Leadership, Center for Demographic Policy.

Hollway, W. 1989. *Subjectivity and Method in Psychology: Gender, Meaning and Science*. London: Sage.

hooks, b. 1984. *Feminist Theory: From Margin to Center*. Boston, MA: South End Press.

hooks, b. 1991. *Yearning: Race, Gender and Cultural Politics*. Boston, MA: South End Press.

hooks, b. 1993. *Sisters of the Yam: Black Women and Self-Recovery*. Boston, MA: South End Press.

hooks, b. 1994a. *Teaching to Transgress: Education as the Practice of Freedom*. London: Routledge.

hooks, b. 1994b. *Black Looks: Race and Representation*. Boston, MA: South End Press.

hooks, b. 2002a. *Communion: The Female Search for Love*. New York: Harper-Collins.

hooks, b. 2002b. *Rock My Soul: Black People and Self-Esteem*. New York: Atria Books

Howitt, D. and Owusi-Bemp, J. 1994. *The Racism of Psychology*. London: Harvester Wheatsheaf.

Hull, G., Scott, P.B. and Smith, B. (eds), 1982. *All the Women are White, all the Blacks are Men, but Some of us are Brave: BlackWomen's Studies*. Old Westbury: Feminist Press.

Huq, S. 1997. 'Acting Locally: Bangladeshi Women Organising as Part of the Global Campaign for Women's Human Rights'. In N. Reilly (ed.), *Women's Rights as Human Rights: Local and Global Perspectives*. Dublin: Irish Council for Civil Liberties.

Hyde, J.S. 1996. *Half the Human Experience: The Psychology of Women*. Lexington, MA: D.C. Heath.

Inglis, T. 2008. *Global Ireland*. Oxon: Routledge.

Itzin, C. (ed.), 1992. *Pornography: Women, Violence and Civil Liberties*. Oxford: Oxford University Press.

Jackins, H. 1977. *The Upward Trend*. Seattle: Rational Island Publishers.

Jacoby, R. and Glauberman, N. 1995. *The Bell Curve Debate*. New York: Times Books.

Jayawardena, K. 1986. *Feminism and Nationalism in the Third World*. London: Zed Books.

Jeffreys, S. 2009. *The Industrial Vagina: The Political Economy of the Global Sex Trade*. Oxon: Routledge.

Jiménez-Domínguez, B. 2009. 'Ignacio Martín-Baró's Social Psychology of Liberation: Situated Knowledge and Critical Commitment Against Objectivism'. In M. Montero and C.C. Sonn (eds), *Psychology of Liberation: Theory and Applications*. New York: Springer.

Jones, R. (ed.), 1991. *Black Psychology*. Hampton, VA: Cobb & Henry.

Jordan, J. 2004. *Women's Growth in Diversity: More Writings from the Stone Centre*. New York: Guilford Press.

Jordan, J., Kaplan, A., Miller, J.B., Stiver, I. and Surrey, J. 1991. *Women's Growth in Connection: Writings from the Stone Centre*. New York: Guilford Press.

Kaschak, E. 1992. *Engendered Lives: A New Psychology of Women's Experience*. New York: Basic Books.

Kasl, C.S. 1989. *Women, Sex, Addiction: A Search for Love and Power*. New York: Ticknor & Fields.

Kasl, C.S. 1992. *Many Roads, one Journey, Moving Beyond the Twelve Steps*. New York: Harper Perennial.

Kasl, C.S. 1997. *A Home for the Heart: A Practical Guide to Intimate and Social Relationships*. New York: Harper Perennial.

Keane, T. 2006. 'Applying Liberation Psychology in a Workshop with Lesbians'. Unpublished Master's Thesis, University College Cork, Cork, Ireland.

Kellegher, M. 1996. *Feminisation of Famine*. Cork: Cork University Press.

Kelleher, C. 2008. 'Documenting Minority Stress in LGBT Youth using PhotoVoice'. Annual Conference, *Psychology Society of Ireland*, November.

Kelleher, P. 1989. *Evaluation Report*. Dublin: Parents Alone Resource Centre.

Kelleher, P. and O'Connor, M. 1995. *Making the Links*. Dublin: Women's Aid.

Kelleher, P. and Whelan, M. 1992. *Dublin Communities in Action: A Study of Six Projects*. Dublin: Community Action Network and Combat Poverty Agency.

Kelly, L. 1988. *Surviving Sexual Violence*. Cambridge: Cambridge University Press.

Kelly, L. 2003. *Rape: Still a Forgotten Issue*. Child and Woman Abuse Studies Unit: London Metropolitan University.

Kelly, L. and Regan, L. 2003. *Study of Attrition in Rape Cases*. London: Child and Woman Abuse Studies Unit.

Kelly, M.B. 1996. 'Women, Credit, Status and Power'. In A. Smyth (ed.), *Feminism, Politics, Community*. University College Dublin: Women's Education Research and Resource Centre.

Kennedy, B. 1996. 'The Relevance of Women's Studies in North County Dublin'. In A. Smyth (ed.), *Feminism, Politics, Community*. University College Dublin: Women's Education Research and Resource Centre.

Kennedy, P. (ed.), 2004. *Motherhood in Ireland: Creation and Context*. Dublin: The Mercier Press.

Kenny, V. (1985). 'The Post-Colonial Personality'. *The Crane Bag*, 9, 70–8.

Keohane, K. and Kuhling, C. 2004. *Collision Culture: Transformations in Everyday Life in Ireland*. Dublin: The Liffey Press.

Keyes, C.L.M. and Haidt, J. 2003. *Flourishing: Positive Psychology and the Life Well-Lived*. American Psychological Association, November 2002.

Kiberd, D. 1995. *Inventing Ireland*. London: Jonathan Cape.

Kiernan, V.G. 1974. *Marxism and Imperialism*. New York: St Martin's Press.

Kinealy, C. 2008. *A New History of Ireland*. Glouchester: The History Press.

King, U. 1993. *Women and Spirituality: Voices of Protest and Promise*. London: Macmillan.

Kirby, P., Gibbons, L. and Cronin, M. 2002. (eds), *Reinventing Ireland: Culture, Society and the Global Economy*. London: Pluto.

Kitzinger, C. 1996. 'Therapy and How it Undermines the Practice of Radical Feminism'. In D. Bell and R. Klein (eds), *Radically Speaking: Feminism Reclaimed*. London: Zed Books.

Kitzinger, C. 1997. 'Lesbian and Gay Psychology: A Critical Analysis'. In D.R. Fox and I. Prilleltensky (eds), *Critical Psychology: An Introduction*. London: Sage.

Kitzinger, C. and Perkins, R. 1993. *Changing our Minds: Lesbian Feminism and Psychology*. London: Onlywomen.

Koedt, A. 1973. 'The Politics of Orgasm'. In A. Koedt, E. Levine and A. Rapone (eds), *Radical Feminism*. New York: Quadrangle.

Laing, R.D. 1961. *The Divided Self: A Study in Sanity and Madness*. London: Tavistock.

Landrine, H. and Russo, N.F. (eds), 2009. *Handbook of Diversity in Feminist Psychology*. New York: Springer Publishing Co.

Lane, R.E. 2000. *Loss of Happiness in Market Democracies*. New Haven, Yale University Press.

Lazreg, M. 1994. *The Eloquence of Silence: Algerian Women in Question*. New York: Routledge.

Leach, D. 2009. *Fugitive Ireland: European Minority Nationalists and Irish Political Asylum, 1937–2008*. Dublin: Four Courts.

Lee, J. 1989. *Ireland: 1912–1985*. Cambridge: Cambridge University Press.

Lentin, R. and McVeigh, R. (eds), 2002. *Racism and Anti-Racism in Ireland*. Belfast: Beyond the Pale Publications.

Lerner, G. 1986. *The Creation of Patriarchy*. Oxford: Oxford University Press.

Lerner, G. 1993. *The Creation of Feminist Consciousness*. Oxford: Oxford University Press.

Lerner, G. 1997. *Why History Matters*. Oxford: Oxford University Press.

Levine, J. 1982. *Sisters: The Personal Story of an Irish Feminist*. Dublin: Ward River Press.

Lindorfer, S. 2008. *Sharing the Pain of the Bitter Hearts: Liberation Psychology and Gender-Related Violence in Eastern Africa*. Lit Verlag.

Lindorfer, S. 2009. 'In Whose Interests do we Work? Critical Comments of a Practitioner at the Fringes of the Liberation Paradigm'. *Feminism and Psychology*, 19(3), 354–67.

L.inC. 2003. *Newsletter*. Cork: L.inC.

L.inC. 2009. http://www.linc.ie/site/news.html.

Lister, R. 2003. *Citizenship: Feminist Perspectives*. Second Edition. New York: New York University Press.

Llorens, M. 2009. 'Liberation Psychology on the Street: Working with Youngsters Who have Lived on the Streets of Caracas'. In M. Montero and C.C. Sonn (eds), *Psychology of Liberation: Theory and Applications*. New York: Springer.

Lloyd, D. 1993. *Anomalous States: Irish Writing and the Post-Colonial Moment*. Dublin: Lilliput Press.

Lorasdagi, B.K. 2009. 'The Headscarf and Emancipation in the Netherlands'. *Feminism and Psychology*, 19(3), 328–34.

Lorde, A. 1984. 'Uses of the Erotic: the Erotic as Power'. In *Sister Outsider*. Freedom, CA: Crossing Press.

LOT. 1992–98. *Annual Reports*. Dublin: Lesbians Organising Together.

LOT. 1996. *Strategic Plan*. Dublin: Lesbians Organising Together.

Lott, B.E. and Bullock, H.E. 2006. *Psychology and Economic Injustice: Personal, Professional, and Political Intersections*. American Psychological Society.

Luke, C. and Gore, J. (eds), 1992. *Feminisms and Critical Pedagogy*. London: Routledge.

Luque-Ribelles, V., García-Ramírez, M. and Portillo, N. 2009. 'Gendering Peace and Liberation: A Participatory-Action Approach to Critical Consciousness Acquisition Among Women in a Marginalised Neighbourhood'. In M. Montero and C.C. Sonn (eds), *Psychology of Liberation: Theory and Applications*. New York: Springer.

Lykes, M.B. 1997. 'Activist Participatory Research among the Maya of Guatemala: Constructing Meanings from Situated Knowledge'. *Journal of Social Issues*, 53(4), 725–46.

Lykes, M.B., Blanche, M.T. and Hamber, B. 2003. 'Narrating Survival and Change in Guatemala and South Africa: The Politics of Representation and a Liberatory

Community Psychology'. *American Journal of Community Psychology*, 31(1/2), 79–90.

Lykes, M.B. and Moane, G. 2009. 'Whither Feminist Liberation Psychology? Critical Explorations of Feminist and Liberation Psychologies for a Globalizing World'. *Feminism and Psychology*, 19(3), 283–97.

Lykes, M.B., Coquillon, E. and Rabenstein, K.L. 2009. 'Theoretical and Methodological Challenges in Participatory Community-Based Research'. In H. Landrine and N.F. Russo (eds), *Handbook of Diversity: In Feminist Psychology*. New York: Spring Publishing Co.

Lynch, K. 2007. 'Love Labour as a Distinct and Non-Commodifiable Form of Care Labour'. *Sociological Review*, 55(3), 550–70.

Lynch, K. and McLaughlin, E. 1995. 'Caring Labour and Love Labour'. In P. Clancy, S. Drudy, K. Lynch, and L. O'Dowd (eds), *Irish Society: Sociological Perspectives*. Dublin: Institute of Public Administration.

Lynch, K. and O'Neill, C. 1995. 'The Colonisation of Social Class in Education'. *British Journal of Sociology of Education*, 15(3), 307–24.

Lynch, K., Baker J. and Lyons, M. (eds), 2009. *Affective Equality: Love, Care and Injustice*. Basingstoke: Palgrave.

McAllister, P. 1988. *You can't Kill the Spirit: Stories of Women and Nonviolent Action*. Philadelphia, PA: New Society Publishers.

McAllister, P. 1991. *This River of Courage: Generations of Women's Resistance and Action*. Philadelphia, PA: New Society Publishers.

McAuliffe, G. and Associates. 2008. *Culturally Alert Counseling, a Comprehensive Introduction*. Los Angeles: Sage Publications.

McAuliffe, M., O'Donnell, K. and Lane, L. (eds), 2009. *Palgrave Advances in Irish History*. Basingstoke: Palgrave Macmillan.

McCarthy, E. 1992. *Women and Work Contexts and Change in Ireland*. University College Dublin: Social and Organisational Psychology Unit.

McCarthy, E. 1995. 'Labour and Education – the Irish Women's Movement Today'. In M. Friese, R. Savioli, and B. Dreyer (eds), *Frauen erobern Europa!?* Bremen: University of Bremen.

McCarthy, I.C. 1991. 'Colonial Sentences and Just Subversions: The Potential for Abuse and Love in Therapeutic Encounters'. Keynote address, *3rd World Family Therapy Congress*, Finland.

McCarthy, J., Quayle, E. and Alwyn, S. 2008. 'Applying Psychology in an Irish Context'. Special Issue in honour of Liz Dunne. *Irish Journal of Psychology*.

MacCurtain, M. 1991. 'Women in Irish History'. In M. MacCurtain and M. O'Dowd (eds), *Women in Early Modern Ireland*. Dublin: Wolfhound Press.

MacCurtain, M. 2008. *Ariadne's Thread: Writing Women into Irish History*. Galway: Arlen House.

MacCurtain, M. and O'Dowd, M. 1991. *Women in Early Modern Ireland*. Dublin: Wolfhound Press.

McGee, H., Garavan, R., deBarra, M., Byrne, J. and Conroy, R. 2002. *The SAVI Report: Sexual Abuse and Violence in Ireland: A National Study*. Dublin: Liffey Press and Dublin Rape Crisis Centre.

McIntyre, A. 2003. 'Feminist Fieldwork and Political Change'. *Feminism and Psychology*, 13(3), 283–6.

McKay, S. 2005. *Without Fear: 25 Years of the Rape Crisis Centre*. Dublin: New Island Books.

MacKinnon, C. 1982. 'Feminism, Marxism, Method and the State: An Agenda for Theory'. *Signs: Journal of Women in Culture and Society*, 7(3), 515–44.

MacLachlan, M. 2004. *Embodiment: Clinical, Critical and Cultural Perspectives on Health and Illness*. Milton Keynes: Open University Press.

MacLachlan, M. 2005. *Culture and Health*. Second Edition. Chichester: Wiley.

McLellan, B. 1995. *Beyond Psychoppression*. Melbourne: Spinifex Press.

MacLeod, C. 2006. 'Radical Plural Feminisms and Emancipatory Practice in Post-Apartheid South Africa'. *Theory and Psychology*, 16, 367–89.

McLeod, J. (ed.) 2007. *The Routledge Companion to Postcolonial Studies*. London: Routledge.

McMinn, J. 1996. 'Same Difference? Principles, Practices and Politics of Feminist and Community Education'. In A. Smyth (ed.), *Feminism, Politics, Community*. University College Dublin: Women's Education Research and Resource Centre.

McPhail, T. L. 1987. *Electronic Colonialism: The Future of International Broadcasting and Communication*. Second Edition. London: Sage

McPhail, T.L. 2009. *Development Communication: Reframing the Role of Media*. London: Wiley-Blackwell.

McVeigh, R. and Rolston, B. 2009. 'Civilising the Irish'. *Race and Class*, 51(1), 2–28.

Madden, S. and Moane, G. 2006. 'Critical Psychologies in Ireland: Transforming Contexts and Political Possibilities'. *Annual Review of Critical Psychology*, 5, 1–24.

Madrigal, L.J. and Tejeda, W.V. 2009. 'Facing Gender-Based Violence in El Salvador: Contributions from the Social Psychology of Ignacio Martín-Baró'. *Feminism and Psychology*, 19(3), 368–74.

Mahon, E. 1995. 'From Democracy to Femocracy: The Women's Movement in the Republic of Ireland'. In P. Clancy, S. Drudy, K. Lynch, and L. O'Dowd (eds), *Irish Society: Sociological Perspectives*. Dublin: Institute of Public Administration.

Mama, A. 1995. *Beyond the Masks: Race, Gender and Subjectivity*. London: Routledge.

Mannoni, O. 1962. (1950) *Prospero and Caliban: The Psychology of Colonization*. New York: Praeger.

Maracle, L. 1990. *Sojourner's Truth and Other Stories*. Vancouver: Press Gang.

Maracle, L. 1996. *I am Woman: A Native Perspective on Sociology and Feminism*. Second Edition. Vancouver: Press Gang.

Marglin, F. and Marglin, S.A. (eds), 1996. *Decolonizing Knowledge: From Development to Dialogue*. Oxford: Clarendon.

Mariechild, D. 1981. *Mother Wit: A Feminist Guide to Psychic Development*. New York: Crossing Press.

Martín-Baró, I. 1994. *Writings for a Liberation Psychology: Essays, 1985–1989*, ed. A. Aron and S. Corne. Cambridge, MA: Harvard University Press.

Masson, J. 1984. *The Assault on Truth: Freud's Suppression of the Seduction Theory*. New York: Farrar, Straus & Giroux.

Masson, J. 1988. *Against Therapy*. London: Fontana.

Matthews, C. 2002. *Singing the Soul Back Home: Shamanic Wisdom for Every Day*. London: Connections Book Publishing.

Meaney, G. 1990. *Gender and Nationalism*. LIP Pamphlet Series. Dublin: Attic Press.

Meaney, G. 1993. 'Sex and Nation: Women in Irish Culture and Politics'. In A. Smyth (ed.), *Irish Women's Studies Reader*. Dublin: Attic Press.

Memmi, A. 1967. *The Colonizer and the Colonized*. Boston, MA: Beacon Press. (Original French edition, 1957.)

Memmi, A. 1968. *Dominated Man*. Boston, MA: Beacon Press. (Original French edition, 1963.)

Merry, S.E. 2006. *Human Rights and Gender Violence: Translating International Law into Local Justice*. Chicago: University of Chicago Press.

Mezirow, J. 1991. *Transformative Dimensions of Adult Learning*. San Francisco: Jossey Bass.

Mies, M. 1986. *Patriarchy and Accumulation on a World Scale: Women in the International Division of Labour*. London: Zed Books.

Mies, M., Bennholdt-Thomsen, V. and Von Werlof, C. 1988. *Women: The Last Colony*. London: Zed Books.

Miller, J.B. 1976. *Toward a New Psychology of Women*. Boston, MA: Beacon Press.

Miller, J.B. 1986. *Toward a New Psychology of Women*. Second Edition. London: Penguin.

Miller, J.B. 1991a. 'The Development of Women's Sense of Self'. In J.V. Jordan, A.G. Kaplan, J.B. Miller, I.P. Stiver and J.L. Surrey, *Women's Growth in Connection: Writings from the Stone Center*. New York: The Guilford Press.

Miller, J.B. 1991b. 'The Construction of Anger in Women and Men'. In J.V. Jordan, A.G. Kaplan, J.B. Miller, I.P. Stiver and J.L. Surrey, *Women's Growth in Connection: Writings from the Stone Center*. New York: Guilford Press.

Miller, J.B. 1991c. 'Women and Power'. In J.V. Jordan, A.G. Kaplan, J.B. Miller, I.P. Stiver, and J.L. Surrey, *Women's Growth in Connection: Writings from the Stone Center*. New York: The Guilford Press.

Miller, J.B. and Stiver, I. 1997. *The Healing Connection: How Women Form Relationships in Therapy and in Life*. Boston: Beacon Press.

Millett, K. 1970. *Sexual Politics*. New York: Avon Books.

Miriam, K. 1993. 'From Rage to All the Rage: Lesbian Feminism, Sado-masochism and the Politics of Memory'. In I. Reti (ed.), *Unleashing Feminism: Critiquing Lesbian Sadomasochism in the Gay Nineties*. Santa Cruz, CA: HerBooks.

Moane, G. 1994. 'A Psychological Analysis of Colonialism in an Irish Context'. *Irish Journal of Psychology*, 15, 250–65.

Moane, G. 1995. 'Living Visions'. In I. O'Carroll and E. Collins (eds), *Lesbian and Gay Visions of Ireland: Towards the Twenty-First Century*. London: Cassells.

Moane, G. 1996. 'Legacies of Colonialism for Irish Women: Oppressive or Empowering?' *Irish Journal of Feminist Studies*, 1(1), 100–18.

Moane, G. 1997a. 'A Womb Not a Tomb: Goddess Symbols and Ancient Ireland'. *Canadian Women's Studies/les Cahiers de la femme*, 17(3), 7–11.

Moane, G. 1997b. 'Lesbian Politics and Community'. In A. Byrne and M. Leonard (eds). *Women and Irish Society: A Sociological Reader*. Belfast: Beyond the Pale Publications.

Moane, G. 1999. *Gender and Colonialism: A Psychological Analysis of Oppression and Liberation*. London: Palgrave Macmillan.

Moane, G. 2002. 'Legacies of History and the Quest for Vision: Colonialism and the Celtic Tiger'. In P. Kirby (ed.), *Reinventing Ireland*. London: Pluto.

Moane, G. 2003. 'Bridging the Personal and the Political: Practices for a Liberation Psychology'. *American Journal of Community Psychology*, 31(1/2), 91–101.

Moane, G. 2006. 'Exploring Activism and Change: Feminist Psychology, Liberation Psychology, Political Psychology'. *Feminism and Psychology*, 16(1), 73–8.

Moane, G. 2008. 'Building Strength through Challenging Homophobia: Liberation Workshops with Younger and Midlife Irish Lesbians'. *Journal of Gay and Lesbian Social Services* 20(1/2), 129–45.

Moane, G. 2009. 'Reflections on Liberation Psychology in Action in an Irish Context'. In M. Montero and C.C. Sonn (eds), *Psychology of Liberation: Theory and Applications*. New York: Springer.

Mohanty, C.T. 2003. *Feminism without Borders: Decolonizing Theory, Practicing Solidarity*. Durham, NC: Duke University Press.

Mohanty, C.T., Russo, A. and Torres. L. (eds), 1991. *Third World Women and the Politics of Feminism*. Bloomingdale: Indian University Press.

Montero, M. 1994. 'Consciousness-raising, Conversion, and De-ideolization in Community Psychosocial Work'. *Journal of Community Psychology*, 22, 3–11.

Montero, M. 1997. 'Political Psychology: a Critical Perspective'. In D.R. Fox and I. Prilleltensky (eds), *Critical Psychology: An Introduction*. London: Sage.

Montero, M. 2007. 'The Political Psychology of Liberation: From Politics and Ethics and Back'. *Political Psychology*, 28(5), 517–33.

Montero, M. 2009. 'Methods for Liberation: Critical Consciousness in Action'. In M. Montero and C.C. Sonn (eds), *Psychology of Liberation: Theory and Applications*. New York: Springer.

Montero, M. and Sonn, C.C. (eds), 2009. *Psychology of Liberation: Theory and Applications*. New York: Springer.

Montiel, C.J. and Rodriguez, A.M.G. 2009. 'Liberation Movements During Democratic Transition: Positioning with the Changing State'. In M. Montero and C.C. Sonn (eds), *Psychology of Liberation: Theory and Applications*. New York: Springer.

Moody, T.W. and Martin, F.X. (eds), 2001. *The Course of Irish History*. Fourth Edition. Cork: Mercier Press.

Morawski, J. 1994. *Practicing Feminisms, Reconstructing Psychology: Notes on a Liminal Science*. Anne Arbor: University of Michigan Press.

Morgan, F. 1991. *Wild Witches Don't Get the Blues: Astrology, Rituals and Healing*. Rio Nido, CA: Daughters of the Moon Publishing.

Morgan, R. 1978. 'Women as a Colonized Group'. In R. Morgan, *Going too Far*. New York: Vintage.

Morgan, R. (ed.), 1984. *Sisterhood is Global: The International Women's Movement Anthology*. New York: Doubleday.

Morrow, D. and Wilson, D. 1996. *Ways of Handling Conflict: Resources for Community Relations Work*. Belfast, Northern Ireland: Understanding Conflict Trust.

Mullaly, B. 2002. *Challenging Oppression, a Critical Social Work Approach*. London: Oxford University Press.

Mulvey, A. 1988. 'Community Psychology and Feminism: Tensions and Commonalities'. *Journal of Community Psychology*, 16, 70–83.

Mulvey, C. 1994. *Evaluation Report on the Allen Lane Foundation's Funding Programme in Ireland, 1989–1991*. Dublin: Allen Lane Foundation.

Murphy, Y. 2009. *Report of Investigations of Sexual Abuse in a Dublin Diocese*. Dublin: Government Publications.

Murphy-Lawless, J. 1993. 'The Silencing of Women in Childbirth, or Let's Hear it for Bartholemew and the Boys'. In A. Smyth (ed.), *Irish Women's Studies Reader*. Dublin: Attic Press.

Murray, C. and Rogers, P. 2009. 'Community Development: A Practitioners' Perspective'. In E. O'Broin and P. Kirby (eds), *Power, Dissent and Democracy, Civil Society and the State in Ireland*. Dublin: A.A. Farmar.

Murray, M. 2007. *Living Our Times*. Dublin: Gill and MacMillan.

Nandy, A. 1980. *At the Edge of Psychology: Essays in Politics and Culture*. Delhi: Oxford University Press.

Nandy, A. 1983. *The Intimate Enemy*. Delhi: Oxford University Press.

Naples, N.A. and Bojar, K. 2002. *Teaching Feminist Activism: Strategies from the Field*. New York; London: Routledge.

Naples, N.A. and Desai, M. (eds), 2002. *Women's Activism and Globalization: Linking Local Struggles and Transnational Politics*. New York: Routledge.

Narayan, U. 1991. 'Finding Our Own Voices: the Need for Non-Western Contributions to Global Feminism'. *Women and Language*, 10, 8–10.

Narayan, U. 1997. *Dislocating Cultures: Identities, Traditions and Third World Feminism*. New York: Routledge.

Nelson, G. and Prilleltensky, I. 2004. *Community Psychology: In Pursuit of Liberation and Wellbeing*. New York: Palgrave Macmillan.

Nicholas, L.J. and Cooper, S. (eds), 1990. *Psychology and Apartheid: Essays on the Struggle for Psychology and the Mind in South Africa*. Johannesburg: Vision/Madib.

Ní Dhomhnaill, N. 1994. 'An Ghaeilge Mar uirlis Fheiminfeach'. In F. Devaney, M. Mulholland and J. Willoughby (eds), *Unfinished Revolution: Essays on The Irish Women's Movement*. Belfast: Maedbh Publishing.

Noble, V. 2003. *The Double Goddess: Women Sharing Power*. Vermont: Bear & Co.

Noor, N.M. 2009. '"Liberating" the Hijab'. In M. Montero and C.C. Sonn (eds), *Psychology of Liberation: Theory and Applications*. New York: Springer.

NWCI. 1995 and 1997. *In Focus*. Quarterly Newsletters. Dublin: National Women's Council of Ireland.

Oakley, A. 1992. *Social Support and Motherhood: The Natural History of a Research Project*. Oxford: Blackwell.

O'Brien, C.C. and O'Brien, M. 1995. *Ireland: A Concise History*. Third Edition. London: Thames & Hudson.

O'Carroll, I. and Collins, E. (eds), 1995. *Lesbian and Gay Visions of Ireland: Towards the Twenty-First Century*. London: Cassells.

O'Connell, M. 2001. *Changed Utterly: Ireland and the New Irish Psyche*. Dublin: Liffey Press.

O'Connor, A. 1991. *Child Murderess and Dead Child Traditions: A Comparative Study*. Helsinki: Suomalainen Tiedeakatemia.

O'Connor, M. 2008. 'Silencing Feminism: Making Sexual Exploitation Invisible and Legitimate'. In U. Barry (ed.) *Where are We Now: New Feminist Perspectives in Contemporary Ireland*. Dublin: New Island Press.

O'Connor, M. and Wilson, N. 2001. *Vision, Action, Change: Feminist Principles and Practice of Working on Violence against Women*. Dublin: Women's Aid.

O'Connor, P. 1998. *Emerging Voices: Women in Contemporary Irish Society*. Dublin: Institute of Public Administration.

O'Connor, P. 2002. *Friendships between Women*. First published 1992. Eastbourne: Guildford/ HarvesterWheatsheaf/ Pearsons Education.

O'Donnell, K. 2008. 'Lesbian Lives and Studies in Ireland at the Fin de Siecle'. In M. McAuliffe and S. Tiernan (eds), *Tribades, Tommies and Transgressives, Histories of Sexualities: Vol 1*. Newcastle: Cambridge Scholars Publishing.

Oliver, M. 1996. *Understanding Disability: From Theory to Practice*. London: Macmillan.

O'Neill, C. 1992. *Telling it Like it is: Poverty in a North Dublin Suburb*. Dublin: Combat Poverty Agency.

Orbach, S. 1986. *Hunger Strike: The Anorectic's Struggle as a Metaphor for our Age*. London: Faber and Faber.

Orbach, S. 2009. *Bodies*. New York: Picador.

Orbach, S. and Eichenbaum, R. 1987. *Bittersweet: Love, Competition and Envy in Women's Relationships*. London: Century.

Orford, J. 2008. *Community Psychology, Challenges, Controversies and Emerging Consensus*. Chichester: Wiley.

Osorio, J.M.F. 2009. 'Praxis and Liberation in the Context of Latin American Theory'. In M. Montero and C.C. Sonn (eds), *Psychology of Liberation: Theory and Applications*. New York: Springer.

Ostrove, J.M., Cole, E.R. and Oliva, G.A. 2009. 'Toward a Feminist Liberation Psychology of Alliances'. *Feminism and Psychology*, 19(3), 381–6.

Owens, R.C. 1984. *Smashing Times: A History of the Irish Women's Suffragette Movement, 1889–1922*. Dublin: Attic Press.

Parker, A. Russo, M. Sommer, D. and Yaeger, P. (eds), 1992. *Nationalisms and Sexualities*. New York: Routledge.

Parsons, S., O'Connor, J. and Conlon, C. 2003. *A Whole New World: A Feminist Model of Community and Lifelong Learning*. Dublin: Women's Education and Research and Resource Centre, University College Dublin.

Penelope, J. (ed.), 1994. *Out of the Class Closet: Lesbians Speak*. Freedom, CA: Crossing Press.

Penelope, J. and Wolfe, S. (eds), 1993. *Lesbian Culture: An Anthology*. Freedom, CA: Crossing Press.

Perez, R.M., DeBord, K.A., and Bischke, K.J. 2000. *Handbook of Counseling and Psychotherapy with Lesbian, Gay, and Bisexual Clients*. Washington, DC: American Psychological Association.

Peters, J. and Wolper, A. (eds), 1995. *Women's Rights, Human Rights: International Feminist Perspectives*. London: Routledge.

Pharr, S. 1988. *Homophobia: A Weapon of Sexism*. Chardon Press.

Pieterse, J.N. and Parekh, B. (eds), 1995. The *Decolonization of Imagination*. London: Zed Books.

Plaskow, J. and Christ, C. (eds), 1989. *Weaving the Visions: New Patterns in Feminist Spirituality*. San Francisco: Harper & Row.

Póirtéir, C. 1995. *The Great Irish Famine*. RTÉ/Mercier Press.

Prendiville, P. 1995. *Developing Facilitation Skills*. Dublin: Combat Poverty Agency.

Prillelstensky, I. 2003. 'Understanding, Resisting, and Overcoming Oppression: Toward Psychopolitical Validity'. *American Journal of Community Psychology*, 31(1/2), 195–201.

Prilleltensky I. and Nelson, G. 1997. 'Community Psychology: Reclaiming Social Justice'. In D.R. Fox and I. Prilleltensky (eds), *Critical Psychology: An Introduction*. London: Sage.

Quayle, E. and Taylor, M. 2005. *Viewing Child Pornography on the Internet: Understanding the Offence, Managing the Offender, Healing Victims*. Dorset: Russell House publishing.

Queralt, M. 1996. *The Social Environment and Human Behaviour*. Boston, MA: Allyn & Bacon.

Quiery, M. 2002. *A Mighty Silence: A Report on the Needs of Lesbians and Bisexual Women in Northern Ireland*. Ballymena: Lesbian Advocacy Services Initiative.

Rahman, A. 2004. 'Globalization: The Emerging Ideology in the Popular Protests and Grassroots Action Research'. *Action Research* 2(1), 9–23.

Randall, V. 1987. *Women and Politics*. London: Macmillan.

Rapping, E. 1996. *The Culture of Recovery: Making Sense of the Self-Help Movement in Women's Lives*. Boston, MA: Beacon Press.

Raymond, J. 1986. *A Passion for Friends: Toward a Philosophy of Female Affection*. London: Women's Press.

Raymond, J. 1993. *Women as Wombs: Reproductive Technologies and the Battle over Women's Freedom*. San Francisco, Harper Collins.

Reason, J. and Bradbury, H. 2008. *The Sage Handbook of Action Research: Participative Inquiry and Practice*. California: Sage Publications.

Regan, L., and Kelly. L with Breslin, R. and Harrison, V. 2001. *Teenage tolerance: The Hidden Lives of Young Irish People*. Dublin: Women's Aid.

Reich, S.M., Riemer, M., Prilleltensky, I. and Montero, M. (eds), 2007. *International Community Psychology, History and Theories*. New York: Springer.

Reilly, N. (ed.), 1997. *Women's Rights as Human Rights: Local and Global Perspectives*. Dublin: Irish Council for Civil Liberties.

Reilly, N. 2008. 'Global Norms and Local Action: Critical Approaches to Women's Human Rights in Ireland'. In U. Barry (ed.), *Where are we Now? New Feminist Perspectives on Women in Contemporary Ireland*. Dublin: New Island.

Reygan, F.C.G. 2010. A*n Interpretative Phenomenological Analysis of the Meaning of Spirituality for Lesbian, Gay, Bisexual and Transgender (LGBT) People in Ireland*. University College Dublin: PhD thesis.

Rich, A. 1976. *Of Woman Born: Motherhood as Experience and Institution*. New York: W.W. Norton.

Rich, A. 1980. 'Compulsory Heterosexuality and Lesbian Existence'. *Signs: Journal of Women in Culture and Society*, 15, 459–65.

Rich, A. 1993. *What is Found There: Notebooks on Poetry and Politics*. New York: W.W. Norton.

Richards, G. 2010. *Putting Psychology in its Place*. Third Edition. London: Routledge.

Richardson, D. 1996. '"Misguided, Dangerous and Wrong": On the Maligning of Radical Feminsm'. In D. Bell and R. Klein (eds), *Radically Speaking: Feminism Reclaimed*. London: Zed Books.

Richardson, D. and Robinson, V. 1993. *Introducing Women's Studies: Feminist Theory and Practice*. London: Macmillan.

Richardson, D. and Robinson, V. 2008. *Introducing Gender and Women's Studies*. Third Edition. Basingstoke: Palgrave Macmillan.

Robb, C. 2006. *This Changes Everything: The Relational Revolution in Psychology*. New York: Picador.

Robertson, A.H. and Merrills, J.G. (eds), 1996. *Human Rights in the World*. Fouth Edition. Manchester: Manchester University Press.

Robinson, M. 1992. 'Striking a Balance'. The Allen Lane Foundation Lecture. Dublin: February.

Rollins, J.H. 1996. *Women's Minds, Women's Bodies: The Psychology of Women in a Biosocial Context*. Englewood Cliffs, NJ: Prentice Hall.

Rooney, E. 1997. 'Women in Party Politics and Local Groups: Findings from Belfast'. In A. Byrne and M Leonard (eds), *Women and Irish Society: A Sociological Reader*. Belfast: Beyond the Pale Publications.

Roper, A. 1992. *Positive Health for Women*. Dublin: Attic Press.

Rosado, R.Q. 2007. *Consciousness in Action: Toward an Integral Psychology of Liberation and Transformation*. Puerto Rico: ilé Publications.

Ross, B.L. 1995. *The House that Jill Built: A Lesbian Nation in Formation*. Toronto: University of Toronto Press.

Rossiter, A. 2009. *Ireland's Hidden Diaspora: The 'Abortion Trail' and the Making of a London-Irish Underground, 1980–2000*. London: IASC.

Rowbotham, S. 1996. 'Introduction: Mapping the Women's Movement'. In M. Threlfall (ed.), *Mapping the Women's Movement: Feminist Politics and Social Transformation in the North*. London: Verso.

Rowland, R. 1996. 'The Politics of Intimacy: Heterosexuality, Love and Power'. In D. Bell and R. Klein (eds), 1996. *Radically Speaking: Feminism Reclaimed*. London: Zed Books.

Ruane, J. 1986. 'Contemporary Irish Culture: A Review Article'. *Studies*, 9, 78–91.

Russell, G.M. and Bohan, J.S. 2006. 'The Case of Internalized Homophobia, Theory and/as Practice. *Theory and Psychology*, 16(3), 343–66.

Ruth, S. 1988. 'Understanding Oppression and Liberation'. *Studies*, 7(308), 434–44

Ruth, S. 2006. *Leadership and Liberation: A Psychological Approach*. East Sussex: Routledge.

Ryan, A. B. 2001. *Feminist Ways of Knowing: Towards Theorising the Person for Radical Adult Education*. Leicester: NIACE.

Ryan, S. 2009. *Report of the Commission to Inquire into Child Abuse*. Dublin: Government Publications.

Sacipa-Rodríguez, S., Tovar-Guerra, C., Villareal, L.F.G. and Bohórquez, R.V. 2009. 'Psychological Accompaniment: Construction of Cultures of Peace Among a Community Affected by War'. In M. Montero, and C.C. Sonn (eds), *Psychology of Liberation: Theory and Applications*. New York: Springer.

Saghal, G. and Yuval-Davis, N. (eds.), 1992. *Refusing Holy Orders*. London: Virago.

Said, E.W. 1988. *Nationalism, Colonialism and Literature: Yeats and Decolonization*. Derry: Field Day.

Said, E.W. 1993. *Culture and Imperialism*. London: Chatto & Windus.

Sapene-Chapellín, A. 2009. 'The Game of War: The Liberating Action of Games in a Context of Political Polarization'. In M. Montero, and C.C. Sonn (eds), *Psychology of Liberation: Theory and Applications*. New York: Springer.

Schaef, A.W. 1987. *When Society Becomes an Addict*. New York: Harper & Row.

Schneider, B. 1993. 'Put up or Shut up: Workplace Sexual Assaults'. In P. Bart and G. Moran (eds), *Violence Against Women: The Bloody Footprints*. London: Sage.

Scott, J.C. 1985. *Weapons of the Weak: Everyday Forms of Peasant Resistance*. New Haven, CT: Yale University Press.

Scott, J.C. 1990. *Domination and the Arts of Resistance: Hidden Transcripts*. New Haven, CT: Yale University Press.

Seager, J. 1997. *The State of Women in the World Atlas*. London: Penguin.

Seager, J. 2003. *The Atlas of Women*. London: Women's Press.

Share, P., Tovey, H. and Corcoran, M.P. 2007. *A Sociology of Ireland*. Third Edition. Dublin: Gill and Macmillan.

Shalhoub-Kevorkian, N. 2009. 'The Political Economy of Children's Trauma: A Case Study of House Demolition in Palestine'. *Feminism and Psychology*, 19(3), 335–42.

Sharpe, S. 2001. 'Going for It: Young Women Face the Future'. *Feminism and Psychology*, 11(2), 177–81.

Sheehan, B. 2005. *Evaluation of the Lesbian Studies and Queer Culture Certificate*. University College Dublin: WERRC.

Sherif, C. W. 1979. 'Bias in Psychology'. In J.A. Sherman and E.T. Beck (eds), *The Prism of Sex: Essays in the Sociology of Knowledge*. Madison, WI: University of Wisconsin Press.

Shiva, V. 2009. *Soil Not Oil: Climate Change, Peak Oil and Food Insecurity*. London: Zed Press.

Smail, D. 1987. *Taking Care: The Limits of Therapy*. London: Dent.

Smail, D. 1993. *The Origins of Unhappiness: A New Understanding of Personal Distress*. London: Harper Collins.

Smail, D. 2001. *The Nature of Unhappiness*. London: Harper Collins.

Smith, J.M. 2007. *Ireland's Magdalen Laundries and the Nation's Architecture of Containment*. Notre Dame University Press.

Smyth, A. (ed.), 1988. 'Feminism in Ireland'. Special Issue. *Women's Studies International Forum*, 11(4).

Smyth, A. (ed.), 1992. *The Abortion Papers: Ireland*. Dublin: Attic Press.

Smyth, A. (ed.), 1993. *Irish Women's Studies Reader*. Dublin: Attic Press.

Snyder, P. 1992. *The European Women's Almanac*. London: Scarlet Press.

Sonn, C.C. and Lewis, R.C. 2009. 'Immigration and Identity: The Ongoing Struggles for Liberation'. In M. Montero and C.C. Sonn (eds), *Psychology of Liberation: Theory and Applications*. New York: Springer.

Spivak, G. C. 1987. *In Other Worlds: Essays in Cultural Politics*. New York: Methuen.

Spretnak, C. (ed.), 1982. *The Politics of Women's Spirituality: Essays on the Rise of Spiritual Power within the Feminist Movement*. New York: Anchor Press.

Stamatopoulou, E. 1995. 'Women's Rights and the United Nations'. In J. Peters and A. Wolper (eds), *Women's Rights, Human Rights*. London: Routledge.

Stanko, E. 1993. 'Ordinary Fear: Women, Violence and Personal Safety'. In P. Bart and G. Moran (eds), *Violence against Women: The Bloody Footprints*. London: Sage.

Starhawk. 1979. *The Spiral Dance: A Rebirth of the Ancient Religion of the Great Goddess*. San Francisco: Harper & Row.

Starhawk. 1982. *Dreaming the Dark: Magic, Sex and Politics*. Boston, MA: Beacon Press.

Starhawk. 1987. *Truth or Dare*. San Francisco: Harper SanFrancisco.

Starhawk. 2005. *The Earth Path: Grounding your Spirit in the Rhythms of Nature.* United States: HarperSanFrancisco.

Stein, D. 1992. *The Women's Book of Healing.* St. Paul, MN: Llewellyn Publications.

Steinem, G. 1992. *Revolution from Within: A Book of Self Esteem.* Boston, MA: Little, Brown & Co.

Stokols, D., Misra, S., Runnserstrom, M.G. and Hipp, J.A. 2009. 'Psychology in an Age of Ecological Crisis: From Personal Angst to Collective Action'. *American Psychologist,* 64, 181–93.

Stone, M. 1979. *Ancient Mirrors of Womanhood: A Treasury of Goddess and Heroine Lore from Around the World.* Boston, MA: Beacon Press.

Stone-Mediatore, S. 2003. *Reading across Borders: Storytelling and Knowledges of Resistance.* Basingstoke: Palgrave Macmillan.

Stout, G. 2003. *Newgrange and the Bend of the Boyne.* Cork: Cork University Press.

Sue, D.W. and Sue, D. 2007. *Counselling the Culturally Diverse.* Fifth Edition. New Jersey: John Wiley and Sons.

Szasz, T. 1972. The *Myth of Mental Illness.* London: Paladin.

Tallen, B.S. 1990. 'How Inclusive is Feminist Political Theory? Questions for Lesbians'. In J. Allen (ed.), *Lesbian Philosophies and Cultures.* Albany, New York: State University of New York Press.

Tavris, C. 1989. *Anger: The Misunderstood Emotion.* Second Edition. New York: Simon & Schuster.

Tavris, C. 1992. *The Mismeasure of Woman.* New York: Simon & Schuster.

Teo, T. 2005. *The Critique of Psychology: From Kant to Postcolonial Theory.* New York: Springer.

Tierney, H. 2008. 'Reality Check' – in Critical Conversation with Fieldwork Supervisors. Training Agencies Group (TAG) Annual Conference, Liverpool John Moore's University, 10–12 July.

Thiongo, Ngugi Wa. 1986. *De-colonizing the Mind: The Politics of Language in African Literature.* London: Heinemann.

Thomas, D.Q. 1994. 'In Search of Solutions: Women's Police Stations in Brazil'. In M. Davies (ed.), *Women and Violence.* London: Zed Books.

Threlfall, M. (ed.), 1996. *Mapping the Women's Movement: Feminist Politics and Social Transformation in the North.* London: Verso.

Tong, R. 2009. *Feminist Thought: A More Comprehensive Introduction.* Third Edition. Boulder, CO: Westview Press.

Torre, M.E. and Fine, M. 2005. 'Bar None: Extending Affirmative Action to Higher Education in Prison'. *Journal of Social Issues,* 61, 569–94.

Torre, M.E. and Ayala, J. 2009. 'Envisioning Participatory Action Research Entremundos'. *Feminism & Psychology,* 19(3), 387–93.

Trask, H.K. 1993. *From a Native Daughter: Colonialism and Sovereignty in Hawaii.* Maine: Common Courage Press.

Trinh, M.T. 1989. *Woman, Native, Other: Writing, Postcoloniality and Feminism.* Bloomington: Indiana University Press.

Tweedy, H. 1992. *A Link in the Chain: The Story of the Irish Housewives Association, 1942–1992.* Dublin: Attic Press.

Unger, R., and Crawford, M. 1992. *Women and Gender: A Feminist Psychology.* London: McGraw-Hill.

Unger, R. 1998. *Resisting Gender: Twenty-five Years of Feminist Psychology*. London: Sage Publications.

Unger, R. (ed.). 2004. *Handbook of the Psychology of Women and Gender*. United States: John Wiley and Sons.

United Nations. 1948. Universal Declaration of Human Rights. New York: United Nations. Reprinted in *Human Rights: A Compilation of International Instruments of the United Nations*. New York: United Nations, Fifth Edition, 1988.

United Nations 2005. *The World's Women 2005: Progress in Statistics*. New York: United Nations.

Ussher, J. 1991. *Women's Madness: Misogyny or Mental Illness?* London: Harvester Wheatsheaf.

Ussher, J. 1997. *Fantasies of Femininity: Reframing the Boundaries of Sex*. London: Penguin.

Valenti, J. 2007. *Full Frontal Feminism: A Young Woman's Guide to Why Feminism Matters*. NY: Seal Press.

Valiulis, M.G. and O'Dowd, M. 1997. *Women and Irish History: Essays in Honour of Margaret MacCurtain*. Dublin: Wolfhound Press.

Veale, A., McKay, S., Wessells, M. and Worthen, M. 2008. Ethics and process in participatory research: Girl mothers and their children from fighting forces. Annual Conference, Psychology Society of Ireland, November.

Vickers, J. 1991. *Women and the World Economic Crisis*. London: Zed Books.

Walby, S. 1990. *Theorizing Patriarchy*. Oxford: Blackwell.

Walby, S. 1994. 'Methodological and Theoretical Issues in the Comparative Analysis of Gender Relation in Western Europe', *Environment and Planning*, 26, 1339–54.

Walby, S. 1997. *Gender Transformations*. London: Routledge.

Walby, S. 2004. 'The European Union and Gender Equality: Emergent Varieties of Gender Regime'. *Social Politics*, 11(1), 4–29.

Walby, S. 2005. 'Introduction: Comparative Gender Mainstreaming in a Global Era'. *International Feminist Journal of Politics*, 7(4), 453–70.

Walby, S. 2009. *Globalization and Inequalities: Complexity and Contested Modernities*. London: Routledge.

Walkerdine, V. (ed.), 1996. 'Social Class': a special issue of *Feminism and Psychology*, 6(3).

Ward, M. 1983. *Unmanageable Revolutionaries: Women in Irish Nationalism*. London: Pluto Press.

Ward, M. 1995. *In their Own Voice: Women and Irish Nationalism*. Dublin: Attic Press.

Waring, M. 1988. *If Women Counted: A New Feminist Economics*. San Francisco: Harper & Row.

Watkins, M. and Shulman, H. 2008. *Toward Psychologies of Liberation*. New York: Palgrave MacMillan.

Watson, D. and Parsons, S. 2005. Domestic Abuse of Women and Men in Ireland. Report of the National Study of Domestic Abuse. Dublin: National Crime Council in association with the Economic and Social Research Institute.

Watts, R. and Abdul-Adil, J. 1998. 'Promoting Critical Consciousness in Young, African-American Men'. *Journal of Prevention and Intervention in the Community*, 16(1), 63–86.

Watts, R.J. and Serrano García, I. (eds), 2003. 'Special Section: The Psychology of Liberation: Responses to Oppression'. *American Journal of Community Psychology*, 31(1/2), 73–203.

Weisstein, N. 1968. *Kinder, Kuche, Kirche as Scientific Laws: Psychology Constructs the Female*. Boston, MA: New England Free Press.

Weisstein, N. 1970. 'Psychology Constructs the Female'. In R. Morgan (ed.), *Sisterhood is Powerful*. New York: Vintage.

Weisstein, N. 1993. 'Power, Resistance, and Science: A Call for a Revitalized Feminist Psychology'. *Feminism and Psychology* 3, 239–45.

West, G. and Blumberg, R.L. (eds), 1990. *Women and Social Protest*. New York: Oxford University Press.

Whelan, P. and Lawthom, R. 2009. 'Transdisciplinary Learning: Exploring Pedagogical Links between Feminisms and Community Psychology'. *Feminism and Psychology*, 19(3), 414–18.

Whelehan, I. 1995. *Modern Feminist Thought: From the Second Wave to 'Post-Feminism'*. New York: New York University Press.

White, A. and Rastogi, S. 2009. 'Justice by Any Means Necessary: Vigilantism among Indian Women'. *Feminism and Psychology*, 19(3), 313–27.

Wieringa, S. (ed.), 1995. *Subversive Women: Women's Movements in Africa, Asia, Latin America and the Caribbean*. London: Zed Books.

Wilkinson, R. and Pickett, K. 2009. *The Spirit Level: Why More Equal Societies Almost Always Do Better*. London: Penguin.

Wilkinson, S. (ed.), 1986. *Feminist Social Psychology*. Milton Keynes: Open University Press.

Wilkinson, S. 1991. 'Editorial'. *Feminism and Psychology*, 1(1), 1–7.

Wilkinson, S. (ed.), 1996. *Feminist Social Psychologies*. Buckingham: Open University Press.

Wilkinson, S. 1997. 'Feminist Psychology'. In D.R. Fox and I. Prilleltensky (eds), *Critical Psychology: An Introduction*. London: Sage.

Wilkinson, S. and Kitzinger, C. (eds), 1993. 'Heterosexuality: A Reader'. Special issue, *Feminism and Psychology*, (1).

Wills, C. 1991. 'Contemporary Irish Women Poets'. In H.D. Jump and J. Briggs (eds), *Diverse Voices: Essays on Twentieth-Century Women Writers in English*. New York: Harvester Wheatsheaf.

Wilson, S., Sengupta, A. and Evans, K. (eds), 2005. *Defending Our Dreams: Global Feminist Voices for a New Generation*. London: Zed Books published in association with the Association for Women's Rights in Development.

Wolf, N. 1990. *The Beauty Myth*. New York: Vintage.

Wolff, L. and Copeland, L. 1994. 'Violence Against Women as Bias-Motivated Hate Crime: Defining the Issues in the U.S.A.'. In M. Davies (ed.), *Women and Violence*. London: Zed Books.

Women's Aid Northern Ireland. 1994. 'Domestic Violence: the Northern Ireland Response'. In M. Davies (ed.), *Women and Violence*. London: Zed Books.

Women of PhotoVoice/ADMI and Lykes, M.B. 2000. *Voces e Imágenes: Mujeres Mayas Ixiles de Chajul/Voices and Images: Mayan Ixil Women of Chajul*. Guatemala: MagnaTerra.

Young, A. 1780. *A Tour of Ireland*. London.

Young, G. and Dickerson, B.J. (eds), 1994. *Color, Class and Country*. London: Zed Books.

Young, I. 1990. *Justice and the Politics of Difference.* Princeton, NJ: Princeton University Press.

Zappone, K. 1991. *The Hope for Wholeness: A Spirituality for Feminists.* Mystic, CN: Twenty-third Publications.

Zappone, K. (ed.), 2003. *Rethinking Identity: The Challenge of Diversity.* Dublin: Joint Equality and Human Rights Forum.

Index